Stepfamily Realities

How to overcome difficulties
and have a happy family

Margaret Newman

New Harbinger Publications

Publisher's Note

This publication is designed to provide accurate and authoritative information in regard to the subject matter covered. It is sold with the understanding that the publisher is not engaged in rendering psychological, financial, legal, or other professional services. If expert assistance or counseling is needed, the services of a competent professional should be sought.

Dedicated to the children of stepfamilies and their parents, stepparents and relatives.

Contents

Acknowledgments

First, I wish to acknowledge the contribution of the following theoreticians, practitioners, authors and professionals to the field of psychology, and in particular to marriage and family theory and therapy, whose wisdom I have drawn upon in writing this book: Murray Bowen for his work on the family; Alfred Adler for his contribution to social psychology; Gregory White and Paul Mullen for their research into jealousy; Frederick Ford and Joan Herrick on family rules; Timothy Leary on interpersonal styles; Clifford Sager and associates on contracts and Sherod Miller, Elam Nunnally and Daniel Wackman for the development of the Minnesota Couples Communication program.

Second, I want to thank David Jansen, my husband, best friend, business partner and stepfather to my children, who worked many extra hours at the Jansen Newman Institute of which we are both directors, to compensate for my absence while writing this book. I also gratefully acknowledge David's powerful influence on my professional development.

I extend my thanks to Joanna Walker, who produced the manuscript for presentation to the publisher; David and Denise Evans, who provided inspiration; my friends and colleagues Millicent Jones and Tony and Christine Trimingham, who took the time to read my initial writings and give valuable comment.

Over the years my clients, students and School of Marriage participants have taught me so much of what I know about marriage, family and stepfamily life. To them I also say thank you.

Thank you, too, to my children Claire, Alison, Barbara and Pamela, who, with me, have journeyed into stepfamily life and continue, with David and me, to work on the process of blending our stepfamily.

Last, my thanks go the editor Liz Halley and Rex Finch and Julie Stanton of Transworld Publishers for their support and encouragement from beginning to end.

Introduction

I was delighted to be asked to write this book on stepfamilies. As a psychologist and marriage and family therapist, as well as a member of a stepfamily, I know that many stepfamilies struggle with difficult and unique problems. The thought of speaking to members of stepfamilies through the pages of a book was very challenging and exciting.

I have written this book for people contemplating leaving a first-time marriage, those in second or subsequent ones, and for the children that are thrust into these families, as well as for extended family members.

The failure rate of second (and subsequent) marriages is higher than that for first-time marriages. This is an indication that the road to happiness for a stepfamily is not an easy one. Stepparents seeking fulfillment and joy in their new union often find disillusionment instead. Their children and other family members, too, all too often experience difficulties and unhappiness in stepfamily life.

Over the years I have discovered in my professional life that information I have shared with clients (and which you will read about in this book) has helped them gain understanding about many of the issues and difficulties that arise in their stepfamilies. This understanding, when combined with the learning of new skills, has frequently helped them get stepfamily life on track.

Some of this information and understanding has its roots in concepts and principles that have been developed by experienced family therapists, psychologists and other such professionals. Research on the family over the last 40 years has provided a basis for much of the material in this book. I am indebted to many researchers and practitioners who have given so unstintingly of their lives by working with families and unraveling some of the complexities of human interaction.

There are instinctual forces and psychological phenomena in all families that determine how they function. In stepfamilies there are added complexities which often contribute to chaos, confusion and conflict.

There are many questions that stepfamily members ask and mostly these go unanswered. Some of the most common ones are:

- Why does stepfamily life so often fail to live up to the hopes and dreams of the couple who initiate it?

- What happens in some stepfamilies to make stepfamily life an unhappy experience for some, or all, of the members?

- What is happening, on the other hand, to make stepfamily life a happy experience for others?

- What do couples need to know to increase their chances of creating a successful stepfamily?

Stepfamily Realities gives a new perspective on why stepfamilies "curdle" rather than "blend." You will discover many hidden causes of discomfort, gain an understanding of unconscious forces that operate in yourself and your family and learn how to constructively change the way your stepfamily functions. At times you might feel discouraged and that it's all too daunting. This is what it means to face the *realities* of stepfamily life!

In presenting these realities, my sincere hope and intention is that you will, however, believe that your stepfamily (and you) *can* reap the rewards of your learning. I hope that you will be encouraged to keep on going when it all seems too difficult. Many people tell me they wonder if it's worth staying in their second or subsequent marriage. These are the times when the going is tough and there seems to be no hope for the realization of earlier dreams.

To illustrate the various issues discussed in this book, I have drawn from the many experiences shared with me by clients at the Jansen Newman Institute (formerly the Relationship Developement Centre). While all the names used are fictitious and some situations are rearranged for reasons of privacy, all the stories are true experiences of stepfamily life.

Stepfamily Realities encourages you to believe that stepfamily life can be a most rewarding experience. Many people do find the joy they seek— but this usually does not happen by chance.

1

This isn't what I expected

An overview of stepfamily realities

Stepfamily life can be wonderful or miserable. There are many reasons for this. While all families are complex and have many difficult challenges and problems to face, this is even more so in stepfamilies.

The simplistic notion that a stepfamily is like a first-time family has trapped countless adults and children who often face, for the second time, the disintegration of their world and their dreams.

> Marlene and Carl were trapped in this way. It all seemed so easy for them. They were instantly attracted to each other when they met and the romance that followed was their dream come true. Their children from previous marriages had fun together, everything seemed to run smoothly and Marlene and Carl decided to get married.
>
> They spent their honeymoon at a luxurious tropical resort following their wedding. As they basked in the sun and enjoyed their romantic evenings, Marlene and Carl anticipated great joy for their new family. In preparation they had read about pitfalls that can be encountered in stepfamily life, but they believed these would never apply to them.

Eighteen months later their joy and optimism had soured, and Marlene and Carl were beginning to think they had made a dreadful mistake. Their initial optimism for the future of their stepfamily was now dulled and destroyed after the past year of conflict and trouble.

Why do hopes dry up and dreams not come true for so many people who, like Marlene and Carl, enter stepfamily life with optimism and joyful anticipation? Why does the "second time around" appear to be even more difficult for many couples than the "first time around"?

It is because stepfamily life presents many *unique and complex challenges*. If these are to be successfully confronted and overcome, people need to have even more knowledge, understanding, skill and maturity than first-time families demand. This is not understood by most people.

(*Note*: The divorce rate for first marriages is now nearing the 40 percent mark in many western countries. For second and subsequent marriages the rate is higher—and increasing yearly.)

A stepfamily is one in which at least one partner has at least one child from a previous relationship. These families come in many different shapes and sizes. They have many different living arrangements and patterns of interaction.

In spite of this, however, many of the problems they face are similar. This is irrespective of whether

- the parents of the stepfamily are legally married;
- the "ex" lives nearby or far away;
- an ex-partner keeps in touch;
- a stepparent was previously widowed or divorced;
- the children live at home or are adults themselves.

Stepfamilies *are* different from other families in many ways. Let's now look at some of these differences.

(*Note*: This book uses the terms "first" and "second" marriage throughout. However, these terms are for convenience and should be taken to include all forms of committed first- and second-time relationships.)

Why stepfamilies are different

- At least one partner has experienced marriage and parenthood before *or* a partner who *is* a parent has never been married.

- Stepparents who have never married or lived with a partner are unaccustomed to family life (apart from their family of origin).

- Adults *and* children come into the relationship at the outset.

- The parent and stepparent often do not have time together alone before having children live with them.

- Stepparents have to live with, care for and/or relate to stepchildren with whom they have no "history." There is a lack of bonding.

- Single-parent family life often precedes stepfamily life.

- There is at least one "intruder" in the stepfamily unit.

- Children often lose contact with a parent from the previous family—sometimes this is a loss of daily contact, other times it is forever.

- Children often have two homes with two sets of rules, conditions, discipline, etc.

- Visiting children/stepchildren have to be accommodated into the stepfamily from time to time.

- Family members may experience relocation of home, school, job, activities, etc.

- New responsibilities may emerge.

- Unfinished business from a past marriage (anger, grief, guilt, anxiety) can come into stepfamily life.

- Suspicion and lack of trust between stepparent and stepchildren may exist.

- Surnames of children can be different and create a sense of not belonging.

- There are more people, all at once, having to get used to each other.

- There is no "legal" relationship between stepparent and stepchild.

- Socioeconomic conditions might change; money can be tight.

- Sibling order might change so the oldest, for example, could now be a middle child.

- There might be less space or territory for each person.

- At least one person has to adjust to living in a different home—with different family rules, etc.

For a stepfamily to reach maturity and its full potential, it typically passes through various stages as the years unfold. These are part of the overall unique process of the growth of a stepfamily. Within this process, the marriage relationship is the pivotal point. It too encounters natural stages which affect the whole stepfamily.

Stages in stepfamily growth

1. The fantasy stage

There is a lack of reality in the shared belief of the husband and wife that with this marriage all dreams of happy family life will come true. In some cases stepsiblings are excited about having each other and look forward to fun times together. Sometimes children look forward to living with a "mother" or "father" again. There is idealism and, to a certain degree, illusion and delusion. In this stage the parent and stepparent do not *really* know each other—they have not lived together long enough for the idealism of their relationship to wane. Many, if not most, of the people involved put their best foot forward so as to be liked and even loved. This is the stage when people tend to be less real and live more out of their pseudo selves. (Chapter 4 talks about real and pseudo self.)

2. The confusion stage

In this stage differences begin to emerge and there is a growing awareness that the happiness and joy that have previously been experienced and expected are slipping away. There is typically a denial of many signs of impending trouble. This stage is characterized by a growing tension. For the parents, the romantic phase of their relationship may have run its course; the novelty for the children has worn off (if ever it was there); there is fear that this family is not going to make it; many issues are unidentified or unresolved.

3. The conflict stage

In stepfamilies, as within marriage, this stage may involve open or hidden expressions of anger and aggression. Either way it creates tension, stress and the breakdown of relationships and family life unless conflict resolution skills are used (discussed in Chapters 17 and 18). In this stage family members become aware that some or many of their own needs are not being met. Up until now these needs might not have seemed important. Power struggles ensue. The conflict stage is a normal and natural stage and has to be negotiated with skill for the maturity of stepfamily life to be achieved. The "blending" or "curdling" of the stepfamily is determined by the way in which this inevitable stage is handled.

4. The coming-together stage

Gradually the stepfamily moves into a stage where emotionality is not as intense, family members are learning how to resolve issues and there is, among stepfamily members, a growing awareness that they are, in fact, a family. Relationships, even if not ideal, are becoming comfortably familiar. The family system is operating smoothly or at least is able to get back on balance after an upset. This stage is an important phase in the growth of a stepfamiy and one where hope is renewed.

5. The resolution stage

When this stage is reached there is relief that the bad times have passed. Optimism returns and the future looks better. Family members are more able to be themselves, to be real rather than pseudo, and to accept each other for better or worse. Family ties are now growing as familiarity develops. Methods for resolving conflict have been learned and will, of course, need to be used again and again. When a stepfamily reaches this stage, the original myths have been dispelled and dreams begin to come true.

(*Note*: Each of these stages may be experienced with elements of other stages present. For example, conflict is usually present to some degree in every stage. Nevertheless, these are identifiable stages that stepfamilies go through and are recognizable by predominant experiences and behaviors.

These stages represent the evolution of stepfamily life, which is always in a state of movement.)

If you are beginning to have a sense of despair and are saying to yourself, "Help! I married for all the wrong reasons. This isn't what I expected!" you are probably going through a stage that most step-couples experience. You are going through a "normal" stage of stepfamily growth.

Myths about stepfamilies

There are many myths about life in stepfamilies that have lured countless couples into forming a stepfamily. The bitter disappointment that can result when these myths are not lived out contributes to unhappiness and, often, separation and divorce. Stepfamily myths are like fairy stories: they may seem true but they aren't. Here are some examples:

- Stepfamilies can function the same way as first-time families.

- Given time, all members of a stepfamily will love each other.

- When a stepfamily is created after the death of a partner, it will be easier than after divorce.

- All the children will be happy together.

- Stepfamilies are better off because parents have learned from their mistakes in their first marriages.

- Part-time stepfamilies have fewer troubles than full-time stepfamilies, where all members live together all the time.

- If the children are treated nicely by their step-parent, they will be happy.

- Partners can love each other so much that the problems will be easily dealt with.

- Relating to stepchildren is the same as relating to natural children (natural children are the biological and/or adopted children of a parent).

Take time

Have you been trapped into believing any of these myths? Which ones? Do you know other people who have fallen into the trap of believing stepfamily myths?

Blending or curdling stepfamilies

Stepfamilies are often referred to as blended families. This term probably refers to the union, or coming together, of three or more people who form a family that is not a first-time family. They have blended to form another sort of family. If, however, the word blended is meant to imply a harmonious union, then the word is a misnomer.

Given that stepfamily life, *like that of any family*, involves an ongoing process, it makes more sense to refer to successful stepfamilies as blending families. If, on the other hand, stepfamily life becomes embroiled in difficulties and unhappiness, the process may well be one of curdling.

A blending stepfamily is one in which the overall experience is one of increasing joy—in spite of the inevitable hurdles along the way.

A curdling stepfamily is one in which the process of blending has become stuck, and the overall experience is one of increasing despair. There is an accompanying inability to resolve the issues and difficulties that are normally encountered in stepfamily life.

The goal is not to be a blended stepfamily as such, but to be able to reach the resolution stage, wherein the blending process is successfully continuing.

The measure of blending is the degree to which family members can resolve their issues and continue to develop their relationships in a positive way.

Positive possibilities for stepfamilies

The image of the "Brady Bunch" type of family is a myth. This television series, and others like it, have led many people to think that stepfamily bliss can be easily experienced. Many couples have been tricked by the happy antics and warm fuzzy feelings of these television families into believing that this joy awaits them once they embark on stepfamily life. Such beliefs are a trap, and one from which many people never escape.

They are unaware of the forces in stepfamilies that, if not dealt with constructively and with skill, create a tangled mass (and mess!) of mixed emotions. This lack of awareness results in misery and confusion for everyone, and leads to the curdling and disintegration of stepfamily life.

On the bright side, these same forces can be utilized for the creation of a unique, united and truly blending stepfamily. You need information, the opportunity to think and learn about yourself and your family, and a willingness to learn new skills.

If you, your partner and your families embark on this journey of blending, everyone will experience happiness along the way. In fact, this is what happiness is all about—succeeding day in and day out in the process of overcoming obstacles, and seeking new joys with each other. While there may be difficult times along the way, the overall feeling can be one of pleasure that you are moving ahead in the blending process.

Summary

In Chapter 1 we looked at:

Why stepfamilies are different
Stages in stepfamily growth
Myths about stepfamilies
Blending or curdling stepfamilies
Positive possibilities for stepfamilies

2

It seems so complicated

Beginning to understand how stepfamilies work

Before you go on to read about stepfamilies and what happens in them, you need to understand some concepts that apply to individuals and families in general. These are referred to throughout this book.

A family system

A family is sometimes referred to as a family "system." This system consists of different parts or persons. It always operates (unconsciously) to maintain a familiarity which keeps it in a state of balance. If this familiarity goes, the family is thrown off balance and strives to find a new balance.

When a family experiences death, separation or divorce, family members have to adjust to the change and find a new balance. This is usually a painful process and may take many years. This balance is really an *emotional balance* which is experienced as security—or a feeling of comfort—in family members.

Some families experience a whole series of profound changes.

Matthew was devastated when Pat left him. While he had been aware that their relationship had been deteriorating for some time, he was, nevertheless, stunned when she walked out, leaving him with their two small children.

The upheaval created when Pat left meant that Matthew had to adjust to a single lifestyle, plus everything that involved taking care of the home and his children. He also had to contend with his own emotional distress, as well as that of the children.

It took two years before Matthew and the children settled down to a contented and balanced family lifestyle—one that was comfortable and familiar to all of them. During that time there were many tears, clashes, and periods of depression and insecurity for everyone.

Pat, too, had to go through a period of adjustment before she found a new balance in her life—and within her family. She was now a part-time mother and she and her children had to adapt to many changes in the way they related with each other.

When Pat eventually remarried, she and her children yet again had to go through a period of adjustment as they sought a new balance in their relationship with each other, and with Pat's second husband and his children, in their stepfamily life.

When Matthew remarried some years later, he and his children started a new family with his second wife and her children. At first everything was very different—for everyone! Another period of time had to pass before this stepfamily unit found its balance.

In contrast to the many profound changes that took place in the lives of Matthew, Pat and their children, smaller changes can also throw a family out of balance. The next story illustrates this.

Rachel, a young mother, decided that she needed to be more assertive and attended a course to learn these skills. Her husband and children noticed the change and, in their individual ways, tried to get the "old" Rachel back. The balance of the family system had changed because Rachel was communicating in a different way.

As you read through this book, you will understand more about the forces that contribute to both the unbalancing and the balancing processes in stepfamilies.

Family and stepfamily genograms

A genogram is really a family tree that uses certain symbols to represent generations of males and females (deceased and living). It enables us to identify clearly the members of a family.

In Figure 1 you will see a genogram showing Matthew and Pat's first-time family and their families of origin (the families in which each of them grew up). It also shows what happened to their family boundaries when each of them remarried. When this happened, two step-families were created. Each one of these comprised Pat and Matthew, their children, their respective partners and their respective stepchildren. You will see how these are now different family systems which have become interwoven and very complicated.

When a stepfamily system forms, it encounters all of the forces that operate in other families, but because of its added complexities, family members usually take longer to find a state of balance within this system.

They also encounter barriers to establishing an identity of their own. For first-time families, upon marriage and with the addition of each child, identities are established naturally. This process is the goal of stepfamily life and yet often proves to be very difficult—if not impossible.

Subsystems in stepfamilies

Within each family (or stepfamily) there are subsystems. These are smaller groups of people who interact within their own "boundary." (You will read about boundaries in Chapter 5.)

Any group of two or more people within the family system forms a subsystem. Here we will look at some subsystems that can exist in step-families:

a. The ex-partners (parents of the children)
b. Husband and wife (one or two step-couples)
c. Husband and his children (from the first-time family)
d. Wife and her children (from the first-time family)
e. The children of the husband (from the first-time family)
f. The children of the wife (from the first-time family)
g. All the children (from parent and stepparent)

(*Note*: Pat and Matthew and their children each belong to many more subsystems in their stepfamily life than they did in their first families.)

These additional subsystems in stepfamilies make the process of finding a balance, and an identity, far more complex than in first-time families.

"Triangling" in the family system

A common interaction between family members is when a third person becomes involved in a matter concerning two other family members. This is called "triangling," and is very dangerous in families.

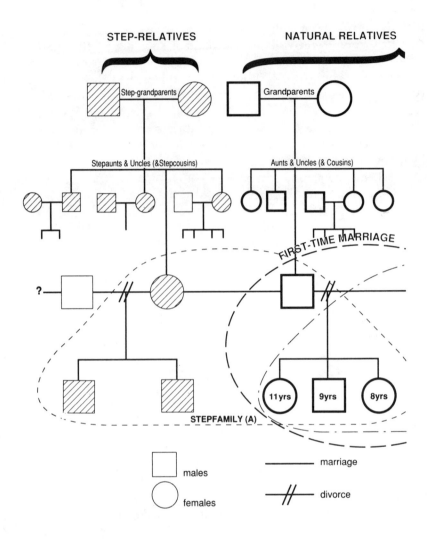

Fig. 1 Genogram showing first- and second-time families

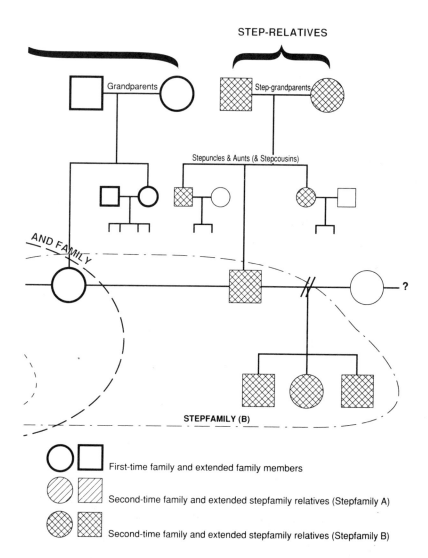

STEP-RELATIVES

Grandparents   Step-grandparents

Stepuncles & Aunts (& Stepcousins)

AND FAMILY

?

STEPFAMILY (B)

○□ First-time family and extended family members

◐▨ Second-time family and extended stepfamily relatives (Stepfamily A)

◕▩ Second-time family and extended stepfamily relatives (Stepfamily B)

A person may "triangle in" on others without permission, or that person may be invited to do it. Here are some examples of the triangling that took place in the lives of Matthew and Pat and their children:

Triangling without being asked

- Matthew heard his daughter on the telephone pleading with Pat to take her out. Pat remained firm. Matthew became angry and took over, accusing Pat of being selfish and uncaring. (Matthew triangled in on an interaction between his daughter and her mother.)

- When Pat left Matthew and the children, Matthew's parents went to see Pat and demanded that she return. (Matthew's parents triangled in on an issue that was between Pat and Matthew.)

- Matthew could not restrain himself in his new stepfamily from telling his stepson that he was ungrateful and lazy and no help at all to his mother. (Matthew triangled in on an issue between his stepson and the boy's mother.)

Being asked to triangle in on someone else's issue

- Matthew and Pat's youngest daughter asked her mother to tell her father to make sure he didn't get her to softball late. (Pat was asked by her daughter to triangle in on an issue that existed between the child and her father.)

- Matthew arranged to meet Pat's second husband and asked him to make sure that Pat kept in regular contact with their children. (Pat's second husband was triangled in by Matthew so that he became involved in an issue between Matthew, Pat and their children.)

- Pat phoned Matthew's brother and asked him to talk to Matthew about the way Matthew spoiled the children. She had tried unsuccessfully herself to do this. (Matthew's brother was triangled in by Pat to become involved in an issue that was certainly not his.)

Triangling is dynamite! Here are two rules to follow if you want to work toward the blending of your stepfamily:

1. *Never* triangle in on anyone else's issue—even if you are asked to do so (unless you think someone's personal safety is involved).

2. *Never* ask anyone to triangle in on your issues. Try to resolve them yourself using the skills outlined in Chapters 17 and 18. Sometimes an impartial person, such as a therapist, is needed to help couples and families resolve conflict.

Defense mechanisms

We have already talked about the way families (and stepfamilies) seek, and then work to maintain, a balance within the family system. Each of us, individually, also seeks to maintain a balance within ourselves. We are helped to do this by our defense mechanisms, which protect us against feelings of anxiety. Otherwise these feelings may prove to be so painful that our vulnerable selves might not be able to cope.

Defense mechanisms are behaviors, thoughts and feelings that serve to protect us from harsh and painful realities about life and ourselves. They protect us from thoughts and fears of rejection and abandonment, and of not being valued by others or even by ourselves.

These defense mechanisms operate unconsciously. We are not aware that we are using them when we do. *All of us use defense mechanisms.*

In spite of the unique complexities and adjustments involved in stepfamily life, it's probably true to say that stepfamily members are no more "defended" than are people in other families or other concentrated social groups. Nevertheless, because of their profound significance, the following brief description of some defense mechanisms will help you understand them better.

Denial

This defense mechanism leads a person literally not to see or accept reality. Many people whose partners tell them they are unhappy in marriage fail to acknowledge and accept what they are being told, and are stunned when the dissatisfied partner leaves. They have denied reality, because to accept it would have been too threatening to that deep, inner vulnerable part of themselves.

Rationalization

This defense mechanism involves making excuses or giving reasons—and believing them. For example, a child tells her friends at school, "Daddy has left Mommy—but it's good, really! Now I can have peace and quiet." This belief protects her from the reality that her father has left the family—and her—forever.

Projection

This defense mechanism is commonly used. It involves believing that other people have the faults that really are our faults! A wife may tell her friends how cold and unloving her husband is—when really it is she who acts this way. Her friends and family may know this, but she doesn't.

Another way that projection operates is to cause us to believe that other people think and feel as we do. For example, many nonassertive people do not set limits because they think people will not like them if they do. What is really happening is that they do not like it when people set limits with them.

Displacement

This defense mechanism protects us from acknowledging the *real* source of our anger (because that would be too threatening) and leads us to displace it onto someone else. For example, a child might be rude and abusive to a stepparent—when really the child is harboring anger toward a natural parent.

Repression

Sometimes events in life are extremely painful and threatening—so much so, that our defense mechanism of repression comes to the rescue and takes them out of our conscious awareness. This way it feels as though a painful event never happened.

Regression

Sometimes children, when presented with a baby brother or sister, want to drink milk from a bottle again or cling to their parents, wanting to be held. They are regressing to behaviors that were only appropriate at an earlier age. These behaviors aim to get the attention these children once had as babies, so they will feel more secure.

Compensation

This defense mechanism serves to cover up inadequacies which would be too threatening for a person to acknowledge. For example, a person has the best garden in the district to compensate for deep-seated feelings of inadequacy rather than for the pleasure of gardening.

Reaction formation

This defense mechanism operates to protect us from painful thoughts and feelings by "making" us feel or think the opposite. For example, a child's father never keeps in touch with him and the child "hates" him—when *really* his love for him is so great he cannot bear to feel it. It feels more comfortable to "hate."

Undoing

When people feel guilty they often do something to make up for it. This defense mechanism of undoing protects them from feeling their guilt. In stepfamilies this is commonly seen when a parent spoils children after having left them, or is overly generous with an ex-partner.

Now that the groundwork is set, you can read on and begin to understand more and more about what makes you and your stepfamily tick.

Summary

This chapter has focused on some concepts and behaviors that exist in all families, including stepfamilies, namely:

A family system
Family and stepfamily genograms
Subsystems in stepfamilies
Triangling in the family system
Defense mechanisms

3

Let's be one happy family

Individual differences and the force of togetherness

When two people and one or more children come together to form a stepfamily, there are three very important factors operating:

1. Individual differences that exist between them.

2. The force of togetherness, or "we-ness"—a natural, instinctual drive which pulls people together.

3. The drive of separateness, or "I-ness"—a natural instinctual drive to be an individual.

These very powerful influences are present in every family, but in stepfamilies they are even more complex. The next two chapters will help you recognize and understand them. Furthermore, you will learn how to manage them in a way that contributes to the success of your stepfamily.

The individual package of each person in the stepfamily

Stepfamily members are very different from each other—much more different than they usually realize. Each person has his or her own individual package of characteristics. The following list shows some of what each person brings into the stepfamily:

- His or her own genetic inheritance.

- Family of origin influences that have been handed down through many generations.

- Values, attitudes, beliefs about all sorts of life issues (for example: health, discipline, loyalty, honesty, family, tidiness, friendship, enjoyment, education, spirituality, punctuality, home ownership, children, finance and so on).

- Traditions and rituals.

- Behaviors that are culturally determined (for example: ethnic, socioeconomic, family, etc.).

- Religious convictions.

- Political convictions.

- Individual traits and ways of thinking.

- Life experiences (from birth to the present time).

- Decisions about how to live life.

- Order of birth (for example: first child, middle child, fourth of five, youngest of nine children).

- Exposure to different role models (mother, father, etc.).

- Experiences and learned behaviors as husband or wife (in first or previous marriage(s)).

- Unfinished (emotional) business from first or previous marriage(s).

- Current situation (for partners) with regard to parental status.

- Unfinished (emotional) business from childhood.

- Communication patterns.

- Conflict resolution methods.

- Expressions of sexuality.

- Degree of comfort with intimacy (verbal and nonverbal).

- Social life, hobbies, interests.

- Educational background and achievement.

- State of health.

- Physical energy and cycles of energy.
- Wealth and social class factors.
- Food traditions and preferences.

And so on...

With all these differences it's a wonder that people get together in the first place. The interesting thing is that instead of recognizing all that is so different between them, when two people enter a relationship they are more inclined to think they are similar.

Take time

Think about your relationship and the differences between you and your partner—especially at the time you met each other. Did you know then that there were many differences between the two of you? In what areas have you become more similar? Are there any factors that apply to you that are not mentioned in the above list? Which of the above do you think applied to the children in your stepfamily at the time it was formed? What differences exist between them now?

The force of togetherness

In every family there exists an instinctual "togetherness force," or drive that pulls family members together. Its "motor" has two elements: one is each person's genetically programmed instinct to do this, the other is the unconscious self of each family member.

This togetherness force operates most strongly between related family members. To a lesser degree, it is also present between couples, in stepfamilies, in groups and even in nations. This drive, or force, pulls people together and gives them a sense of we-ness through similar belief systems, attitudes, values, desires, ways of behaving and even similar emotional reactions to different life situations. This "seeking sameness" behavior is one aspect of the togetherness force.

The other aspect of the togetherness force is that it binds families emotionally with what can be referred to as "emotional glue."

Each of these will be described in more detail in this chapter. First, though, we'll take a look at the unconscious self and how it controls our lives.

The unconscious self

The unconscious part of us can be likened to that part of an iceberg which is hidden under the surface of the water and which is by far the largest and most powerful section. (See Figure 2.)

When the *Titanic* came to disaster many years ago, it was the hidden, submerged section of the iceberg that determined her fate. So it is with us. Our unconscious self—the hidden part of our mind—is the part with the greatest power and influence that determines *our* fate. We do not have any conscious awareness of why we do so many things that we do in our lives, or why we often think and feel as we do.

That is why, for instance, people often try to make others the same as they are, but don't *really* know why they are driven to do it. The conscious need in family members, especially in the parent and stepparent, to "feel like a family" actually comes from the unconscious and instinctual drive to be together "as one." The unconscious factor is associated with early experiences of closeness and bonding to parents and family, and the feeling of security that this gave. Hence, this is sought again in adult life.

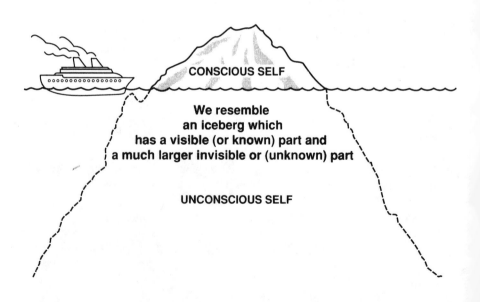

CONSCIOUS SELF

**We resemble
an iceberg which
has a visible (or known) part and
a much larger invisible or (unknown) part**

UNCONSCIOUS SELF

Fig. 2 Our conscious and unconscious selves

Seeking sameness: one of two aspects of the togetherness force

First of all we will look at what happens in marriage relationships with respect to seeking sameness.

Even though people are so different from each other, at the start of their relationship they become focused on their similarities. This involves denial and is what makes them believe they are made for each other. Some or all of their differences are hidden or unknown. This is because it is more comfortable for them if they seem to "be the same"—operating out of their pseudo selves and agreeing about all sorts of things (even if they don't!), thus gaining the approval (and love) of each other.

Even if differences are noticed in these early days, there is a denial of these—so great is the need to seem to be the same. This is why romantic love is often referred to as being blind.

Sooner or later, when the illusory romantic phase of the relationship has waned and differences are now being acknowledged, the drive for togetherness or *the need to be the same* gets into gear. Each partner now operates more out of his or her real self. Bit by bit pressure is applied by each one to *make the partner the same as him or her.* "Why don't you pick up your clothes?" (the way I do); "Gosh, don't you like curry? Try it." (my family loves curry); "For goodness sake, close the door!" (the way I was taught to).

If the differences between partners create discomfort, either the togetherness force begins to operate between them or, alternatively, they distance themselves from each other.

Battles often result as people try, in so many ways, to create a world that is comfortable for them. Marriage breakdown is caused, in part, by this powerful drive.

Remember, this drive to achieve sameness is one aspect of the togetherness drive. Our anxiety is lessened and we feel more comfortable when the people in our lives are like us.

Take time

Think about yourself and how well you tolerate differences in other people—especially those who are closest to you. What do you do to try to make your partner and other family members be like you? What pressures do other people place on you to be like them? How do you feel about this? What pressures were placed on you when you were a child to be like others?

Let's take a look at this seeking sameness behavior and how it is influenced by experiences of childhood or a previous marriage.

Family of origin and/or previous marriage and the togetherness force

In first marriages, there is a great deal for partners to get used to, but eventually life in the marriage takes on a familiar pattern. Many family-of-origin influences may weaken as time goes by and partners adapt and change in the process of living with each other. Partly this comes about because of the force of togetherness. This gives rise to behaviors that may be constructive or destructive to the relationship. If they are constructive, this contributes to the blending of the marriage so that partners resolve many of their differences: for example, they agree, or agree to disagree, on various issues, or create together a new way of doing and thinking about things. When the force of togetherness is expressed by destructive behaviors, as so often happens, the marriage fails and often ends in divorce.

> Frances grew up in a family in which she was taught to take great care of her possessions. She learned to handle books carefully, polish her shoes daily, keep electronic equipment covered so that dust would not ruin it, close doors gently, and frequently clean and polish furniture. She was taught that most things last forever if they are looked after.
>
> In her first marriage Frances tried to make her husband look after their possessions as she wanted him to (that is, her way). He, in turn, found her compulsivity very irritating and tried hard to make her change to his way. He was not successful. Eventually, because of many reasons (although this was a major one, over which they frequently argued), he left her.

When one or two people enter a second marriage, they have experienced life in two families: their family of origin and their first marriage. In each of these families the togetherness needs have shaped the personality and behavior of these people.

Here is a story about John, whose first marriage (rather than family-of-origin) experience has come back to haunt his second marriage:

> John does not like the way his second wife, Barbara, keeps the kitchen doors wide open when she is cooking. Funny thing is that he used to do the same himself, but in his first marriage he was "taught" by his wife that this was unsightly and unhygienic. He changed to become a "door-closer" himself. Now, he tries again and again to get Barbara to close the doors. She gets very irritated at being picked on and refuses to oblige.

The two stories above illustrate how destructive the togetherness force can be to a relationship. We will now see how children, too, are affected by this force when they enter stepfamily life.

Seeking sameness with children in stepfamilies

Much like adults, children who enter stepfamily life usually find that they have to adapt to a new set of rules, values, beliefs, behaviors and so on. They frequently resist any attempt to behave as their stepparent wants them to. "Mom doesn't make me eat my peas." "Dad used to clean my shoes." The greater the enforcement of rules by these newcomers in their lives, the greater might be their resistance.

What often evolves in stepfamilies is an "I'm going to win at any cost" attitude. This cost is often the marriage and stepfamily. For many people the thought of giving in is unthinkable. On and on they go, trying to make people be the way they want them to be. They are driven by unconscious forces, seeking security in the name of sameness or togetherness.

(*Note*: If this is what you do, it will be constructive for you and your stepfamily if you think deeply and try to find out what drives you to push this way. Your conscious mind can do a lot of thinking and exploring, and maybe in the process will retrieve some information out of your past which may shed light on what your behavior is about.)

Here is what one stepfather did when he became aware that his attempts to get his stepchildren to do as he asked were unsuccessful and causing much conflict in his stepfamily:

> Bruce was constantly at war with his stepchildren, Amy and Eliza. He wanted them to sit up straight at the dinner table, to finish everything on their plate, and not to interrupt when he or his wife were speaking. Furthermore, he expected them to clear the dinner table and help their mother in the kitchen every night.
>
> For quite a while he blamed his new wife for not having raised these children "correctly" and was determined to "teach" them the right way. Many awful fights had erupted over these issues, and still Bruce continued to try to make his stepchildren behave the way his own children had been taught to behave. In reality, when he started to think deeply about all of this, he was trying to make them behave as he had been made to behave when he was a child. He now realized how he had hated his father for controlling him in this way!
>
> He began to realize he had a lot of anger toward his father about this, which he was taking out on his stepchildren (displacement). He also realized that he felt guilty that he wasn't with his own children, and this was affecting his behavior too.

Once he had these realizations, he was able to "own" the problem as his and gradually was able to relax and allow his stepchildren more freedom.

Take time

Think about the pressures you put on others to do things your way. Ask yourself: "Where did I learn that this (value, behavior, attitude) is important?" "What would be the worst thing that might happen if I don't get my way?"

Teenagers in stepfamilies

When small children come into stepfamilies, they are more likely to adapt to new rules and family behaviors than are older children. When teenagers enter stepfamily life, additional problems are likely, however skilled the parent and step-parent are at parenting and relating.

This is because at the very time that the togetherness force begins to exert its strength in the creation of the new family, the teenager has reached the natural developmental stage in life when he or she seeks to separate in order to seek his or her identity. The question "Who am I?" becomes a burning psychological issue, and original family *and* stepfamily values are frequently challenged and flaunted. (It's interesting that often the adolescent does this by striving to be the same as his or her peers at school.)

This can be a very difficult time for parents, step-parents and children. In many ways, however, the difficulties are no different from those in first-time families when children enter the teenage years, although it is probably true to say that stepfamily life, together with unresolved issues from the family of origin, combine to make this time quite turbulent for many adolescents and their families.

Some strategies that are used in stepfamilies to force togetherness

It is common for people to live with the delusion that their second marriage will give them an instant happy family. To make this dream come true, family members (especially parent and step-parent) often engage in behaviors that actually force other family members to comply with their private wishes.

Marjory and Dennis decided to marry in a romantic vacation place, and took all their children away with them for the big event. So confident were they about the instant success of their new family that they invited all the children to remain with them on their honeymoon. Three declined (wisely as it turned out) and two decided to go along. These two created havoc and completely ruined the so-called honeymoon. They wanted their father to themselves and resented everything their new stepmother tried to do for them. Gone was the newlyweds' dream of one (instant) happy family!

The force of togetherness made Marjory and Dennis thrust their children into their new stepfamily life from the moment it began. Each one longed for the security they believed they, and the children, would experience if they were all together for their honeymoon and holiday. In a way, they tried artificially to create togetherness and closeness.

Many people try to do this, even if they don't invite their children to come on the honeymoon! Rarely, however, do such strategies work. In fact, they are more likely to inhibit the coming-together process.

Here are some of the things that people might do to force together-ness in stepfamilies:

- Mealtimes all together, all the time (terrible for most teenagers).

- Disagreements not allowed.

- Children told to "be nice" to other members of the stepfamily.

- Family outings *together*, even if a child wants to do something else.

- Insistence that a child kiss his or her stepparent goodnight.

- Dressing stepsiblings alike so they look as though they belong to each other.

- Stepparent told by partner to inquire after his (her) child's day.

- Over-involvement in many areas of children's life—especially by stepparent who wants to be involved.

- Name change so that all family members match.

- Stepparent to be called "Mom" or "Dad."

- Stepchildren to call step-grandparents "Grandma," "Grandpa" or whatever the natural children call them.

- Stepsiblings sent to the same school, so as to be together.

- Pressure put on children to play happily together and *love* each other.

- Encouraging sameness (in all the ways that are talked about in this chapter).

And much more...

While some of these strategies might contribute to stepfamily happiness, depending on how they are implemented, they might just manipulate stepfamily members to fit in with someone's dream of being one happy family. Usually the effects of this are damaging to the stepfamily and contribute to the curdling process.

Many different strategies evolve in a stepfamily to pull its members together. Everyone can be part of this process—often not realizing that when forcing strategies or other damaging behaviors are used, the process of blending is inhibited.

Some characteristics of stepfamilies where damaging negative sameness behaviors are predominant

- Family members lose their sense of who they are. Their "self" gets lost as they are pressured to become like the rest of the family.

- Differences between family members are discouraged.

- The pronouns "we" and "us" are used instead of "I."

- Family members assume responsibility for others (for example, a parent says to a child of voting age, "Of course you'll vote the way we do!").

- Family members blame each other if something goes wrong, and see the reason as others behaving or thinking differently from themselves.

- Family members are not liked, and are even rejected if they are different.

- When a family member seeks to become an individual and be different from the family, there is conflict as pressure is applied for him or her to be the same as the others, and he or she rebels against this.

- Triangling in on a situation involving two other family members creates conflict and confusion. (See Chapter 2.)

- Family members gossip about each other.

- Family members feel guilty when relationships in the family appear to have (or have already) broken down, asking themselves, "Where did I go wrong?"

- Anxiety about differences in family members produces destructive behaviors such as aggression.

- Family members fail to develop their own potential, because of the fear of being different and therefore not being "one of the family."

- When family members do develop their potential it is in keeping with their family programming. It's as though they need the approval of their family to do what they do.

- Family members do not think for themselves.

- The family is enmeshed (see below).

Family enmeshment

Enmeshed families are those in which family members stay "stuck" to other members of the family. They "live in each other's pockets," do things together, live for each other. They often feel smug about their closeness and may think, "Our family is better than others—we all love each other so much."

This type of family may be quite psychologically damaging to the individuals within it, as it may become difficult for them to develop a sense of identity and separateness. If this is the case, they might always cling to their family or, if they marry, their partners might be expected to join in their family life.

Enmeshment is at one end of a continuum of family closeness (disengagement is at the other).

Now we shall look at togetherness behaviors that are constructive in stepfamilies and contribute to the blending (rather than curdling) process.

Some characteristics of stepfamilies where positive togetherness behaviors are predominant

- Family members know each other and accept differences between themselves.

- There is a feeling of security because family members care for each other by nurturing each other in a nonthreatening way.

- Family members are interested in the lives of each other but do not interfere.

- Family members give support and comfort to each other.

- There is love, devotion and compassion between family members.

- A sense of belonging, but having freedom at the same time, is experienced by family members.

- Family members are there for each other: for example, at times of crisis or rejoicing.

- Cooperation rather than competition exists.

- Family members communicate honestly with each other.

- There is a working together toward the goal of blending.

- There is enjoyment at being together.

- When family members experience conflict between themselves they are able to resolve it.

- Family members share rituals, traditions and family celebrations.

- There is respect for each other.

- A strong sense of trust and loyalty exists.

- There is a lack of gossip about each other.

- Family members are united, yet retain a strong sense of their own identity.

We will now look at the second aspect of the togetherness force.

The emotional glue of togetherness—the other aspect of the togetherness force

Not only do family members bond and develop a sense of we-ness when they have similar values, beliefs, behaviors, rules and so on, but they are also bound to each other because of the shared and familiar emotional experiences of their family life.

This is the "emotional glue" that holds families together. This glue is really the emotional environment which is created in the family by the habitual (learned) emotional responses that each member of a family has to each other member. The emotions that family members experience in their relationship with each other may be pleasant or cause much discomfort. In either case, they are familiar and automatic (coming out of the unconscious) and that is what gives them their power to hold people together.

This is why, even though thousands of miles and many years may separate family members, when they get together again it's as though the clock turns back to earlier times. After much time apart, when families reunite, it takes only about eight hours for all the old, familiar feelings and interactions between family members to surface.

Negative and positive effects of the emotional glue of togetherness on stepfamily growth

The emotional glue of togetherness has positive and negative effects on stepfamily growth. There are three negative aspects:

1. The emotional glue of the family of origin binds children emotionally (and unconsciously) to the people in that family. These earlier relationships, involving immediate family members as well as extended family members, have shaped their personalities and the way they relate to others. They have a deep sense of belonging to their original family which will be with them for the rest of their lives.

   This longing can prevent them from bonding with stepfamily members whom they never accept as family.

2. Partners who had a previous marriage bring into stepfamily life their emotional connectedness to their children, their ex-partner and their ex-partner's extended family members (in-laws, nephews, nieces, etc.)

   It is quite common for people to enter their second marriage when they have not resolved the emotions they feel toward their first partner. This is dynamite ready to explode. Unless and until these emotions are worked through and resolved, neither the second marriage nor the stepfamily itself can thrive.

   There is often an intense and destructive emotional bonding between partner and ex-partner that contaminates the lives of their children, so that children are used as weapons for retaliation.

   When adults are no longer members of their first family, they may have a deep sense of loss—akin to that felt by children who lose their family-of-origin connectedness. This, too, can inhibit a free and full involvement of a partner in his or her stepfamily.

3. Sometimes family members from the previous marriage try to sabotage relationships in stepfamilies. This is because they are still emotionally connected to the people (adults and/or children) who were once members of their families.

   The positive effect of the emotional glue of togetherness in stepfamilies involves family members getting to know each other and establishing familiar ways of relating to each other. When this happens within a blending process, the emotional environment in the stepfamily is more likely to be predominantly one of happiness and security. Parent, stepparent, children, stepchildren and members of their extended families have a sense of belonging to each other and knowing each other, as well as having a strong sense of "Now we are a family."

Be encouraged

In spite of the many differences between people and the instinctual and unconscious ways in which the force of togetherness operates to make people the same and bind them together emotionally, many people find great joy in their stepfamilies. These *can* and *do* succeed!

If you are thinking about entering stepfamily life, or are already in it, there is much you can do to make it successful for you and the other people in it. It *is* possible to use the positive togetherness behaviors and, at the same time, help yourself and the other members of your stepfamily be the individual people you are. The next chapter will tell you about this.

Summary

In Chapter 3 you have read about:

The individual package of each person in the stepfamily
The force of togetherness
The unconscious self
Seeking sameness: one of two aspects of the togetherness force
Family of origin and/or previous marriage and the togetherness
    force
Seeking sameness with children in stepfamilies
Teenagers in stepfamilies
Some strategies that are used in stepfamilies to force togetherness
Some characteristics of stepfamilies where damaging nagative sameness behaviors are predominant
Family enmeshment
Some characteristics of stepfamilies where positive togetherness behaviors are predominant
The emotional glue of togetherness—the other aspect of the togetherness force
Negative and positive effects of the emotional glue of togetherness on stepfamily growth

4

Let me be me

The force of separateness in stepfamilies and the search for self

In the last chapter we looked at a very powerful life force which operates, in an unconscious way, to pull people together. We are now going to take a look at another powerful life force, which works against this. This is the drive for individuality or separateness.

These two forces of togetherness and separateness push and pull against each other and underlie your interactions in relationships at home, at work and at play. In stepfamilies that are striving for a sense of togetherness, each member is also striving to maintain or achieve a sense of being a separate person, with his or her individual way of thinking, feeling and being in the world.

The challenge in living with others and getting along with them is trying to achieve a balance between these two instinctual drives. It is natural to seek closeness, that feeling of we-ness, at the same time that you seek to be your own separate person, with a sense of "I-ness."

The force of separateness

The two-year-old's tantrum demonstrates the power of the force of separateness. This behavior is well-known to many parents and often to other family members as well. The two-year-old is asserting him- or herself to get his or her own way. This is very interesting, because no one teaches a toddler to have a trantrum. It is instinctual and the drive is so strong that no one has any control over it, let alone the child.

Even before the age of two, children have learned that they are separate human beings. This is one of the first major lessons that babies instinctively learn: that they are not part of mother but that they exist alone in the world.

When children have pressure put on them to be as others want them to be, they often rebel.

> Melissa, age eight, had recently started to live in her new stepfamily with her father and two brothers. Her stepmother did not like the way she spoke to her brothers. She wanted her to "be respectful and polite". The more she insisted that Melissa change her ways, the more Melissa had to fight for her own sense of self. She did this by being even more disrespectful to her brothers—and her stepmother!

(*Note*: Melissa's stepmother is driven by the togetherness force to make her stepdaughter conform to her values, and Melissa is driven by the separateness force to resist. This resistance helps her retain and even reinforce her sense of who she is: her identity or sense of self.)

Older children often rebel, too, when they experience pressure from others to conform.

> Albert and Jenny sat around the dinner table with their respective children discussing politics. One of the children, now at voting age, was explaining why she would vote differently from her stepfamily at the next election. All hell broke loose. She was criticized as being ignorant, foolish, rebellious.... But (fortunately for her) she remained steadfast and true to herself in the face of this onslaught.

(*Note*: In seeking a sense of I-ness a certain amount of rebellion in children is healthy. Some children, however, learn to be more compliant than rebellious. This is because they feel safer—perhaps because of punishment, conflict or rejection (or the fear of these) should they present a challenge to the authority figures. Children who are overly compliant often grow into adults with a more poorly defined sense of self.)

The greater the pressures are in a stepfamily (or any family for that matter) for a family member to conform to the thoughts, desires or behaviors of other family members, the more likely it is that this person will fight to be different and separate.

Lynn and Eddie have been married for 14 months. Lately, Eddie has been staying out after work with his friends for a drink or two and getting home quite late. Lynn is not at all happy about this and has made demands of Eddie that he come home early. It has made no difference. Eddie seems determined to do what he wants to do.

(*Note*: Lynn and Eddie need to use assertive communication skills to resolve this issue. If they fail to do this, they are almost certainly headed for disaster.)

Eloise decided in her early forties and second marriage to go to college to study history. She had always wanted to do this, and now that the children were older and she had settled into her second marriage, she decided that the time had come. At first everyone opposed her. She stood firm, however, thinking it all through for herself and deciding that no one would suffer. She spoke with her husband and family members and helped them understand her, explaining that the need to fulfill her life goal was very important to her, and helping them see her point of view.

(*Note*: Eloise and her family were able to use assertive communication skills to resolve this issue.)

Brian's son Patrick came home from school one day with cropped, bleached hair and two earrings on one ear. He had left that morning with an ordinary haircut and no earrings. At 16 years of age, this was his way of saying, "I am me, and you'd better all get used to it!" It might seem that this was rather a drastic way to assert this sense of I-ness, but perhaps it was necessary for him to go to this length to make the statement clear to everyone that he, Patrick, was Patrick.

(*Note*: The members of Patrick's family were at first threatened by this behavior but eventually they were able to accept his need to assert his individuality.)

Each of us is unique: Mozart (composer), Picasso (artist), Albert Einstein (mathematician), Midori (violinist), Charles Dickens (author), Margot Fonteyn (ballerina), Christopher Columbus (navigator and explorer), Winston Churchill (politician), John Lennon (musician), Chuck Yeager (aviator) ... and *you*. And so is each member of your stepfamily.

The above stories illustrate the power of the force of separateness. We will now look at why and how this force can be so disruptive to stepfamilies. Then we'll look at the positive aspect of this force in step-family life.

Why the force of separateness creates extra difficulties in stepfamilies

While the force of separateness operates in all relationships and families, in stepfamilies it seems to create more problems. This is because of the added complexities of stepfamily life—especially the fact that, in some instances, *all* stepfamily members have lived in other families beforehand. They have, therefore, been influenced by the togetherness force in those families, so that certain ways of behaving, thinking and so on became familiar to them.

If both partners have lived as single parents for some time prior to the marriage (and this is often the case), not only do they and their respective children have a history of their first-time families with *two* natural parents, but there is also a history of family life with only *one* parent. Each of these family experiences will have been quite different.

And now, when the stepfamily forms, there is another type of family to get used to, with different people as well. With all the changes and accompanying confusion, it is little wonder that the people in it have to try extra hard to retain (or regain) their sense of who they are.

The added numbers of people put extra pressures on everyone. If a mother with children marries a father with children and they all then live together, the striving for separateness and individuality versus pressures to be together and conform can erupt into war.

Unfinished business from the first family may have lain dormant within the single-parent family, only to erupt within the stepfamily. Children who long for the reunification of their original family (and most of them do) often displace their grief, which they unconsciously mask as anger, onto stepparents and stepsiblings. They do not want to be part of this family. They want to pull away from it. And, if they can't do that, they behave in ways that they know are unacceptable. This is what they have to do to feel separate.

Children, who naturally resist parental authority, might be even more resistant toward stepparents. Their need to be and feel separate from these intruders, who they probably didn't want anyway, can lead them to behave defiantly. This defiance might be acted out at school, at home or in society (if they are older children).

Adults, too, have a natural need to be separate. Many of them feel swamped in their stepfamilies.

Clifford married his third wife, who had two children. They lived with him and his two children. Sometimes he felt overcome by everything that was happening in his home. His wife asked him to help her, his children wanted him to themselves and his stepchildren also wanted him to be their "father" and spend time with them. How did he cope with this? He bought a bicycle and took himself on long rides—alone!

(*Note*: Clifford's identity (and sanity) were threatened at times by his step-family life. He felt as though he was losing himself in it. The force of separateness within him led to the solution which helped him get away from it all and reestablish a connectedness with himself. As long as Clifford's bike rides are kept in balance with his home and family involvement, he has found an appropriate solution to his need for separateness.)

Partners who have lived as single parents with their children before they remarry often find it very difficult to adapt to married life again. Gone are the days when they alone make decisions about family life; gone are the nights when the evening is spent the way they like; gone is the autonomy many of them enjoyed as single parents. Now there is someone else to consider who, even without children in the home, shares the decision-making with them. How does such a parent hold onto his or her identity and individuality, which is so often only discovered and developed during those single-parent years?

And how does the partner who marries a "family" keep his or her individuality? As the only "foreigner" in this alien place, he or she usually has to go along with the traditions, rules and contracts of the family in which he or she is now living. Much inner pain and struggling is often experienced by these people, who feel despair, anxiety and anger at not being able to live life in their customary way.

Dean married Doris, who had five children. From the very beginning he felt "out of it." This family had its own set ways of operating and, try as he did to do some things his way, he met with opposition. For example, he really enjoyed eating dinner on his lap instead of always having to sit at the table, but Doris would not allow it. She said it was not good training for the children. He also enjoyed watching late-night television, but Doris and the children complained that it woke them up. He liked pastries and junk food, but that was not allowed in this house. It "set a bad example."

What was Dean to do with himself? To start with, he got nasty and there were some terrible fights. After a while he gave up on this and his anger started to come out in other ways. He stayed out late, got in touch with old friends and brought home his junk food anyway!

(*Note*: Dean's passive aggression was his way of saying: "Hey, you're not going to stop me from being me!")

There are countless ways in which every stepfamily member natural-ly and instinctively strives to be him- or her*self*. Sometimes this striving is of a positive nature and other times the behaviors are damaging or negative. Before we go on to look at these, it's time for inner thought and reflection.

Take time

What do you do in your stepfamily to resist the force of together-ness? What do you think the other family members do? To what extent do these separateness behaviors affect your stepfamily life? How have you tried to resolve any difficulties that have arisen because of them?

Negative and positive separateness behaviors

Given that each one of us is driven to be our own separate and individual person, there are many ways we try to bring this about. We have not been given lessons but instead have developed, in our own unique and creative ways, many different strategies to fulfill this life task. Some of them have had positive outcomes for us and our partners, families and friends and others have had negative outcomes. These outcomes are on a continuum, so that you will probably be able to identity items that apply to you in each of the next two lists. First, here are the *negative outcomes*:

- Self-centeredness.
- Isolating self by pulling away from others (physically as well as with behaviors that push people away).
- Rebellious attitudes and behaviors.
- Creating disunity (through isolation and rebellion).
- Disrespect for others.
- Lack of interest in the well-being of others.
- Selfishness.
- Being emotionally dead or overemotional.
- Fear of intimacy or close friendship.
- Emotional cutting off.
- Being pseudo rather than real.
- Finding it difficult to trust others.
- Lack of respect for the uniqueness of others.

- Likely to be jealous.

- Discomfort when people disagree.

- Difficulty in giving and receiving love.

- Fearful of losing self (arguing, being defensive).

- Fearful of rejection.

- Low self-esteem as a result of the above.

- The family is disengaged.

Here are the *positive outcomes*:

- The ability to think, feel and act for oneself.

- The ability to be alone, and to enjoy aloneness.

- Speaking for oneself (comfortable with the use of the word "I").

- Being emotionally separate from family. This means that emotional issues with the family of origin have been resolved. (Although it is said that no one ever completes this task.)

- Being real (true to self) rather than pseudo (seeking approval from others).

- An ability to trust oneself.

- A sense of inner freedom.

- An ability to trust others (many people find this difficult).

- An ability to respect the individuality of others and not try to make them be the same (as oneself).

- Working at the positive aspects of togetherness without losing a sense of self.

- Acting on the basis of thoughts rather than feelings.

- Taking responsibility for oneself (not blaming others).

- Exploring one's life philosophy, courses of action, values, etc., and not relying on what other people think.

- Not minding if someone disagrees.

- Being self-disciplined.

- Not being rebellious—cooperating and compromising when appropriate.

- An ability to love others for who they are.

- An ability to be intimate without fear of losing oneself.

- Developing high self-esteem as a result of all of the above.

Take time

Which of the above behaviors, in either list, do you think apply to you? Which ones apply to your partner? Your children? Your step-children? What can *you* do to make changes in yourself? Do you want to behave in more positive ways to develop your own individuality and enhance your self-esteem?

Now that we have looked at negative and positive outcomes of the separateness force, we'll take a look at two negative outcomes in more detail. Each of these involves distancing in extreme ways so as to ensure separateness. The first is "emotional cutting off" and the second is "disengagement."

Emotional cutting off and disengagement

When people are overwhelmed by relationships, life's pressures and their own emotions, they may distance themselves physically and/or psychologically. This is what Nathan did.

> Nathan left home at 18 years of age, boarded a ship as a deck-hand, and traveled to the other side of the world. He wanted to be as far away as possible from his family. He put them out of his conscious mind and ceased all contact—forever!

(*Note*: Nathan, in cutting off emotionally in this way, reacted in an extremely negative way to the separateness force. Not only was his family brokenhearted but he, too, paid the (emotional) price for his inability to resolve his unfinished business. In running away and thinking this would solve his problem, his health, subsequent marriage and family life were all adversely affected.)

Disengagement is the term used to describe what happens in families when all the members remain distant and separate from each other. A disengaged family is one in which, for example, family members don't tell each other where they are going or what they are doing. They may grab a bite to eat instead of having dinner together and go off to their rooms without saying goodnight. When they are together, conversation might be stilted or they might hardly talk at all.

Disengagement is the opposite of enmeshment, which we talked about in the last chapter. This way of relating in families is another extremely negative outcome in response to the force of separateness.

Now that we have looked at what the force of separateness is and how it operates, we shall look at what makes you the way you are, and how you can enhance the self-esteem of yourself and your family members.

What makes you the way you are?

There are three components that operate to make you the way you are today.

1. Your genetic inheritance

This determines your physical appearance, as well as certain aspects of your personality. Studies of identical twins who have been raised apart have shown how remarkably similar they can be, not only with respect to appearance, but with respect, for example, to the way they think, the things they enjoy or the way they like to dress.

2. Lessons learned in your family of origin and society

Everyone is raised to learn certain values, behaviors, rules to live by and so on. The earliest lessons you had about life took place in your families, where your parents (or primary caregivers) almost certainly put much effort into trying to make you as they wanted you to be.

There were other lessons you learned in your family of origin (and outside it, too). You learned (often just by observing) about relationships: how people interacted and how they dealt with conflict, intimacy, nurturing, enjoyment and much more. These experiences, or lessons in human behavior, helped shape you and make you the person you are today, so that you may, for instance, behave similarly or have made a conscious decision to behave differently because you did not like what you saw or heard. Either way, these early experiences influenced you.

3. Your strategies for reducing anxiety

You have developed, from a very early age, your own unique strategy for coping with life itself. In a way, you have created a survival kit of countless behaviors (most of them operating out of your unconscious self) to help you feel more secure in the world.

Some of these might be: avoiding conflict (because you learned that conflict is scary); never getting close to people (because you learned not to trust); working hard (because that way you got recognition); keeping very busy (because that way you didn't have time to feel); being helpless or sickly (because then other people will look after you); or being possessive in relationships (because you believe you will feel more secure this way). People are very creative in the ways they try to feel more secure—and in different ways, we all do this.

These three components have contributed to make you the unique person you are. You become *you*! But do you *really* know who you are?

The search for self: pseudo and real selves

"Who am I? I want to find out who I really am!" is a request heard by many therapists in their counseling rooms. Why is it that so many people are driven to go on this search? What has happened to them in their lives to "de-self" them?

There are many answers to these questions. One reason is that when people are continually indoctrinated and conditioned to be as others want them to be, their sense of self gets lost.

Another reason lies in an individual's need for approval. A strong need to be approved of and valued—in the family, among peers and elsewhere in life—can make people, sometimes from a very young age, sacrifice their own individuality and instead live so as to please others.

In living this way, always seeking to gain the approval of other people in order to feel secure, they deny themselves the growth opportunity of developing their *real* selves. What does develop in them is a sense of self that is a *pseudo* self, or a pretend or phony self.

You may find it difficult to believe, but most people live their lives, to a large extent, out of their pseudo selves. It's very likely that you do this, too! Ask yourself, as you read through these *pseudo self-behaviors*, whether you:

- Agree with others so you will be liked.

- Ask yourself, "What will people think of me?" (and behave so they will apprrove of you or like you).

- Are nonassertive in some or all situations in your life (see Chapter 17).

- Feel insecure about yourself—what you think, feel, want.

- Want other people to love you to boost your self-esteem.

- Ask other people what you should do or think.

- Find it difficult to make decisions because of being fearful of displeasing other people.

- Find it hard to accept a compliment.

- Avoid conflict whenever you can.

- Behave aggressively to hide your inner fear and insecurity.

- Do not enjoy your own company and need to be with other people to really feel okay.

- Get jealous.

- Are critical of yourself (see Chapter 17 for more about this).

- Want everyone to like you.

- Fail to be open and honest in your relationships.

While some of these characteristics may seem positive to you in that they make life easier for you in many ways, they really prevent you from being known to others as the person you *really* are. This is because, in a way, you live your life behind a mask—which hides what you really think, feel and want. Here are some *real self behaviors*:

- Satisfaction with self-approval (rather than seeking it from others).

- Awareness of the difference between thoughts and feelings and behaving because of what you think, rather than because of your emotionality (Chapter 7 talks more about emotionality).

- Having the confidence in your own convictions, beliefs, ideas— even if these are in disagreement with those of other people.

- Refusing to compromise your values and behaviors just to be accepted by others.

- Asking yourself, "What do *I* think?" rather than "What do (or will) other people think of me?"

- An ability to compromise or agree, but not in order to gain approval.

- An ability to accept that differences between people are natural and not be threatened by them.

- A willingness and ability to resolve conflict constructively.

- An ability to communicate honestly and openly (assertively).

- An ability to give compliments in a genuine way and not in order to be liked.

- An ability to receive compliments—and believe in them!

- An ability to make your own decisions and live by them, taking full responsibility for the outcome.

- Having integrity, so that you say what you really think, feel and want, when that is appropriate.

Take time

Ask yourself, "Which behaviors in the above two lists apply to me?" Now think about (or write down) all of the things you do out of your pseudo self to get the *approval* of others—in your family, with friends, people at work, at church, in the neighborhood and anywhere else—maybe even with a stranger on the bus. (This is different from being pleasant to people out of respect.)

What would it be like for you if you expressed honestly what is happening in the real part of you (to your partner, children, stepchildren?) How do you think you would feel being so honest? What would it be like for you if they related to you out of their real selves.

Before you can be real in your relationships, you have to know more about yourself. This means you need to develop your self-awareness so that you can tell people what is really happening in you.

Developing your self-awareness

With respect to your *thoughts*, ask yourself such questions as: "What is my opinion about this?" "What do I really believe in?" "What do I value in life?" "What do I think is the best way to do that?" Search yourself and get in touch with the ideas, beliefs, opinions, values, attitudes, expectations and assumptions you have.

You can help yourself get more in touch with your *feelings* by asking yourself: "How do I feel about that?" "What feelings did I have when ...?" If you answer sometimes that you feel hurt, ask yourself again whether you really feel angry. (Many people, especially women, are unaware of their angry feelings and mask them by saying they feel hurt.) If you answer sometimes that you feel angry, ask yourself again whether you feel sad. Many people, especially men, are unaware of their sad feelings and mask them with anger. (See Chapter 7 on emotions.)

Many people find it difficult to know what they want for themselves. Help yourself get in touch with your *wants* (or *needs*) by asking yourself: "What do I really want in this relationship?" (perhaps more time together or intimate sharing); "What do I want for me in my life?" (a successful marriage or a university degree); "What need do I have that is not being met?" (this may be a cuddle, time to relax, or your self-development).

In addition to the above become more aware of your *senses*—especially what you *see* and *hear* happening around you. You may find that you have been unobservant and not noticed teary eyes, the birds singing, a kind word, a face that is pale and drawn or even a warm wink! When you notice such things, you are becoming more tuned in to yourself—and your world.

There is another dimension of your awareness that is important in helping you get to know yourself, and therefore be able to be more real in your relationships. Begin to think about and notice your *patterns of behavior*. How do you react to certain situations? Ask yourself: "If I was looking at me, what would I see me doing?" For example, do you always withdraw when someone is angry with you? Do you look for an argument when you are tired? Do you push your partner out of the way, perhaps by being unpleasant, when your own children come to visit?

(*Note*: In Chapter 18 the self-awareness wheel is used to help you see more clearly the six dimensions of your self-awareness. This wheel provides the framework for conflict resolution as well as the development of intimacy.)

These above strategies for your personal growth are part of the process of seeking your identity and of answering the question, "Who am I?" But you may be wondering what this has to do with the blending of your stepfamily.

The answer to this is that *real people make real families!* If you develop yourself, you are helping your partner, children and stepchildren relate honestly, in a real way, and in so doing creating an emotionally healthy environment for everyone.

As you begin to live your life in a real way, using assertive communication skills (see Chapters 17 and 18) and developing your self-awareness, your self-esteem will be enhanced as you develop a much stronger sense of *who you are*.

This does not mean that you become self-centered. *The goal is to achieve a healthy balance between the we-ness and I-ness of your existence.*

Enhancing your self-esteem

Your self-esteem is the extent to which you value yourself. This aspect of human behavior, too, is on a continuum: from low to high self-esteem. More people have low or middling self-esteem than those who have high self-esteem.

Your self-esteem comes from your "self-concept," or how you see yourself. This refers more to how you see your unique self in your head rather than in the mirror. It has a lot to do with what we have been talking about in this chapter: searching for your *self*, knowing who you are and being real. Another way to develop your self-esteem is to learn and use the assertive communication skills covered in this book.

How to help your family members develop their unique selves and their self-esteem

- Encourage them to have their own ideas and to express them, even if they differ from your own.

- When someone disagrees with you about an idea or opinion, feed back to that person what you heard him or her say so they know that they were heard.

- Let your partner, children and stepchildren know that you care about and/or love (take your pick!) them.

- As much as possible give children the freedom to arrange their room, dressing table, shelf, cupboards, etc. as they wish.

- Allow children (and partner) to select clothes they want to wear (if not all the time, at least some of the time).

- Do not force children to eat what they don't like.

- When your child or stepchild comes to visit, do not try to force him or her into the family pattern or way of doing things (encourage if you like, but don't force).

- Examine your own values and try, unless it is absolutely necessary (for example, with moral or safety issues that are important to you), not to force them on other family members.

- Remember, your way is not the only way—just one of many!

- Give all children (visiting ones as well) a place of their own, whenever possible (see Chapter 5).

- Look for signs of uniqueness in children and encourage this in whatever way you can.

- Avoid a "children are to be seen and not heard" mentality (believe it or not this still exists).

- Respect children, whatever age they may be. Treat them as you would like to be treated.

- Give children (and partners) permission to express anger toward you (see Chapters 17 and 18 on communication).

- If punishment is required, use constructive methods (see Chapter 11).

- Use positive separateness behaviors.

Be encouraged

You can do a lot to help your partner, children and stepchildren develop their self-esteem, be real in their relationships and respond positively to the force of separateness that instinctively resides within them.

The more encouragement you give them to be themselves, the more likely it is that your stepfamily life will be a source of joy for you and the other people in it.

This does not mean that the children in your stepfamily will rule the roost. Limits must be set and there are many important lessons that you will want to teach them. That, too, is part of helping them find themselves as individuals, and involves finding a balance between the forces of togetherness and separateness in your stepfamily.

With respect to your own growth, this is within your grasp if you *want* it. People can and do make changes in themselves—and you can too!

Summary

This chapter has dealt with:

    The force of separateness
    Why the force of separateness creates extra difficulties in step-families
    Negative and positive separateness behaviors
    Emotional cutting off and disengagement
    What makes you the way you are?
    The search for self: pseudo and real selves
    Developing your self-awareness
    Enhancing your self-esteem
    How to help your family members develop their unique selves and their self-esteem

5

Leave me alone

Boundaries and personal space in stepfamilies

Along with the instinctual drive for separateness, discussed in the last chapter, there is a need in all of us to have space—physical and psychological. We will now take a look at this need and how, in stepfamilies in particular, this can create conflict.

Boundaries

The idea of a boundary can be applied in many ways. Nations have geographical boundaries, and so do national parks, football fields, schools, houses, bedrooms and even cupboards and shelves. These are physical boundaries.

The are other boundaries which are invisible. There is the boundary between warm and cold streams of water in our oceans, or between the lower and upper levels of our atmosphere. These may not be as sharp or definite as the physical boundaries mentioned above but, nevertheless, they are there.

There are also boundaries within relationships and between groups of people. If you go to a restaurant and sit with your friends at a table, you have, by doing that, created a visible boundary around your group which gives you and your friends your own personal space. There may be many other separate groups in the restaurant who also have, by socializing in this way, created a boundary around themselves as if to say, "This is our territory: keep out!"

Teenagers group together within invisible boundaries of special groups. These boundaries are defined by membership of acceptable friends only. Members of these groups can be very cruel at times and often expel members if they are not wanted in this personal space any longer.

Sometimes a close friendship between two friends develops, to the exclusion of anyone else. This really means, "We want to be alone together."

This is, of course, what happens when two people form a relationship and want to marry. By marrying and being together, they create an invisible psychological boundary which keeps other people out and gives them an identity as a couple.

When any family reaches the stage of having an identity of its own, an invisible boundary has been created which says, "This is *our* family." This is what the blending process of a stepfamily is all about—aiming for this goal.

Physical and psychological boundaries define and protect our physical and psychological personal space. We seek to protect ourselves within these boundaries so we feel more secure.

These boundaries can be wide, close, strong, weak, rigid or loose, and each one of us instinctively uses them in countless areas of life.

Our boundaries operate on automatic in many different ways and in many different situations. This way we have developed our own use of boundaries and our personal space needs over our lifetime is absolutely unique. It is represented in our personality and in everything that we are.

We have boundaries that contract and expand to keep us close to others, distant from others, boundaries that we put up when we want peace, silence, privacy, time alone or time with someone else.

Some people, for example, have a fear of closeness (they often don't realize this) and protect themselves by sitting alone at social gathering, failing to "keep in touch," spending time alone and being noncommunicative. In doing this, they put a tight and close boundary (like an invisible wall) around themselves which stops other people from getting close, even when these people try to.

Other people who fear closeness may create a different sort of boundary. They may be aggressive, talk too much, monopolize relationships or engage in other behaviors that invade the unseen psychological boundaries of other people. This "turns others off" and these other people, in turn, construct their own boundaries against the invader by, for example, not talking to him or her—or, at least, not being friendly.

This has the effect of isolating the invader, whose desire to be alone and distant is realized. In this case the one who feared closeness has invaded the personal space of others, who have tightened their boundaries and repelled the unwanted intruder.

We will now look at the needs stepfamily members (and all people) have for physical space, or territory, *and* psychological space. In both cases, physical and psychological boundaries define and protect this personal space.

Physical boundaries and personal space in stepfamilies

We all need to feel safe within the confines of our home. The much loved song "Home, Sweet Home," which has as its last line "There's no place like home," was written by someone who knew this. It is a special place, which we all seek, within which we can be ourselves and express ourselves in a way we cannot do elsewhere.

A home is a place with visible and invisible boundaries. External walls are visible boundaries, and rooms and hallways, too, are defined this way. Some areas of homes are defined by other sorts of visible boundaries, such as furniture, benches, screens and so forth.

Invisible physical boundaries in homes are more difficult to define, but the people who live there usually know them. A special place in the living room where someone usually sits, or on the shelf where the person likes to put belongings, are some examples.

But there are other sorts of invisible boundaries in homes, too. For example, when someone is dressing, other people in the home know not to enter the room or the territory; when someone is sitting quietly and reading, that person may not want anyone to talk to him or her or to play loud music; when someone is on the telephone, the person may not want anyone listening in.

When one partner moves into the home of the other, with or without his or her children, difficult times usually lie ahead—for everyone. Children already living there can be very cruel to these newcomers, who not only do not know the "rules of the house" but are seen by them to be invaders of their space.

People who have lived in the home are threatened by the changes brought about by having different people living there. For them, all that was familiar, the way the home was run and the familiar interactions between the people within it, are no more. Boundaries that were previously acknowledged and respected are often violated and encroached upon, usually because the newcomers are not aware of them. The house or apartment itself has not changed but life within it becomes very different.

Partners who move into the existing home of their new partner and stepchildren also have many things to get used to—and put up with. They are in a foreign place, and often feel uncomfortable. This is not their territory and they are not psychologically connected to it. If their children are with them, the added stress involved in helping them adjust can take its toll on the marriage relationship.

It is not uncommon for stepparents, having gotten to know and relate well with their stepchildren-to-be, to discover that when stepfamily life begins things do not go that smoothly at all.

Ziggy, father of two, married Wilma five years after the death of his first wife. Wilma had two grown-up children of her own who had embarked on their own lives elsewhere. Ziggy's children, both in college, were delighted at the prospect of their father marrying Wilma, as were her own children.

Over the past five years, since the death of their mother, Ziggy's children had lived at home with him. A very strong bond had developed between the three and there were lots of good times together. It was a home of happiness in spite of the loss of a loved wife and mother. They all looked forward to having Wilma live with them after the wedding.

Once Wilma moved in everything started to change. She had broken into their boundaries. This was now her home, too, and naturally she wanted to put her mark on it. Gradually, objects, such as a vase, were put somewhere else or disappeared altogether to make way for her own belongings; new furniture was moved in; pictures on walls were changed; and the food in the kitchen cupboards and refrigerator was different. Wilma needed to feel "at home" and this was her way of making this place her home.

She played "strange" classical music and cooked meals that were unfamiliar. Furthermore, she didn't like anyone in the kitchen, especially when she was cooking—she said she was in charge. In doing this she created another boundary—the kitchen was out-of-bounds to other family members.

After a while Ziggy's children left home to live elsewhere, quite embittered about the way in which their home life had changed because of their stepmother. From their point of view, their home had been taken over by Wilma and was no longer the place they knew and loved.

Many stepparents are not comfortable with stepchildren in their home. For them there is something about having the child or children *in* the home that creates the tension. "This is my space and I don't want you here!" their inner voice is saying.

It is important to realize that this need for our own space is instinctual. We are, by nature, territorial creatures who go to great lengths to protect our territory. There is no one to blame for wanting or creating boundaries. It just *is*. It is a reality which we all have to learn about, accept and learn to live with.

Within the confines of the house or apartment (home), there are smaller areas with boundaries, too. A bedroom, a cupboard, a drawer or objects such as a favorite chair, a special book or compact disc will be guarded—at times as though our life depended on it. So much of our sense of self is tied up with these objects and these places. We derive comfort from them. They help us feel secure.

We often see tragic pictures of refugees escaping from their own land and carrying with them a pitiful bag of all that they own. These possessions might seem to us to have no monetary value at all but, to the refugees, the contents represent their lives and, as such, are of considerable value.

When fires sweep through homes and everything that has been familiar is lost, the victims are devastated. For many of these people it is as though a lifetime has vanished. Our homes, what is in them and all that they mean are very important to us and our journey through life. Even people who do not have homes or are forever traveling own some items that have significance and value for them.

All of this means that it is very necessary to respect the space and possessions of others if we are to live happily together. Everyone needs to be aware of this and to remember that *boundary-setting is a normal and natural human behavior.*

Another common problem in stepfamilies occurs when the child or children of one of the partners come to visit or stay. These children are sometimes referred to as "access children" and for them these times can be very difficult. They are often very aware that this is not *their* home and this makes them feel uncomfortable.

> Charles lives with his mother and every so often went to stay with his father, stepmother and stepsisters. While he actually enjoyed the company of his new stepfamily, he never felt comfortable in their home. His bed was a couch in the daytime and the family room was his bedroom at night. He always had a sense of being in the way, and that was one reason why he did not go there often. He also knew that he had to be careful not to upset his stepsisters by going into their rooms, playing with their basketball or turning on the television whenever he felt like it. He always felt like an outsider.

It's like this for many visiting children. The physical boundaries of the home and the boundaries imposed by family members on certain rooms, spaces and objects prevent them from feeling like members of their step-family unit. There are countless ways in which children can get this message of not belonging.

> Tim loved ice cream. In his home it was quite all right for him to go to the refrigerator during study break time and have one or two scoops of ice cream. The first time he did this at his dad's new home he really got to hear about it. "Never do that again!" he was told by his stepmother. Home was certainly not like this. His stepmother's reprimand contributed to the curdling of this stepfamily.

Visiting children often consider the home to be their home because their mother or father lives there. Young children might consider toys that are lying around the place to be there for them.

For the children who live there, however, visit days often present a threat and they struggle to protect their own territory and possessions. "Dad, she keeps coming into my room!" or "Mom, tell him not to ride my bike, it's mine!" are exclamations all too familiar in their circumstances.

Children are not the only ones in stepfamilies who wrestle with territorial issues.

> Helen persisted in putting her handbag, mail and bits and pieces onto her second husband's bedside table. She did not do it deliberately—it just seemed a natural thing to do, as his bedside table was nearest the door. He became increasingly irritated about this and (lacking conflict resolution skills) eventually took them off and hurled them across the room. He was guarding his personal space. "Get your things off my table!" he shouted. Helen's first husband had not worried about such things and it certainly was not easy to adapt to this new husband, who was so territorial.

In varying degrees we are all this way. Some people are more comfortable with loose boundaries and others with rigid boundaries. One of the challenges of marriage and family life is to adapt to the differences between us. People are shaped by the experiences in their families, whether these are in the family of origin or in first or subsequent marriages. This means that values, attitudes and behaviors of stepfamily members with respect to their personal space are likely to be in conflict when a stepfamily is created.

> Harry knew Carla for two years before they decided to marry. It was not long after they moved into their new home with their combined families including seven children, an Alsatian

dog, two cats and a furry white rabbit that they began to real-ize they had some serious problems. Harry had always allowed children, the dog, the cats and anyone else who happened to be around to go wherever they wished in his home. His at-titude was that they were all his "nearest and dearest" and what was his was theirs.

Carla did not share his attitude about personal space. She was more inclined to have rigid boundaries and to set defined areas for children, the dog, the cats and the rabbit. Fortunately for Harry and Carla, they had learned some assertive com-munication skills and were able to resolve this potentially ex-plosive issue.

These two people came into their second marriage with very different attitudes about personal space. Harry was comfortable with loose boun-daries and Carla with rigid boundaries.

Each member of a stepfamily has a right to his or her own space, but if the people in their lives feel totally excluded by them, it is almost impossible for relationships between them to flourish.

If the step-couple commence their married life with one or more children living with them, it may be very difficult for them to find either the time or the space to be alone together. The opportunity to cuddle on the sofa or kiss in the kitchen, in private, is often hard to find.

Creating a boundary around the bedroom when there are children around is often difficult. Many couples are inhibited when their bedroom is close to their own children's, or to their stepchildren's. Some couples feel uncomfortable locking the door and prefer an open-door policy. This is all right for management in business but not in a family. Sometimes partners lock the door, only to hear children banging to get in or calling out: "Mom (or Dad), where are you? When are you coming out?"

Needless to say, this creates tension which affects the marriage relationship. Opportunities for time together *alone* are essential for two people to build a strong marriage.

(*Note*: This is an example of another invisible boundary that people try to maintain, both for themselves and for the children. The resulting in-hibition can create conflicts, which need to be openly and honestly dis-cussed with each other.)

Children need their own space, too. Some children have their own bedroom in the home, regardless of whether they live there permanently or not. This is probably not possible in most stepfamilies, where space and financial resources are stretched to the limit. It is, however, a good idea if visiting children have some place and/or object that is theirs.

In some stepfamilies, visiting siblings share a room and sleep in their own beds. This helps give them a sense of belonging, but if this is not possible, there are other ways to help visiting children have a sense of belonging.

Maybe a section of a room can be cleared and the stamp of ownership put there with a special lamp, bookshelf and belongings. If that is not possible, a cupboard can be emptied and become the property of absent children who could be given a lock and key if old enough. Small children might have a toy box and toys that are theirs. Some people put drawings or paintings that children have done on a bulletin board or the refrigerator. This helps children feel connected to this second home.

There are many ways in which parents can be creative and help their children feel as though they belong in their "visit" homes, for example: favorite meals can be served, the child can contribute to home decoration ideas, a friend of the child's can be invited to stay over, or the child can choose what he or she wants to do. When children feel as though they belong, they are less anxious and are able to participate more fully and happily in stepfamily activities and lifestyle.

Take time

In your stepfamily, what problems have arisen over territorial issues? How are these issues dealt with? How do you feel when your stepchildren or children come to stay? How do other people in the family react? How do the children react? Do they raise issues over *your* house and *my* house? If they do, are you able to talk it through constructively?

Psychological boundaries and personal space in stepfamilies

There are two aspects to psychological boundaries and personal space. The first applies to *relationships* and the second to some specific *human needs*.

One aspect of personal space has to do with invisible psychological boundaries that exist in relationships and involve the closeness or distance that people seek between themselves and other people.

To understand this we need to look first of all at the early years of human life.

From the day children are born they are not alone in the world. If they are, they perish, so dependent are they as infants on being cared for by someone else. For some, their early experiences with their primary caregivers were very positive, and for others they were quite negative.

Irrespective of how these early experiences were, by the age of about seven months to nine months most children experience what is known as separation anxiety.

This is a normal stage of child development and is the anxiety (usually shown as crying and screaming) that children feel when they are separated from their mother (usually). When they can no longer see her, for example, when she walks out of the room, they don't realize that she's coming back, and interpret the situation as one of being abandoned or rejected by her—hence, the panic.

Another normal stage of child development is referred to as stranger anxiety. You can recall times when some stranger (or a person you did not know well) wanted to kiss you or take you by the hand when you were small, and you cried and pulled away. Or perhaps now, as an adult, you remember times when you wanted to cuddle or talk to someone else's cute baby, only to be met with screams and withdrawal.

When we were children we felt safer when we were close to some people and safer when we were distant from others. As adults these behaviors persist in all of us to some degree. There is a sense of the appropriate distance we need to maintain to maximize our comfort. Sometimes we even learn to feel safer with people outside our immediate family than we do with people within it.

What happens to determine these behaviors? What is the underlying fear that makes children (and adults) seek closeness or distance so they feel more secure? It is the *fear of rejection*. We shall now take a look at the profound effect this fear has on every one of us.

Fear of rejection

To a greater or lesser degree, all of us fear being left, rejected or abandoned. We may fear being rejected by our partner, parents, children, friends or even our employer.

This fear is usually not even in our conscious awareness. It is primitive and instinctual and exists from the moment of birth, maybe before. We all live with it—whatever our childhood experiences might have been.

Unconscious strategies to reduce the fear of rejection

In order to reduce the anxiety that the fear of rejection gives us, we develop certain (unconscious) strategies as we grow up. Some of these strategies are *behavior that create distance or closeness* between us and other people.

These strategies are on a continuum of human behaviors, so that the greater the fear of rejection that a person has, the greater the distance *or* closeness that person needs between himself and others.

Some children, for example, when believing they are not liked or loved, seek to get closer and closer to the person they perceive as rejecting them.

Many parents know what it is like to have a child clinging to them, refusing to let go, or to have a child banging the door to get in, or screaming when being put to bed at night. This behavior indicates that the child is very fearful of being left, or abandoned, and is seeking to be comfortable and reassured that he or she is loved and will not be left.

Other children, however, do the opposite. They create a distance between themselves and the rejecting person or people. This way they feel safer. It's as though they are thinking, "If I get away from you, you can't reject me because I'm not there to be rejected."

Each of these instinctual strategies of drawing close or distancing is carried into adulthood in an endless variety of ways—by each one of us. They involve our *psychological boundary* which serves to pull us close to, or away from, other people, to protect us. This boundary is mobile, in that we seek closeness with some people and distance from others.

Some people have a wide psychological boundary. They have need of more space between themselves and others than do other people. The ways they create this may be by:

- Not having too much time to spend with others.

- Not wanting to talk much.

- Not talking about their real self.

- Not letting people know them.

- Avoiding conflict, or creating it so as to create distance.

- Not kissing, hugging, having sex.

- Pushing people away by being uncooperative.

- Rude and aggressive behaviors.

- Never joining in.

- Not even trying to relate.

Other people have a boundary that only puts a little space between them and others. The ways they create this may be by:

- Being compliant.

- Wanting everyone to like them.

- Touching, hugging, clinging.
- Confiding, having secrets with other people.
- Focusing attention on one person.
- Being possessive
- Keeping other people away from the loved one(s).
- Wanting to spend all their time with the loved one(s).
- Constantly making contact.
- Needing constant reassurance.

(*Note*: It is important to realize that people usually do not have any conscious awareness that these behaviors are strategies to reduce their fears about being rejected.)

To some extent we all get close to or distant from the people in our lives. Depending on the people and situation, our behavior can vary, as it did with Heather in the next story.

> When Heather's children seemed displeased with her, Heather became quite depressed. Sometimes the older ones, who lived away from home, didn't contact her for weeks. She thought, "They really don't love me," and this made her feel very tense and depressed. She tried to contact them so as to feel closer to them.
>
> On the other hand, when Heather and her husband had a disagreement, she didn't talk to him for days. The psychological distance that this behavior created between her and her husband felt more comfortable to her. (See Approach and Avoidance in Chapter 12.)

In both situations Heather's behavior was because of her need to have the appropriate psychological space between herself and her family members in order for her to feel more secure and comfortable.

In a stepfamily all of these intra- and interpersonal dynamics are operating and frequently cause misunderstanding and unhappiness.

Sometimes a parent tries to get a child to kiss a stepparent or talk with him or her and the child does not want to do it. The child needs time (space) to get used to this person and for a relationship to develop gradually. The stepparent may need this too.

Sometimes when visiting stepsiblings come to stay or play, a parent or stepparent may force the resident children to play with them—and they don't want to. The more that children's personal space, or freedom to do as they wish, is threatened in this way, the less likely it is that the parent's request will be met. The "at home" children have put a psychological boundary around their small group and in different ways exclude the others. "Go away!" "No, you can't play with us!"

(*Note*: In situations like this, it is probably best to allow the children to sort it out themselves. If you wish, you might talk later with the resident children and ask them what the reasons are for not wanting the other children to play. By inviting disclosure and bringing the reasons out in the open you are more likely to help sort out this problem.)

Sometimes children refuse to have anything to do with a parent who leaves home, remarries and perhaps has stepchildren living with him or her. When this happens, children are helping themselves feel more secure. The pain of the family separation, and possible anger at the parent for what has happened, is so great that an emotional cutoff seems the best way to cope. This is an extreme example of distancing and withdrawal.

There are parents, too, who distance themselves from their children. It's as though trying to maintain a relationship with them involves so much pain that it is easier to forget them.

Alice and Debbie were two and four when their father left their mother to go and live with another woman. Once he walked out of the family home he never again had any contact with his children. They grew up not knowing him at all.

Why would a father do this? Why do some mothers do this? One reason is because the thought of maintaining partial contact with their children creates a deep uneasiness and anxiety. It might constantly remind them of their loss—and perhaps their failure. Perhaps their need for acceptance by their children, together with a deep-seated belief that they will be rejected by them, is so great that they feel better if they continue life as though these children never existed.

Early life experiences, and the development of a distancing strategy to reduce the fear of rejection, determine this behavior.

(*Note*: Defense mechanisms may be unconsciously used in such cases. For example, "It really is better for my child if I have nothing to do with him/her" (rationalization); or "I don't miss my children at all, and I know they don't miss me" (denial). (See Chapter 2 on Defense Mechanisms.)

We have looked at invisible psychological boundaries that exist in interpersonal relating. The other aspect of personal space applies to space that people *need* or *want* so as to feel better: for example, happier, more relaxed or less tense, more confident. This space is created in may ways, including having time, privacy, freedom, silence or solitude.

Within all families, there are times when family members want this sort of space for themselves. They may long, for instance, for the opportunity to do just what they want to do for themselves. When stepfamilies are formed, these individual needs are usually not known to people who have not lived together before.

> Steffani was desperate. She needed a day to herself, all alone in the family home to get things done and to enjoy the peace of solitude. It took some talking to convince her husband and their children that she *had to have it*!
>
> Her husband felt quite rejected and unloved and the more she insisted the more anxious he felt. This lead to a fight. Eventually, in anger, he cleared out of the house with children in tow.

There are times when many of us are like Steffani. When that sort of space is needed, it is not necessarily because we do not love those people near us. Sometimes, though, they may interpret our request that way and feel rejected by us. This can stress our relationships and, unless some constructive communication enables mutual understanding, can have negative effects.

Occasionally children want to be alone, perhaps in their room or somewhere else. Children need their space, too, and in fact it can be beneficial for them to become accustomed to being alone some of the time. (This does not mean that young children should be left entirely alone in the home.)

For adults coming into stepfamilies it can be very difficult at times to have space needs met and to make them known.

> Gary enjoyed listening to music in the evenings and was dismayed to discover, as soon as stepfamily life began, that his stepchildren played their music so loudly that he couldn't enjoy his own music. His "enjoyment" space was invaded by the noise of their music.

> Angie's efficiency was something she prided herself on. When her husband made suggestions about how to do something, she became very resentful. He had invaded her psychological space—her invisible "efficiency" territory.

> Carrie and Jake were settling in to stepfamily life. Carrie's daughter, Nancy, felt betrayed by her mother when she discovered that Carrie had told Jake something about her which she considered to be very private. Her "privacy" space had been invaded by her new stepfather.

> Wade loved playing golf and, prior to his second married, played twice each weekend. He knew when he married that

this probably wouldn't be possible, but had hoped for some time to enjoy his favorite pastime. Once stepfamily life began, however, he had pressure put on him by his stepson and wife to spend the weekend with them. He was unhappy and frustrated when he realized his days of golf were numbered. His "relaxation" space was threatened.

People need both physical and psychological space. The degree to which different people need this varies and has been determined by life experiences that go way back to infancy.

Because a stepfamily is an instant family, some members of which have not experienced a bonding or "getting to know each other," it can go through a difficult transitional stage as members learn to live with their differing needs for personal space.

How to reduce conflict and dissatisfaction involving personal space needs in your stepfamily

- Acknowledge that all stepfamily members have the right to their personal space—physical *and* psychological.

- Get to know (by talking and asking) what needs different family members have: for example, what is, or what do they want to have as, their personal physical space.

- Be prepared to negotiate if conflict over physical space arises. Also find out as much as you can what psychological space needs people have: for example, time alone, privacy, silence, relaxation and so on.

- Assertively state *your* needs.

- Allow visiting children to have some place that is theirs (a room, a bed, a section of a room, cupboard, shelf, toy box, etc.).

- If you have moved into the previous home of your stepfamily, go slowly and sensitively with changes you make. Communicate with your new family about changes that could be made and your need to have this as your home with your own mark on it.

- Tell your ex-partner that you do not want him or her coming into your home (if it creates problems). Use assertive communication to set your boundaries.

- Parent and stepparent need to make time to be alone together.

- Acknowledge that everyone has an instinctual fear of being rejected or abandoned or left.

- Understand that some people instinctively come closer and others distance themselves when they experience anxiety.

- Give assurance to family members, especially children, that just because you are not living with them, or seeing a lot of them, does not mean you do not love them.

Be encouraged

It takes time for people to learn about the personal space needs of others. It is normal and natural for people to need and protect their personal environment—visible and invisible.

While some behaviors may seem excessively territorial to some people and other behaviors might suggest that "anyone is welcome anywhere, anytime," the important thing to remember is that each person's needs are unique. As such, they need to be respected.

It is also natural for people to keep their distance or draw close to family members at different times and in different ways.

With time, patience, good communication and understanding, situations involving conflict and misunderstanding about boundary issues between family members can be resolved.

Summary

In Chapter 5 we have looked at:

Boundaries
Physical boundaries and personal space in stepfamilies
Psychological boundaries and personal space in stepfamilies
Fear of rejection
Unconscious strategies to reduce fear of rejection
How to reduce conflict and dissatisfaction involving personal space
   needs in your stepfamily

6

It's how I've always done it

Individual habits, attitudes, values and rituals that come into stepfamilies

In Chapter 3 we looked at the force of togetherness and how people are driven to make others become like them. In this chapter we'll look at what it *is* that people try to change in others.

We all have our own package of habits, attitudes, values and rituals which are part of what make us who we are. We started to put this package together in childhood, as the result of experiences in our families of origin, at school, with friends and so on, and we have added to it as the years have gone by. Sometimes we have discarded an item and replaced it with another. These contents have provided a "map" for the way in which we have lived our lives.

When a stepfamily is formed and the people in it have to become accustomed to living with each other, these individual packages, which to a large extent are a representation of who each person *is*, are unfamiliar to those people who have not known or lived with each other before. There's a lot of truth in the saying "You don't know a person until you have lived with him or her."

This lack of familiarity is threatening or, to put it another way, makes people feel uncomfortable, irritated, impatient and so forth. That is why, as you read in Chapter 3, people often try to destroy the uniqueness of each other and attempt to make everyone in their groups, marriages, families and stepfamilies the same as they themselves are (or at least as much as they can).

In so doing they challenge the habits, attitudes, values and rituals of these different people—sometimes in extreme ways. This is what contributes to the curdling process that is (regrettably) so common in stepfamily life.

Some of you may be asking, "Why is this such a problem in stepfamilies? Doesn't this happen in first-time families as well?" The answer to these questions is that yes, it is common in all families, but is a real problem in many stepfamilies because of the added numbers of people involved at the *beginning* of that family life, each of whom come into it with a different package.

We shall now look at each of the unique human qualities that comprise these different packages.

Habits

A habit is a behavior or sequence of behaviors that an organism repeats and which is determined by the situation or goal at hand. Ants have habits, so do birds, dogs, babies, children and adults.

> Paul married Yvonne after having lived alone for two years following his divorce. His children lived with his ex-wife and Paul had regular contact with his children. When he met Yvonne he was sure that she was the one for him and, having met her three daughters who lived with her, he felt very confident about the idea of marriage. They seemed to be very congenial children with whom he felt very relaxed.
>
> Paul and Yvonne had not been married two months before tension appeared in the family home. The girls seemed to distance themselves from him and complained to their mother that Paul irritated them and they hated having him live with them. They didn't like the way he held his knife and fork (even though they had sat at the table together many times before the marriage).
>
> They also didn't like the way he walked around the house in his pajamas until 10 o'clock on Sunday morning. Once or twice one of their friends had stopped by and they felt very embarrassed. Another thing: he burped and they had been taught not to do that, and so on … and so on …
>
> On the other hand, Paul had his gripes, too. One of his stepdaughters kept turning her radio up too loud; another left

the screen door open so that the flies came in, and Yvonne, his wife, put her cosmetics all over the bathroom (or so it seemed).

All of these habits—so natural to each person and familiar to those who had always lived together—became a constant source of irritation in these new and developing relationships.

Habitual behaviors can serve to remind us how different we all are, and when two families are in the process of merging, it can be these that create enormous stress. A habit, however insignificant it may seem, may be so irritating to someone else that a stepfamily can be turned upside down because of it.

People are often unaware of the habits they have. This is because each of us has a blind spot: that part of us that other people know about and we don't. Many people, when told about their blind spots (or even the habits they know they have), feel confronted.

They may react angrily or nurse an inner resentment toward the giver of the information. They might also, at times such as these, unconsciously use defense mechanisms, such as denial or rationalization (see Chapter 2). This stops them from acknowledging that there may be some truth in what they are being told, and thus having to look at themselves.

For example, if the stepdaughters of Paul (in the story above) confront him about his burping, he may say: "I don't burp. That's nonsense!" (denial); or "I have to burp otherwise I get indigestion!" (rationalization). These responses indicate that Paul is unwilling and unlikely to change.

On the other hand, his stepdaughters may respond, when he mentions that loud music bothers him: "It's not loud! It's just that you're not used to it."

You may be thinking these responses are rather typical for all families—and they probably are. However, if stepfamilies are going to get off to a good start (and keep on that track), people in them need to be able to say constructively what bothers them *and* be open to honest feedback.

This doesn't mean that everyone immediately has to change. It just means that gripes and complaints about habits come out into the open and strategies for individual change can now be explored—or, at least, family members can *understand each other's point of view*. That way people open themselves to honest communication. This is the only path toward successful relationships.

Sometimes people know that their habits are irritating to others and deliberately engage in them. Needless to say, this aggressive behavior sends stepfamily life on the downhill track.

Some habits are quite idiosyncratic. All of us, in our own way, have idiosyncrasies—those habitual behaviors (habits) that are peculiar to us. To others they might seem very peculiar, if not irritating, but for us they are comfortable, even if we really don't know why we have them.

Andrew had the strangest way of eating an apple. He would wash it thoroughly, dry it on a dish towel, peel it, cut it into quarters, remove the core, slice each quarter in half, put it all onto a plate and dip each piece in salt. Everyone who saw him eat an apple this way thought it very odd. Did he? Of course not. For him it was the only way to enjoy it.

When we find it difficult to accept and live with people and their unique habits, it is ourselves we need to look at, not the unfamiliar behaviors of others. The more irritated and impatient we are, the greater the problem within *us*.

Acceptance of others and their own uniqueness is a challenge for all of us. The more stepfamily members are able to accept others and *not* try to change them, the more *blended* their family will become. This might sound contradictory but it's true.

Take time

What habits do you think *you* have? Do you know whether they annoy other people? If so, what do you do about this? Do the habits of your partner, family and stepfamily members irritate you or amuse you or drive you crazy? If so, what do you do about your reaction?

Attitudes

Our attitudes are how we think and feel about or toward something. They come from many sources and can change over time and in different life situations. The attitudes that children have about certain things, for instance, are different from those of their parents. They might think that chocolate before going to bed is a good idea, whereas their parents might not.

Attitudes are often associated with different stages of life and are affected by many factors. They cannot be seen, heard or felt, and yet we can know the attitudes of others, just by what they tell us or the way we see them behave.

Attitude changes might occur, for example, in families in which a marriage has ended and one partner becomes a single parent. Extended family members who previously have derided single parenthood may now find that their attitude toward it is different. A woman who said she would never marry again after her failed first marriage may change her attitude later, when a loving relationship has developed with a partner. A man might have scoffed at his male friends who became stepfathers, but when he becomes one himself, his attitude is usually quite different.

Attitudes hold groups together. When people have the same attitudes about aspects of life, it is easier to get along with them and it is this way, too, in family life. When our family members have the same or similar attitudes to us, life seems so much easier. Parents of rebellious adolescents know how differences in attitude between themselves and their children create distance and conflict.

Of course it is not necessary for all family members to have the same attitudes about everything. If this ever existed, it would be an indication of an extremely enmeshed family. What needs to be remembered is this: differences between people are natural and healthy. *It is learning to live with these differences that presents the problem.*

It is interesting how in one family different attitudes can develop (and coexist).

In this next family story you will see how the *mother's attitude* toward sickness affected her two children who, in turn, developed *different attitudes*, which they took into their families when they married.

> Edith was a nurse before she married. When her first child was born, Edith was alert to any sign of a sniffle or probable illness in her baby son, and imagined that he was heading for a bout of pneumonia or some other serious illness. She was sure he would end up in the children's ward of the hospital. She therefore became very protective of him.
>
> When he grew older he decided that he didn't want to be fussed over anymore. He began to ignore signs of sickness in himself and in others, too. As a father he said to his children when they were sick, "You'll be all right, just ignore it." If sick himself, he went off to work however dreadful he felt, and managed to get through his day. He used to boast to his family and friends, "I never get sick."
>
> His attitude was, "It's best to ignore signs of sickness, and get on with life."
>
> On the other hand, his younger brother, who was at the hands of this same overprotectiveness, grew up to be anxious about his own health and that of his family members. A sick child was promptly put to bed, and he always took a day off from work if he felt unwell.
>
> This brother's attitude was, "It's best to be careful and always take every precaution when any sign of sickness is present."

In the example given earlier of Paul and Yvonne and her children, it is possible that Paul's attitude toward the complaints of his step-daughters was, "They have to get used to me." Their attitude toward him might have been, "He has come to live with us and therefore should learn to live as we do."

In raising children, parents usually have similar attitudes about descipline, eating habits, schooling, play, manners and so on. Although parents have been influenced by the attitudes of their family of origin, because of the gradual evolution of their own marriage and their family life over a long period of time, they mostly adapt to each other and change some of the ways they think. This is a normal and healthy process.

Because stepfamilies are instant families, there has been no time for people gradually to get used to each other's attitudes let alone develop similar ones.

One parent believes that children should never be smacked, and his or her partner believes "spare the smack and spoil the child." One child's attitude is that homework is for goody-goodies, and a stepsibling believes that it is actually fun to do. One family's attitude is that a variety of experiences makes life interesting, and the new stepfamily members think that people who always do different things are peculiar—or even unstable.

When a marriage ends—and with it a first-time family or stepfamily—it is often because the attitudes of partners toward many life situations have come into conflict. Sometimes it seems as though separation and divorce is the only solution.

In fact learning to live with others who have different attitudes from ourselves can make life interesting and challenging. We do *not* all have to be the same.

Take time

What attitudes do you have that come from your family of origin? What attitudes have you thought out for yourself in your adult life? What differences in attitudes cause conflict in your stepfamily Would you say you are rigid and inflexible about exploring your attitudes and perhaps about changing some of them? How could you become more flexible? How tolerant are you of other people's attitudes?"

Attitudes are linked to our values, and we will now look at these and the effect they have on our lives.

Values

Our values are the thoughts we have that identify what is important to us and give us the frame of reference for how we live our lives. As with attitudes, we cannot see, hear or feel them.

Sometimes people have difficulty differentiating between attitudes and values. Here are some examples to help you make the distinction:

Attitude: "I will not tolerate untidiness."
Value: "Tidiness is important."

Attitude: "When my stepdaughter wants to talk to me, I always try to be available to talk with her."
Value: "Open and caring relationships are important.

Attitude: "I hate it when you're late."
Value: "Punctuality is important."

Attitude: "We must spend time together."
Value: "My relationship with you is important."

Parents give their children lessons about their own values. These are mostly taught by example or implication. Some commonly held values are honesty, cleanliness, good health, education and friendship.

In stepfamilies it is inevitable that values about some life issues will be different. For example, one person might value family times together, try to arrange such times, and meet with opposition from family members who place no value on this at all. A child might desperately want (value) a dog, only to find himself or herself with a stepparent who wants (value) a pet-free home. A partner might value the occasional vacation away from his or her partner, only to find that a primary value of this partner is to "be together all the time."

Children who come into stepfamilies have values that are primarily those of their previous family unit. Parents and stepparents, too, have been influenced by their first-time marriage and family. While it is true that conflict over values is inevitable between partners, it is also true that it is largely because of a perceived matching of values that they married in the first place. This is what is meant when people say, "We have a lot in common."

Values have varying degrees of strength. We all have a hierarchy of values ranging from those that are major or the most important to those of little or no real importance. When different values of the least important kind exist between people, they are often able to live together quite happily. It is virtually impossible, however, for two opposing sets of "must" values to coexist in a marriage or family with any degree of harmony.

If group or family members do not have major values in common, they will find it difficult to resolve conflict or even stay together as a group.

When major values are shared among family members, they serve as a unifier or bond. They help provide the family with a common direction, common goals, mutually acceptable ways of behaving and even a reason for being.

When we are clear about our values we are clearer about our goals and what we want out of life. We also have a better idea of who we are and what we stand for.

As mentioned in an earlier chapter, some people lack a sense of identity: they don't know *who* they are. For many of them, a lack of major, or "must," values by which to live their lives means they are like corks adrift on the ocean—swept along this way, that way, without any direction.

Values are so significant to us and the meaning of our lives that some people face death—and even die—because of them. Viktor Frankl, in his famous book, *Man's Search for Meaning*, wrote about the role that personal values had with respect to the survival of prisoners in concentration camps during World War II.

Here is a list of values that have been expressed by various people:

education	punctuality
short fingernails	clean feet
pressed shirt	dinners that are meant to be hot to be *hot*
healthy food	freedom
white teeth	straight teeth
fidelity	trust
privacy	order
sharing	a home that looks lived in
cooperation	competition
integrity	the top job in the company
holidays	a hot bath
knowledge	books
jazz	sacred music
spiritual faith	belief in God
relatives	friends
and much more ...	

The list is endless. Some of these values rank highest in a person's value system, and others are of lesser value.

Values and decision making

It is on the basis of our values that we make decisions. Here are two examples:

Keith was finding his third marriage difficult. His wife urged him to attend counseling and at first he refused because he placed a high value on his *privacy*. He did not want to talk to anyone else about his problems. On the other hand, he valued his *relationship* and when he weighed these two values, he decided that of the two, the most important was the relationship. He phoned the next day to make an appointment.

Linda had visions of her new family all spending Christmas together: her husband, his children and hers too. However, as December approached, it became clear that her husband's two oldest children planned to go away for a camping trip the day before. At first she was very upset and put pressure on her husband and his children to do as she wished. Then she explored herself and her values so as to see the situation more clearly and objectively.

When faced with the choice of her values of *family togetherness* and the value of *personal freedom* she had to accept that it was this second value that she valued more highly. Her stepdaughters were delighted when their stepmother told them that she understood their excitement about their trip and their desire to get away before Christmas. She wished them a happy holiday. By doing this, she was helping build positive relationships within this family.

Take time

What do you value most in life? Is there any value you would die for? What similar values do you and your partner and family members have? What differences are there? Is there conflict in your stepfamily over values? Do you get caught up in this? Now ask yourself: "What do I value most: my relationship with X *or* my value with respect to what I want to change?"

It was by asking herself this last question that Linda, in the story above, was able to resolve the issue. Here is another example:

Katie, a new stepmother with no children of her own, could not conceal her agitation when her young stepson put his sticky fingermarks all over her polished furniture. She tried to stop him but that made no difference. She spoke to her husband about it and he said, "Children will be children, he'll grow out of it one day. Leave him alone." What was she to do?

She used the formula above, saying to herself "What do I value most, my relationship with my husband or clean polished furniture?" She decided that the quality of her marriage was far more important than her furniture.

(*Note*: Katie and her husband could also have used conflict resolution skills to help them resolve this issue. (See Chapters 17 and 18.))

The value of peace

Many people are uncomfortable with conflict and do anything to avoid it. They do this for various reasons, but perhaps the most common is that they value peace. This so-called peace is often obtained at a great cost. Frequently this is the cost of a marriage which has failed to function and grow in an honest relationship in which conflict is dealt with openly and constructively using conflict resolution skills.

Rituals

One of the ways in which families hold together and develop an identity is to engage in family rituals. These can become very important and familiar to family members, and are highly resistant to change.

Family rituals may be handed down through many generations. One of the challenges for two people who start to share their lives is to blend all that they bring with them into the relationship—including the rituals that are familiar to them.

> Vivienne was staying with her father for her tenth birthday and woke early in the morning, excitedly anticipating the cup of hot chocolate and toast with jam that would be brought into her while she was still in bed. The whole family would be there, so she thought, and there would be lots of fun as she opened her presents
>
> This was how birthdays were always celebrated in her family. Vivienne waited and waited and nothing happened. Then she heard the rest of the family getting ready for the day and slowly she began to realize that her expectations would not be fulfilled. She was very, very upset. She started to cry. "It's my birthday," she sobbed, "don't they know?" Little did she know that her stepmother had planned a special breakfast for her which was being prepared in the kitchen at that moment. Her stepmother always treated her own children this way on their birthdays.

December holidays are a time when differences between stepfamily members often come into focus. Different ideas about when to open gifts, what sort of meal to have, when to have it, with whom to have it and even which holidays to celebrate can create great distress.

For many people, especially children, holidays are *not* holidays unless experienced in the same familiar way. For them it can be quite traumatic to break with traditions that have been a part of their family life.

There are other rituals, too. Perhaps at the end of each day it has been a ritual in your family to ask, "How was your day?" Or perhaps everyone knows that the first person up is to turn the kettle on, let out the dog and set the table. Day-to-day rituals and special-event rituals all serve to give order and familiarity to individual and family life. Our rituals also give meaning to our lives by being a part of how we live them. That is why it is so hard to let go of them.

When a stepfamily is formed there are more people programmed to value certain rituals—especially extended family members, who often play a part in them. Where both partners live with their children in the stepfamily home, the blending of rituals familiar to each family presents a challenge.

Stepfamilies have many different ways of sorting out these issues. They may decide to do something one way one time and another way another time; for example, "This year we'll have hot turkey in the middle of the day for Christmas and next year we'll have a cold salad." Or they may compromise and decide, "Let's have hot turkey on Christmas Eve and cold salad on Christmas Day."

There needs to be much compromise, discussion, negotiating and communicating to create harmony. At first there may be underlying resentment at having to "give in," but unless members of families are prepared to do this, they are heading for hard times.

For some people, these situations present an "I'll beat you" situation. With that approach there will be no gain, only pain. Stepfamilies need to strive for successful outcomes for all concerned, bearing in mind the dictum: "Give a little to get a little."

Take time

What rituals existed in your family of origin? In your previous marriage(s)? In your current marriage? What do you know about the rituals in your partner's family of origin? Or previous marriage(s)? How does your stepfamily go about sorting out the different rituals and coming to a comfortable agreement about them?

Now that we have looked at the individual packages of habits, attitudes, values and rituals that come into stepfamilies, we can look at some positive ways for you and your family to use these differences for blending—rather than curdling your stepfamily.

Guidelines for living with different habits, attitudes, values and rituals

- Assertively communicate and discuss your differences with family members (using the skills in Chapters 17 and 18). At first this may be very difficult for you to do, and for the others, too, but with practice you'll get used to it.

- Develop an awareness about your package and the history of it.

- Acknowledge that you, too, have habits, idiosyncrasies, attitudes, values and rituals that might be strange or even difficult for others.

- Ask yourself, "what would it be like to live with/be married to me?" (The answer might astound you.)

- See if you can begin to value the uniqueness of the people around you—accept them for who they are, and as they are.

- Learn to compromise—aim for an outcome that satisfies everyone.

- If all of this is too hard and you still want to get your own way all the time, you may need to talk about it with a skilled professional who will probably be able to help you deal with this situation.

In conclusion, take time to reflect upon the reason that people fight so hard to retain and preserve their habits, attitudes, values and rituals. They are what makes us who we are. To relinquish them arouses in us a deep anxiety, "Who will I be without them?"

Be encouraged

All of us can change as we go through life. In fact, that is part of the fun and challenge of living. In stepfamilies there are many challenges, changes and opportunities for growth.

It *is* possible for you and your stepfamily members to get used to each other. With patience and perseverance and the acknowledgment that it takes time, you can reach a point where your stepfamily has an identity of its own, with values, attitudes and rituals unique to it. It is a cliche, but true, that "times does fly by" and if you stay focused on your goal and use new awareness, knowledge and skills, you will get there.

It is this that can encourage you. You have opportunities to contribute to the growth of yourself, others and your stepfamily as well. Believe that!

Summary

In Chapter 6 you have read about what it is in relationships that people try to change. The topics covered were:

    Habits
    Attitudes
    Values

Values and decision making
The value of peace
Rituals
Guidelines for living with different habits, attitudes, values
    and rituals

7

It's all one big mess

Emotions in stepfamilies

Different emotional responses

All of us experience emotions. These are the responses to thoughts and events in our daily lives that we know as grief, joy, fear, anger, hate or love, and which are described by many different words. Here are some words that people use to express their emotions or feelings:

Grief: I feel sad, devastated, bereaved, depressed, down, upset, distressed, distraught, broken-hearted, miserable, dismal, melancholy, dejected, grief-stricken...

Joy: I feel excited, happy, elated, ecstatic, content, delighted, exhilarated, cheerful, glad, joyful...

Fear: I feel terrified, scared, anxious, uneasy, petrified, concerned, worried, frightened, horrified, fearful, misgiving...

Anger: I feel furious, irritated, annoyed, mad, outraged, resentful, hostile, incensed, infuriated, rankled, exasperated, angry...

Hate: I loathe, hate, detest, abhor, am disgusted...

Love: I like, care for, love, adore, admire, respect, idolize...

These six basic emotions are experienced in varying degrees of intensity and they are in a way a "barometer" of what is happening (or has happened) in our lives.

Depending on how we are feeling at any particular moment or period of time, we evaluate the quality of our lives, for instance, "I'm so happy—life is great!" or "I feel so upset—life is not worth living."

What we *do* with our lives is often determined by how we feel, for instance, "I feel so down—I can't go to work," or "I'm so angry—I'm going to leave him," or "I love her so much—I'm going to marry her."

Unless we are unconscious, or mentally incapacitated, we feel something. We can even be emotional in our sleep! Sometimes we have no control over our emotions and may cry uncontrollably, laugh hysterically, be gripped with fear, filled with loathing, be overcome with passion or explode in anger.

Some people are more emotional than others. This is part of their inherited character. They are more sensitive to what is happening in and around them, and they experience emotional responses more frequently than do other people, and/or with greater intensity.

On the other hand, there are people who are almost feelingless or emotionless. Again, this is partly inherited or they may have unconsciously suppressed their emotions, because to express them was too threatening or more than they could bear. For example, some children know that it is not safe to express their anger and rage, and instead hold it in— sometimes for the rest of their lives. Some people hold in grief after the loss of a loved one. *When people stop one emotion from being released, they actually inhibit all of their emotions.*

(*Note*: The "love" goes out of many marriages because of unexpressed anger between partners.)

Emotions are often referred to as being positive or negative. This idea infers that love and joy are positive (because they feel good and do no harm) and fear, anger, grief and hate are negative (because they don't feel good or can harm others).

In fact, *every* emotion is positive, and needs to be acknowledged and expressed because when this doesn't happen, people lose part of themselves.

It is the way in which emotions are expressed that can be positive or negative—not the emotions themselves. For example, anger can be released destructively so that people, relationships or objects are damaged (negative outcome). Or it can be expressed constructively, using assertive communication skills (positive outcome).

We will now look at different ways in which anger is destructively dealt with in stepfamilies, and thus hinders the blending process.

How anger stops stepfamilies from blending

The failure to deal constructively and honestly with anger is the cause of most relationship breakdowns: between friends, marriage partners and family members.

In stepfamilies, unexpressed or unresolved anger from a previous marriage or family is likely to prevent new relationships from thriving.

This anger is sometimes displaced onto new stepfamily members, who don't realize that the anger that is directed at them is really not *meant* for them. The person displacing this anger often does not realize that he or she is doing this either.

Partners, natural children and stepchildren may be the senders *and/or* receivers of these displaced expressions of anger. The cat or dog can also be on the receiving end of this unfinished business!

There are many ways in which unresolved anger from the first-time family can affect members of stepfamilies. For example, an ex-partner or ex-relative may take out his or her anger by hassling over visiting times for children, who are often caught in the cross fire between adults.

Many parents and children know the arguments that can ensue over making arrangements for visit days and holidays.

Ex-partners go at each other in many different ways to deal with their anger. Sometimes money is withheld, plans are sabotaged, or a partner refuses to constructively discuss the welfare of his or her children.

There is an especially damaging way in which anger (of an ex-spouse) is often used against a former partner.

Rita was devastated when, 15 years ago, her husband Leo left her to live with another woman. At that time her four children were from ages 10 to 16. After a while, her 15-year-old son went to live with Leo and his new partner, who subsequently married each other.

Occasionally the other children stayed in their new stepfamily home and enjoyed the company of their new stepsiblings. After one year of marriage Leo and his second wife had their own child—a half-brother for the two sets of children.

This filled Rita, Leo's ex-wife, with rage and jealousy, and she started a campaign to "turn the children against their father." Now, after many years of this campaign, out of Rita's four children only one daughter has anything to do with Leo or his family.

The sadness that has come over Leo because of the way his own children have rejected him has adversely affected his marriage and stepfamily relationships. He has plunged into a depression he cannot shake off.

(*Note*: Depression is often the result of anger that is turned inward and about which a person has no awareness. People are often helped by getting professional assistance when they cannot shake off a depressed state of mind.)

Other members of Leo's family have also been affected by Rita's actions. His young son by his second marriage misses the half-siblings he grew to love (perhaps this is why he is misbehaving at school). The children in this stepfamily have cut their own father out of their lives.

Rita has tried to deal with her own anger by manipulating her children to reject their father. In so doing she has sacrificed the emotional well-being of her own children to try to help herself feel better.

(*Note*: What Rita did is evidence that she has not emotionally let go of Leo. (Remember the emotional glue?) If she is to get on with her life and find happiness and peace of mind, it is necessary for her to deal with her own unfinished business.)

Children often bring anger into stepfamilies because they, like Rita, have not let go of their emotional involvement with their first family.

The fact that they are taken into a stepfamily situation following a parent's remarriage brings home the reality that their original family has gone forever. Their anger often masks great sadness.

It is very common for children to take out their anger on a new stepparent—even if prior to the marriage the relationship seemed to be going along well.

Children can make life very difficult for their stepsiblings, too, whom they may see as rivals for their own parent's affection. This is one way they can mask their fear of losing their own parent's love or recognition.

(*Note*: Anger is like this. It is not always as it seems. It can mask sadness, fear and hate in many different ways, or can be masked by other emotions, especially by what appears to be grief.)

Stepparents, in learning to live with their new stepchildren, often find themselves angry because these children do not behave as they want, or do things the way their own children have been raised to do, or the way they were reared themselves. (Remember the negative behaviors of the togetherness force.)

Another reason for anger in stepfamilies is because of guilt. It is not uncommon for partners to be troubled and ashamed, sometimes for years, about having left a former partner and children. The accompanying guilt is often masked (unconsciously) by anger, which may be directed at a partner and stepchildren—or anyone else, for that matter.

In stepfamilies there are often situations in which stepfamily members feel left out. In Chapter 5 we looked at psychological boundaries and how people can be excluded or pushed out of groups.

Parents often pull together with their own children, or take their side. This can leave a stepparent feeling excluded, especially if he or she doesn't have children living in the stepfamily home. At times like this, a stepparent may feel quite angry—often not knowing why.

Stepfamilies can be adversely affected if the relationship between a partner and his or her "ex" threatens the current partner. Some ex-partners maintain a congenial relationship (often "for the sake of the children") and this sometimes arouses jealousy in a new partner, whose anger hides the real emotion—fear.

Extended family members, too, may be angry toward a son-in-law or daughter-in-law who they see as the cause of the breakup of the original first family. This often affects their relationship with their grand-children, nephews, nieces and cousins.

The way in which this anger is expressed may alienate them from the parent of the children, who decides to stop the children from seeing them or speaking to them.

(*Note*: When anger is dealt with aggressively, everyone loses. In Chapters 17 and 18 you will learn more about anger and how to deal with it con-structively.)

Take time

In your stepfamily, who gets angry? How do you know this? In what way do these people show their anger? What do you do when you are angry? What situations seem to cause anger in your stepfamily? What strategies, if any, have your stepfamily members taken to resolve anger constructively? How do you handle anger in yourself and in others?

Now that we have looked at some of the ways in which anger stops stepfamilies from blending, we shall take a look at another emotion which wields great power in stepfamilies. This is the emotion of fear.

The role of fear in stepfamilies

There are many fears and anxieties that people bring into stepfamilies. Some of these are in their conscious awareness, others are not. For in-stance, a partner may *know* that she or he fears another failed marriage; another person may avoid conflict, unaware that the reason for this is because of an *unknown* fear of a failed marriage. In either case, the effect on stepfamily life can be devastating.

Jenna and Barry had been married for nine years—each for the second time. Jenna's son, age 17, and their own daughter, age 7, lived with them. Since about the sixth year of their marriage,

Barry had directed frequent bouts of aggression at his family members—as well as at the doors, furniture and other possessions! Jenna was close to the breaking point and seriously thinking of leaving Barry.

After much searching and professional counseling, Jenna and Barry realized that their marriage had never really been successful. They rarely had any fun together. They had never engaged in honest communication, and issues were rarely resolved. Instead, they were afraid to be honest for fear of upsetting each other and thereby destroying their marriage.

Barry was also afraid to relate honestly and assertively with his stepson (for example, if he wanted to ask him not to do something), because he was afraid that Jenna would get angry.

All of this resulted in a family of four "strangers" living together in one house. They did not know each other or relate well with each other. This was not the dream of a happy family that Barry and Jenna had when they married. Their fear that this marriage and family would fail, as each of their first ones had, made them behave in ways that almost *did* bring about the failure of their second marriage.

(*Note*: Our fears are often linked to *self-fulfilling prophesies*. These are beliefs we have that something is going to happen, and about which we are afraid. They are often based on a belief that what happened in the past will repeat itself. Our fear makes us behave in certain ways that are supposed to prevent this thing from happening but actually *make* it happen!)

Ivan married his second wife believing that his stepchildren would never get used to him. This made him awkward around them and he decided to keep his distance and not bother them.

This belief became a self-fulfilling prophesy because, as time passed, his stepchildren gave up trying to be friendly with him. He made it too difficult and eventually they decided it wasn't worth trying to relate to him.

Children and adults often come into their new stepfamilies feeling anxious and wondering how everything is going to work out. Many stepparents wonder of they are "up to the job" of parenting children who are not their own. If things go badly from the start, their anxiety is heightened: "What have I gotten myself into? How am I going to do it?"

Children are less likely to realize that the strange and uneasy feelings they have are those of fear. Change, or even the thought of it, commonly brings out feelings of anxiety in most of us.

Children are often anxious about further loss of contact with the absent parent now that they have another "father" or "mother." If their new home is further away from their absent parent, their anxiety may be very realistic.

Children's divided loyalties between parent and stepparent

One of the reasons that stepchildren do not relate favorably to their stepparent is because they are emotionally torn between this person and the natural parent of that sex. The idea of being true to both of these people can create great anxiety. It's as though the child reasons: "If I love my stepmother, then that will mean I don't love (or can't love) my own mother." The way a child deals with this dilemma is often to reject the stepparent. Sometimes children are rejecting of their natural parent in favor of their stepparent.

> Anna lived with her mother and stepfather up to the time of her wedding and had, over the previous 10 years, developed a strong relationship with her stepfather. They were really good friends and spent many hours discussing mutual career interests. She saw very little of her father, who lived far away. She often told her family that she loved her stepfather more than her father.
>
> However, when the plans for her wedding were being made, she decided that not only did she want her father to give her away, but she did not want her stepfather to participate in the wedding celebrations at all. She became cold and distant toward the stepfather she had loved so much for many years.

The issue of divided loyalties is one that often bewilders and hurts parents and stepparents. Children, too, are troubled by the complex emotions that they experience and which drive them to behave in this way. It helps if adults understand this process and are patient and nonjudgmental. When time and space are allowed and force not applied, children usually sort these things out and learn to relate comfortably to both parent and stepparent.

If the parent with whom they live seems to be paying more attention to his or her new partner than to them, children may feel left out, alone and scared. (Of course, the reality is that whenever a stepfamily is formed and children have had a parent to themselves for some time within a single-parent household, they have to relinquish the exclusive access they had to this parent.)

On the other hand, there are partners who enter into stepfamily life with someone who has children living with them and come to an early conclusion that they are outsiders and can never belong to this existing family. Panic may overcome them as they think, "Help! Get me out of here!" This reaction usually passes, but at the time it can be very frightening.

If conflict is unresolved in stepfamilies, especially between partners, the tension that results can arouse deep anxiety in children who, like in the family of Barry and Jenna, fear the end of another family. Deep feelings of insecurity can make children withdraw, rebel or behave in other ways that reflect distress.

One of the reasons that people don't deal with issues in their relationships is that they are frightened of conflict. This fear of conflict often means that people become conflict avoiders, and in avoiding conflict they actually create more of it. Barry and Jenna did this. Do you?

The failure to deal with anger because of fear of the consequences is one of the major causes of relationship failure.

Marriage therapists can tell countless stories of couples who seek help for their marriage and, while sitting in the therapist's room, tell of all the things they have been angry about in their relationship.

Have they honestly told each other these things? Have they tried to talk these issues through? You probably know the answer to these questions.

Take time

Are you aware of anyone in your stepfamily being afraid of anyone or anything? Are you afraid? If you have fears or anxieties, what do you do to deal with them? Think about yourself and whether or not you are aware of being afraid of anger. Think very carefully and ask yourself the questions: "In my childhood, how did I react when people were angry with me?" "How do I feel inside now, when people are angry with me?" "What do I do when I am angry with others?"

(*Note*: There is another reason why people don't deal constructively with anger in their relationships. It is because they don't know how to go about it. Specific communication skills are necessary for conflict resolution, and in Chapters 17 and 18 you will learn how to use them.)

The effects of grief on stepfamily life

Stepfamilies are families that are born of loss. At least one of the partners has lost a previous partner because of death or divorce. Children are involved in these losses, too.

The blending of stepfamilies is often made more difficult because of the grief that stepfamily members still feel about their earlier losses. This unresolved and resurfacing grief, which can manifest itself in many different ways, prevents new stepfamily members from entering wholeheartedly into new relationships.

As we have seen, grief can be masked by other emotions, as well as by behaviors. Children, for instance, may show anger (a feeling or emotion) or keep distant from a new stepparent (behavior). There are many different ways in which grief or sadness inhibits the blending of stepfamilies.

Children nearly always hope for reconciliation between their separated or divorced parents. When one of them remarries, children often feel sad as they face the reality of the family breakup.

Stepfamily life may bring out sadness in children who, because there are now two "parents," may be painfully reminded of a parent who is absent—especially if he or she has died. They may long deeply for the old times.

Sometimes, when a child hopes or expects a stepparent to fill the void, grief and anger follow when the child realizes this can never happen.

Other times, when a stepparent moves into the family home of the deceased parent and starts to make changes in the way the home is furnished and decorated, children (of all ages) are confronted again with the reality of their parent's death. The accompanying grief, even if the parent died years earlier, can be very painful for them.

When children have to say goodbye after spending time with a parent who does not live with them anymore, it is very common for them to feel upset. Small children may cry, older children may act tough, but all of them, especially in the early days, find this a very difficult time.

Even though these "goodbye" experiences become a familiar part of life, if the parent remarries and has stepchildren living with him or her, they often feel sad when they realize that other children are living with their own parent.

Parents, too, can experience overwhelming sadness when they have to part from their own children at the end of visiting times. Whether or not this stepfamily life is happy, these times can always be wrenching.

Stepfamily life frequently involves leaving *many* parts of life behind. Homes, schools and jobs may change, relatives who were once part of life fade into the distance, friends are left behind and a door closes on much that was familiar.

This is something that most people feel sad about. Usually time takes care of these emotional responses, which are, in most cases, healthy and part of the healing process.

Now that we have looked at some of the ways anger, fear and grief affect stepfamilies, we are going to take a further look at anger. This emotion often controls our lives, and a better understanding of how it operates gives us the opportunity to control it—rather than it controlling us!

Understanding more about anger

Some of you may be thinking, "I never get angry." If this is so, it is probably because you were trained by others, or yourself, to block out awareness of your anger. As a child you may have lived in a family that had a spoken or unspoken rule (or injunction): "don't be angry" or "don't feel" or perhaps you lived in a family riddled with anger and had made a childhood decision to deny and avoid it.

> Austin grew up with three sisters, all older than himself. He used to hate it when they fought—it aroused all kinds of anxiety in him. This was mainly because his father used to get very angry and send all the children off to bed, and his mother used to cry and withdraw when this happened.
>
> This left Austin feeling very worried about his mother and scared of his father *and* of anger! He made a childhood decision never to feel angry himself and to avoid conflict at all cost.
>
> His first marriage failed because he was so emotionally dead that his wife never felt connected to him (remember that when one emotion is stopped the others are inhibited) and he avoided conflict so that issues were never resolved.
>
> Austin subsequently remarried and his second wife, too, found that she could not raise issues with him or express her anger to him. She felt emotionally distant and this made her isolated in her marriage, and more angry than ever.

When different stepfamily members start to live together or get to know each other, they usually discover that each one has different ways of dealing with anger. Some seethe for days, some explode like a summer thunderstorm, some use aggressive behaviors, some use assertive communication skills and others are like Austin: they don't seem to get angry at all.

Children who are not used to explosions of anger often feel very frightened if a stepparent deals with anger this way. They may recoil when they are confronted by, or witness, these unfamiliar outbursts of anger. Their parent may become protective of them and scared of, and/or angry toward, the new partner.

Emotional outbursts such as these are often "knee-jerk" reactions and are sometimes referred to as "twitches."

Emotional overreactivity

The following examples illustrate how suddenly emotion can take over and control a person's behavior. This *emotional overreactivity* usually has its origins in childhood experiences that have long since been forgotten. It's as though we are computers and an old program is reactivated when the right (or wrong) button is pushed. That is why people sometimes say, "You pushed the wrong button."

> Kate tried to tell her husband, the stepfather to her sons, that she was nervous about them going away with him on a camping trip. As he was an experienced scout leader, he took this as an insult and exploded with rage at what he interpreted as a suggestion that he was incompetent and careless.

(*Note*: Kate's husband grew up with an irresponsible father and had resolved to be super-responsible himself when he grew up. Kate's remarks suggested to him (at an unconscious level) that he was irresponsible like his father. One of Kate's husband's major twitch reactors is when he interprets a situation as one in which he is judged or thought to be irresponsible.)

> Al decided to make an apple pie—the sort his mother used to make. When his wife corrected him as he rolled the pastry, he suddenly let out a string of angry words. He twitched.

(*Note*: As a child Al was always picked on by his older sister for not doing things the right way. When his wife gave him advice about his pastry making, his unconscious self hurtled back to childhood and the rage he used to feel toward his sister, who used to be so critical of him. Al often twitches when he is criticized or *thinks* he is being criticized.)

Here is another story that illustrates how unfinished business from childhood comes back to haunt people and their relationships:

> Linda and Max had been married six years and lived alone. They each had children who lived with their respective ex-partners. Once a month each set of children came to stay, and once a year they all had two weeks' vacation together.
>
> Things went fairly smoothly, except on the occasions when Max's 12-year-old son made a funny face when dinner was placed before him. When that happened Linda could not contain her fury. It just welled up inside her!
>
> She tried to tell herself that she was immature, that it didn't matter if occasionally one 12-year-old boy was critical of her cooking, or that he was only with her for a short time.

(*Note*: She was a victim of unfinished business from her childhood. Her reaction seemed out of all proportion to the event. That is what emotional overreactivity is all about.)

Linda sought professional help and learned that the reason for her extreme behavior lay in her childhood. She brought to her conscious awareness, by talking and thinking, the fact that as a child her younger brother often taunted her by making a funny face. Her reaction to Max's son was really the reaction she had to her brother some 30 years earlier.

From a therapeutic point of view, this unfinished business needed to be dealt with for Linda not to twitch anymore in this situation.

Take time

Do you ever react with a sudden surge of anger? (This may be irritation, annoyance or even rage.) Do other people in your stepfamily twitch? Can you detect themes to your twitching pattern? What about emotional triggers in other members of your stepfamily?

How to deal with your emotional twitches

1. Think about all the times you twitch emotionally and try to find a pattern. For example, in Linda's case, did she have a similar reaction whenever people seemed to make fun of her or tease her? These reactions might all be connected to the same situation with her brother, when she felt belittled and unvalued.

2. Ask yourself: "When did I feel this way as a child? Who was there? What was happening?"

3. Then say to yourself, "The emotion I feel when I twitch is ..."

4. Think about what happens when you twitch. How do you behave?

5. *Resolve* to stop and think next time you find yourself in a situation in which your twitch button is pressed.

6. Then (and this is the hard part) next time you feel these familiar emotions surging, *stop and think* and act out of your thoughts rather than your feelings. Say to yourself something like, "I'm reacting to old history—this is *here* and *now* and I have the power to respond differently."

Transference

Transference is a term used to describe a type of displacement of emotional reaction which contaminates our feelings toward other people. We are all inclined, at times, to displace positive or negative emotion onto someone who reminds us (unconsciously) of someone else from our past life experiences.

Our emotional responses of the past are deeply ingrained. Every part of our being is trained to react automatically. For that reason we have very little control over these responses until we become conscious of where these emotional overreactions originated. Furthermore, taking control of these automatic knee-jerk reactions takes a long time.

In stepfamilies we often see a husband responding to his new wife as he would to his mother or previous partner. Wives do the same sort of thing. A certain kind of behavior, even a look or body gesture, can be the stimulus that unconsciously triggers an old emotional reaction.

Jason is a good example of how transference can be devastating to a new relationship. His first wife was always on the lookout for a sign or cue that he did not really love her. When they went to a party she watched how other women related to him. If one of them was overly friendly from his first wife's perspective, there would be a flood of distrustful accusations on the way home from the party.

In his second marriage, to Sheila, he would become anxious if he saw her glancing at him even fleetingly at a party. The fear that he would be confronted by her on the way home flooded him. The result was that he distanced himself from other women, talked only to men and then built up resentment for no reason at all. Later, an argument often occurred due to the buildup of tension based only on his unnecessary fear.

This is a typical way in which transference operates. The significant persons of the present are unconsciously perceived as being like key people from the past. Instead of seeing the important persons of the present as unique and different, there is a damaging contamination which prevents people from starting out with a clean slate and forgetting past hurts.

Most stepfamily situations have times when this unfortunate kind of anxiety arises and there is unnecessary misunderstanding. This highlights the true fact that it takes a long time, in many cases, just to understand why things go wrong between two people who love each other and have no ill intent at all.

Parents sometimes take out emotions on their children because they remind them of someone else—a father, mother, sibling or, especially in stepfamilies, an ex-spouse. Stepparents, too, may do this to their stepchildren who remind them of their parent's ex-partner.

Emotional responses can take people unaware. The more you do some thinking and try to discover *why* you react as you do, the better off everyone will be.

When we understand why we overreact emotionally, we can control our emotions rather than them controlling us.

Guidelines for dealing with emotions in your stepfamily

- Acknowledge and accept that emotions are real—and that *everyone* in your stepfamily has them.

- Encourage family members to express their emotions, preferably by talking about them, even if this is after the emotion itself has been openly expressed.

- Do not be judgmental of the emotional responses of others.

- Know that emotions are about something—try to understand what is behind the emotion you feel yourself, or you perceive in others.

- Accept and believe that anger does not cancel out love—it is part of loving.

- Be patient with the emotional pain of others.

- Be aware that one emotion can masquerade as another.

- Do the "Take time" assignments in this chapter.

- Acknowledge emotions in family members by saying such things as "You really are angry that Dad forgot your birthday. I can see that and I understand that must feel dreadful for you." "I know it's hard to say goodbye, it's hard for me too. I'll be thinking of you and look forward to being with you again." "My children are really giving you a hard time. I don't blame you for feeling upset and angry." "I can imagine how scary it must be for you to have stepchildren when you've never had anything to do with children before."

Be encouraged

Our emotional responses reflect and influence our relationships. In stepfamilies, as in all families, different expressions of different emotions are part of what makes that family the way it is.

Although this chapter hasn't talked about the emotions of love and joy, many adults and children in stepfamilies feel this way, some of them often! There can be lots of laughter, fun times and much affection and warm caring, all of which is evidence of, and contributes to, a blending stepfamily.

This chapter talked about emotions that are evidence of, and contribute to, a curdling stepfamily *if they are not recognized and constructively dealt with.*

The best way to deal with these emotions in our relationships is to learn to talk about them. Skills are required to do this in a way that is constructive and, in the case of stepfamily life, contributes to the blending process.

Reference has been made already to Chapters 17 and 18, which set out assertive communication skills to help you talk about your own emotions. These skills also help you to help others deal with their emotions by assertively talking things through.

If both partners learn how to use these skills, stepfamily life is greatly enhanced. It's not that you and your family cease to *feel*; it's just that feelings or emotions of family members need not inhibit the growth of your stepfamily.

Summary

In this chapter we looked at emotions that commonly are experienced in stepfamilies:

Different emotional responses
How anger stops stepfamilies from blending
The role of fear in stepfamilies
Children's divided loyalties between parent and stepparent.
The effects of grief on stepfamily life
Understanding more about anger
Emotional overreactivity
How to deal with your emotional twitches
Transference
Guidelines for dealing with emotions in your stepfamily

8

I thought when we married...

Spoken, unspoken and hidden contracts; family rules

Most people know that in many areas of life, contracts are drawn up and signed. This means that certain conditions have been agreed to and are legally binding.

Most people, however, are unaware that apart from the legal contract of marriage, there exists contracts in every couple relationship. (They also exist between people in other types of relationships.) These contracts are either spoken, unspoken or unconscious.

Three different contracts in relationships

1. The *spoken contract* involves a verbal agreement between the people making the contract. Negotiation and compromise are often necessary before agreement is reached.

2. The *unspoken contract* is not talked about and instead involves an assumption on the part of one or both partners that there is a particular contract or agreement. These contracts frequently cause conflict and unhappiness in relationships, because people believe they are as legitimate as spoken contracts. They often involve unrealistic expectations.

3. The *unconscious contract* lies hidden, unbeknown to the person who has it. It is the underlying cause of many behaviors, many of which destroy a relationship. When this contract comes to conscious awareness (usually involving an "insight" experience), it loses its power.

Spoken contracts in stepfamilies

By the time a stepfamily is created, most step-couples have done some talking about how they will live together. Whether they have verbally *agreed* to certain aspects of their stepfamily lifestyle is another matter. Nevertheless, there are usually at least some spoken contracts between them and, to a lesser extent, between them and their children and stepchildren. Here are some spoken contracts that may exist in stepfamilies:

- When we marry we'll share the household duties.

- Your children will come to stay every second weekend.

- I'll discipline my children myself—you are not to do it.

- When your children stay they can choose what they want to do.

- We'll have a child of our own once everyone has settled down.

- We'll each put in equal amounts of money for housekeeping.

- You'll pay the electricity and telephone bills and I'll pay the insurance.

- If we feel unhappy, we'll tell each other and talk about it.

- We'll present a united front to the children.

- When your children have special days, such as birthdays, graduation, sports days, concerts … you will go without me and be with your ex-wife/ex-husband on those occasions.

- We'll make arrangements to get away alone for two weeks every year.

Spoken contracts between partners and children may be:

- You can go to stay with your father the first weekend of every month.

- Once we are settled, I'll buy you a new bed.

- You don't have to change schools unless you want to.

- Your stepmother will not come into your room.

- I'm not trying to take the place of your father.

- Tell me the foods you don't like and I won't give them to you.

Even though spoken contracts have been discussed and agreed upon, many couples find, with the passage of time and all that happens in it, that contracts between stepfamily members are too hard to keep, are forgotten or turn out to be the wrong contract! In other words, these contracts are broken. And, of course, it only takes *one* person to break a contract.

> Walter and Sharon were in total agreement prior to their marriage. They would share household duties when they started their stepfamily life. They agreed that, after all, it was only fair, as each one of them would have their two children living with them and both had long and tiring days at work.
>
> At first things went well. There was equitable sharing between Walter and Sharon of all the jobs that had to be done. The children were young but did their bit to help. Six months later, however, things changed. Sharon seemed to be doing much more than her share and her resentment and anger were escalating by the day. The contract she had made with Walter was broken.
>
> What did she do about this? She talked to Walter and told him how she was feeling about this, but all that happened was that he got angry. No conflict resolution here!
>
> She went on strike, thinking that would shake him, but all it did was make things worse. The house got messier and the jobs piled up.
>
> She threatened to leave if he didn't shape up. All she got from him was an angry tirade and a list of reasons why he had to work late at the office, how exhausted he was, how her kids were more work than his and so on...

Walter and Sharon had a lot of work to do to get their marriage and stepfamily life on track—in addition to the housework!

Let's consider their situation: is their conflict really about housework and sharing of duties? Probably not. The issues probably go a lot deeper than this and need to be understood before they can live happily together.

For example, Walter might have a deep (unconscious) fear of becoming unmanly if he engages in household tasks; he might have an unconscious contract that wants him to be looked after by his wife; he might want to take out all the anger on Sharon that he still has toward his first wife; or he might want to get the promotion at work and want to be seen as working extra hours. There are countless possible reasons for Walter's breaking of the contract.

In a case such as this professional help may be needed, unless Walter and Sharon learn, and use, conflict resolution skills. This will involve Walter and Sharon in making a spoken contract to learn and then use these skills.

(*Warning*: Never try to analyze other people and say, for example, "I know the real reason why you don't help me around the house, it is because you..." This only leads to more trouble.)

If you want to explore anyone, explore yourself. For instance, Sharon could ask herself, "What reasons might there be for my angry reaction to Walter when he doesn't help?" This way, Sharon is on the way to developing self-awareness and being involved in her own personal growth.

Sharon might also say to Walter, "We made a contract. What do you suppose is the deeper reason why it is so difficult for you to keep your word?" By doing this she is inviting him to *think* rather than *emote* (over-react emotionally).

Some people write down the contracts they make with each other. They review them from time to time, maybe amending them by mutual consent or replacing them with new ones. This strategy ensures commitment and can be a beneficial building block for a relationship.

Take time

What spoken contracts do you have with your partner, children, stepchildren? How successfully are these adhered to? If they are not, what do you think happens to stop this?

Unspoken contracts in stepfamilies

- I'll be the best stepmother/stepfather a child could have.

- I'll teach him/her (my stepchild) how to behave.

- I'll be a better husband/wife to you than your first one was.

- I'm not going to put myself out for these kids.

- I'll make it up to the children now that I am remarried.

- My partner is not going to have any say in how I raise my children.

- I will stick by my own children no matter what happens.

- My children are more important to me than my partner is.

- You'll learn to do things the way I like them done.

- You'll learn to parent my children the way I want you to.

- If things don't work out, I'll leave.

- You will look after me and provide for me.

- You will maintain my house the way my first husband/wife used to.

- I'll marry you and inherit all your money when you die.

- I'll marry you and live in your nice house.

- You'll love me even more than you loved your first partner.

- You won't drink as much when I am married to you.

- I'll cook healthy food when we are married, and you'll lose weight.

- Your children will learn manners when I'm their stepmother/ stepfather.

Many of these are potentially explosive! Some of them involve hidden agendas (secret plans that a person has) to meet his or her own needs. They can result in manipulating behaviors that are not understood by a partner, and create distance and distrust. Unspoken contracts frequently involve assumptions that certain things will happen. If they don't, there is often bitter disappointment with accompanying anger.

> Nadia had the unspoken contract, "You will love me more than you loved your first wife," when she married Hans. She had heard about Hans's first marriage and the way his wife had left him. Hans still grieved over the loss of his wife and children and Nadia often noticed him looking sad and withdrawn. She was sure he was thinking about his ex-partner and was determined to help him get over this loss.
>
> It seemed to her that the best way to help him was to try to get him to love her more than he loved his first wife. Actually, the real reason she had this hidden agenda, or unspoken contract, was that if she believed that Hans loved her more than he loved his first wife, that would mean to her that she must be a "better" person.
>
> However hard she tried to be a perfect wife, she failed to shake Hans out of his depression. She became angry. Her unspoken contract was not being fulfilled and she felt like a failure.

Many (maybe most) stepparents try to earn the affection and respect of their stepchildren. Sometimes, though, they want to show the absent natural parent of these children and even their partner that they can fill a *parental* role. Some stepparents have a hidden agenda to "win" their stepchildren by showing that they are better parents than the other natural parent. This usually backfires.

In other cases, stepparents know all along, deep inside, that their stepchildren will always take second place to their own children. (This is an unspoken contract.) This may be a reasonable and honest attitude, but when a spoken contract is made with a partner, such as, "I will love and care for your children in the same way I do for my own," these conflicting contracts can lead to confusion and conflict.

Many unspoken contracts involve plans to change people. Countless couples are in conflict because one is trying to change the other. (Remember the force of togetherness.) These unspoken contracts are kept very secret in the courtship stage of a relationship and are only acted upon when the relationship is older. When efforts are made to change people, they usually resist. Adults and children usually resist when they perceive that pressure is being put on them to change. (Remember the force of separateness.)

Take time

What unspoken contracts do you have with your partner, children, stepchildren? What stops you from bringing these contracts out into the open? What conflict do they cause?

Unconscious contracts in stepfamilies

- I'll lose respect for you if you are not nice to my children.
- I want you to be the kind of mother/wife that my mother was.
- I want you to be the kind of father/husband that my father was.
- I'll make love to you if you spend time with me, and me alone.
- I want you to prove to me you love me.
- If your child monopolizes our relationship, I'll leave.
- My house is mine and don't ever think it is yours.
- I need to have time alone.
- If you try to control me, I'll try to control you.
- If you are kind to my children, I'll love you all the more.
- You will like my friends and they will like you.
- I will always be closest to my own children.

- When it really comes down to it, I'll do my own thing, whatever you might want me to do.

- I'll resist any attempt on your part to make me the same as you.

- Deep down I don't really trust men/women, so I'll be cautious with you.

- I'll never have conflict in my home the way my parents did.

- I'll never get so close to you that I could be hurt.

Our unconscious contracts are not known to us, yet they can come into our conscious awareness in different ways and at different times. People may become aware of them quite suddenly or after much thinking and exploration. When people seek professional help for difficult life situations, they are often amazed to discover that their lives have been directed by hidden and unknown life decisions and beliefs.

> Marie was very pleased for Glenn to move into her home when they married. He had moved out of his own family home, where his ex-wife and children still lived. Marie was a widow, her husband having died 10 years earlier. When Glenn moved in, there were many maintenance jobs that needed to be done around the house and garden. She was delighted to see him so eager to help and assisted him whenever she could. After 10 years of being alone, it was wonderful to have a partner again and life seemed to be full of joy.
>
> She was shocked, therefore, to find herself feeling very angry when she discovered that Glenn had cleared out the old shed and taken all the junk to the garbage dump. She realized that she had an unconscious contract: "Everything that is in this house and garden is mine and my permission must be granted if any changes are to be made." Until Glenn had cleared out the junk without asking her, she had not realized she had this contract.
>
> Now that it was out in the open, she explained to Glenn why she was angry, and they were able to establish a spoken contract that would guide future behavior with respect to this issue.

Unconscious contracts can often only be detected by thinking and observing patterns of behavior and what you *do* in your relationships.

Take time

What unconscious contracts that you have had have come into your awareness during your life? Have you become aware of any in your closest relationships? If you have, how have you dealt with them once you became aware of them?

Children and contracts in stepfamilies

Children, too, make contracts. Some of these may be:

- I'll make it so difficult for you that you'll leave (unspoken).
- I want you to love me like my mother who died loved me (unconscious).
- You'll never take the place of my father (unspoken).
- I'll make you pay for leaving us (unspoken).
- I'll keep in touch even though we don't live together (spoken).
- I'll be good and then I'll get what I want (unspoken).
- If ever you neglect to keep in touch, I'll reject you (unconscious).
- I want you to love me more than you love my brothers and sisters (unconscious).
- I'll phone you whenever I have something important to tell you (spoken).
- I'll act out at school and wherever I can, and that will make you pay attention to me (unconscious).
- I will be nasty to my stepbrother (unspoken).

Samuel, age 11, expected to hear from his mother the day before he was to give his speech at school. He waited by the phone until late into the evening expecting her to call. He tried to phone her but there was no answer. The next morning he set off for school anticipating seeing her there with all the other parents. During the ceremonies and afterwards as well, he looked everywhere for her. She was not there.

His disappointment was impossible to contain. His inner pain was acute and, as he held his tears back (boys don't cry!), he kicked and kicked the post in the schoolyard. An onlooker might have thought he was angry, but this was really only covering his deep grief. He had expected his mother to be there and she wasn't.

Samuel was the victim of his unspoken contract: "My mother will always be interested in me and my life even though I don't live with her."

All types of contracts exist in relationships and families. In step-families, however, there are more people and therefore more contracts to contend with. These contracts are just one more of the many complexities that exist in stepfamilies. It is the unspoken and unconscious contracts, however, that frequently contribute to the curdling process in stepfamilies.

Using the Johari Window to understand contracts

One way to get a picture of how these contracts work is to use the framework of the *Johari Window*. This was developed by Joseph Luft and Harry Ingham in 1969, and helps us understand that there are different parts of ourselves that function in our relationships with others. These parts also have relevance with respect to our spoken, unspoken and un-conscious contracts. (See Figure 3.)

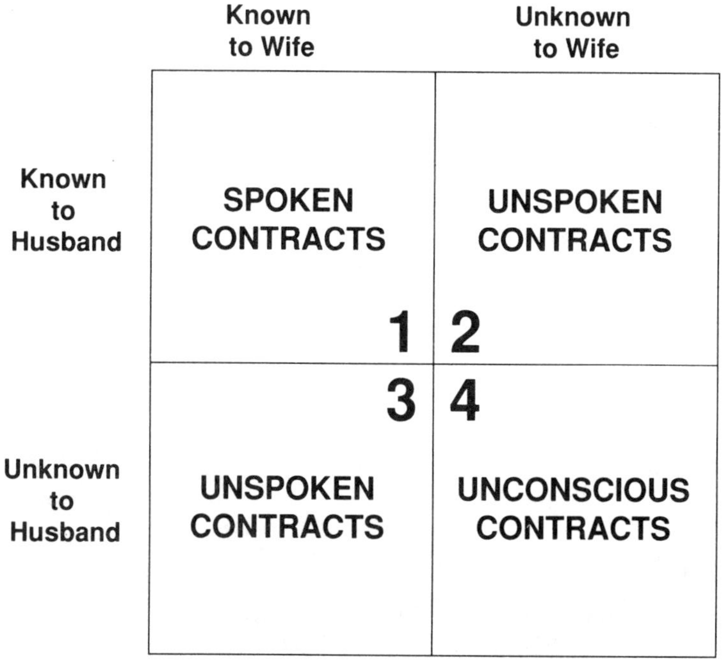

	Known to Wife	Unknown to Wife
Known to Husband	SPOKEN CONTRACTS **1**	UNSPOKEN CONTRACTS **2**
Unknown to Husband	**3** UNSPOKEN CONTRACTS	**4** UNCONSCIOUS CONTRACTS

The blending of a stepfamily is helped when window 1 enlarges through honest self-disclosure and negotiations, making windows 2, 3 and 4 smaller.

Fig. 3 Window showing spoken, unspoken and unconscious con-tracts in a marriage. (Note: This diagram is based on the original "Johari Window" of Joseph Luft and Harry Ingham, 1969)

In this diagram you will notice four windowpanes. With respect to contracts in your relationships, windowpane 1 represents spoken contracts, which are known to yourself and the other person. Windowpanes 2 and 3 show unspoken contracts: those that are known to the other person and not to you and those that are known to you but not to the other person. Windowpane 4 shows the unconscious contracts that are known to neither you nor the other person.

The fewer spoken contracts there are between partners, for example, the smaller is windowpane 1. The more spoken contracts there are, the greater is the area of windowpane 1. The same rule applies to the other windowpanes.

If the two windowpanes that represent unspoken contracts are bigger than the first one, the relationship is either in trouble or heading for it. If this applies to you, you need to begin patiently and honestly to talk about the hidden unspoken contracts that you each have, so that they come out into the open and can be dealt with constructively. This has to be done for the blending of your stepfamily.

With respect to your unconscious contracts, if they surface, follow the suggestions given above. If your relationship and stepfamily are in real trouble, a professional therapist may be able to help you uncover contracts that drive you to behave as you do.

Guidelines for dealing constructively with contracts in your stepfamily

1. Each member (especially partners) makes a list of what he or she wants or is (or is not) prepared to do, be, etc.

2. Check the items of agreement, and verbally acknowledge them.

3. One by one, discuss the remaining items, using conflict resolution skills. You will need to negotiate and compromise. Do not rush. It's better to go slowly and be thorough. Write down your final agreement(s).

4. Search yourself for your unspoken contracts. Be honest! Write these down.

5. Now (here is the challenge), select those that you can talk to your partner about. Many of them will have to be converted into statements or requests, for example:

> "I want to request that you not get involved in telling me how to raise my children. If I want to discuss it with you, I'd like to feel free to ask." (This spoken contract is far more construc-

tive than the unspoken one— "You'll have no say in how I raise my children.")

If one of your unspoken contracts reflects a deep insecurity in you, it is better to express that. For example, the unspoken contract, "I will leave you if you ever stop loving me," is better dealt with in an honest, self-disclosing way: "I want you to know I'm scared that you might stop loving me. Sometimes I think that if that happened, I'd want to leave you." This way, when it is out in the open, the couple can talk about it with mutual understanding and cooperation.

(*Warning*: There are some unspoken contracts that should remain that way and should never be disclosed! An example is: "I'll stay with you as long as you keep your figure." This also applies to some of the "I'm going to change you" unspoken contracts.)

If you discover unspoken contracts that fall in this category, you will benefit and so will those around you if you take a good look at *yourself* and try to find out what your dissatisfaction is all about. You may even need to seek professional help.

6. If and when you become aware of previously unconscious contracts, first of all think of what they mean to you and where they came from. Talk to your partner or family about them, if that seems appropriate. Use this awareness for your personal growth.

7. Remember that all people make contracts, and that children make them, too.

8. Always check out the assumptions that are linked with your unspoken contracts.

Family rules in stepfamilies

In all families there are rules. Some of these are rules or laws that must be obeyed and which are explicitly stated so that there is no mistake about what they are. Children learn to live by rules such as: wipe your feet before you come in the door; say "please"; kiss Mom and Dad goodnight; don't fight with your sister; make your bed before you go to school. The law enforcement agents who make these rules are usually the parents (or stepparents).

There are also rules that exist between partners, such as: if you're running late, you'll phone to let me know; be careful with money; we'll never go to bed with an argument between us.

Some families are so aware of certain rules that they say, for example, "In our family we have a rule that children are given the icing on the cake" or "In our family we have a rule that everyone comes to dinner when there is a birthday in the family."

Needless to say, with the many different family rules that come into stepfamilies there is a need for them to be understood, compromised, learned and sometimes changed!

The family rules that we are going to talk about in this section, however, are different from these. They are family rules that are unspoken. These are usually unrecognized by family members and are very powerful in the way they affect family life—and the lives of people long after they have left their family. In fact, all of us are affected by the unspoken rules that existed in our families of origin. Some of these unspoken family rules are:

- Children come first.

- Father know best.

- Do the right thing.

- Follow the leader.

- Don't let anyone know what you think or feel.

- Don't ask questions.

- Don't give yes or no answers.

- Don't listen to what anyone says.

- Don't argue.

- Make sure you know the answer before you ask a question.

- Don't talk about the past.

- Always look to yourself before you blame anyone else.

- Always blame others.

- Change the subject (or crack a joke) if things become serious or intimate.

and many more...

(Note: All families have unwritten, implicit rules.)

A family system is held together by many factors. One of these is the complex system of unspoken rules which, over a period of time, become established and fixed. One of the reasons family members slip into old patterns of interacting after years of separation is these rules. They are seldom explicit and are rather governed by unwritten law.

How can you identify these implicit, unwritten rules in your family or stepfamily? The answer is that it may be difficult for you to do so because you are too close to your own family to see clearly what happens within it.

Outside observers are more likely to be able to recognize these rules by stepping back and observing familiar interactions and behaviors. These rules can be identified by observing repetitive behaviors and interactions within a family. What people argue about often gives signs and clues.

These unconscious family rules are an expression of the family philosophy and are consistent over time. It is important to realize that usually family members are not aware of them, unless, perhaps, they are students of family therapy or engaged in some therapeutic endeavor and have been alerted to this phenomenon.

When a stepfamily is created, there is a coming together of people who have been raised in, and lived in, families which had their own unique set of unwritten rules. No wonder these people can have difficulty getting along!

Even if the same rule, for example, "father knows best," governed in the first-time family and in the stepfamily, because of the changes in the members of the family system, the rule has a different effect and the family dynamics are different.

It is especially complex when older children are involved, because they have lived long enough to become accustomed (without knowing it) to these rules in their own families.

> Jason, Jenny and Benjamin went to stay with their father every second weekend. Their father, Bob, had moved into an apartment and, although it was small, they enjoyed being there. He took them to the beach, the park, or the movies and in some ways, it was better being with him this way than when he had lived at home. There were no more fights between him and their mother and they certainly spent more time with him.
>
> One day a lady came along for the outing too. Her name was Celia. Six months later their father told them that Celia and he would soon get married.
>
> One year later the three children decided that they didn't like going to stay with Dad anymore. They didn't really know why—they just knew they didn't want to and that it had something to do with Celia.

They didn't know that an unconscious family rule had been broken now that Celia was a member of their family. The rule had been—"children come first." Now it seemed to the children that their father paid more attention to Celia than to them and frequently considered her wishes before theirs.

(*Note:* This is a good example of how conflict can exist in a family and people don't know the real reason for it.)

Of all the rules that can exist, the most emotionally laden issue in a family is: *who makes these rules?* For example, if a husband was raised in a family in which the unspoken rule was, "father makes the rules," and he marries a woman who lived in a family with the rule, "mother makes the rules," there will clearly be much sorting out to do!

When these rules become explicit, that is, if they are spoken or written, they lose their power. For instance, a family might have the rule, "always blame others." In such a family, no one is actually taught to do this, they just do! A child in such a family learns, for example, that Mom, Dad, older brothers and sisters always blame somebody when something goes wrong for them. It is natural, then, for the child to do the same.

If these family members become aware of what they do, the rule will probably lose its power and in fact cease to operate altogether. It is not uncommon for people to say, upon learning about their family system and the rules it has, "I never realized that this is what happens in my family!"

Take time

Think carefully about the family rules you grew up with. First, think about the spoken rules. Are these rules still important to you? Have you taken them into your present relationship or family? What new rules have you introduced?

Second, see if you can identify some of the unspoken rules that operated in your family of origin. Then, see if you can identify implicit rules in your present or past relationship and/or family life. This can be very difficult to do. Some people use this strategy: "If I were a fly on the wall in my family home, what would I see happening?"

Be encouraged

This chapter has provided you with a lot to think about. Take your time, there is no hurry, and gradually you are likely to find that you understand much more clearly what is happening in your marriage and stepfamily. When you make a discovery, try to use your information constructively, never as a weapon.

With patience, tolerance and growing self-awareness, your stepfamily will reap the benefits.

Summary

In this chapter you have read about:

Three different contracts in relationships
Spoken contracts in stepfamilies
Unspoken contracts in stepfamilies
Unconscious contracts in stepfamilies
Children and contracts in stepfamilies
Using the Johari Window to understand contracts
Guidelines for dealing constructively with contracts in your step
     family
Family rules in stepfamilies

9

He's my father not yours

Jealousy in stepfamilies

When jealousy enters any relationship it can be very destructive. Unfortunately, in stepfamilies it is a most common experience. In this chapter we'll first of all look at what jealousy is and then at how it can affect individuals and different relationships within the stepfamily—as well as the emotional environment of the entire stepfamily.

Three types of jealousy

There are three types of jealousy:

1. The first is instigated by actual or potential loss and is called *normal* jealousy. For example, a husband whose wife leaves him for another man may feel very jealous of this man.

   Or a boy might go to live with his father in his new stepfamily and his sister is jealous of him because she has to stay with her mother. She perceives her brother as taking her father's love from her.

2. The second type involves *projection*, whereby a person projects onto someone else the desires or intentions that he or she may have. This is a defense mechanism that serves to protect a person from feelings of guilt.

An example of projection is when a teenager feels jealousy toward his stepsister, believing that she, and not he, is going to be given a special privilege; but actually, he (unconsciously) wishes that he would get this treat and she would miss out. In this case it is guilt that his jealous feelings hide.

3. The third type of jealous experience involves *delusion*. This is when there is no real basis for the jealousy—it is really based on imagination. Children are often jealous of a new baby brother or sister who comes home to live and imagine that this means that mother and father won't love them anymore. This delusional type of jealousy is probably the most common and it is mostly this type of jealousy that creates unhappiness in stepfamilies.

Insecurity is always at the root of jealousy. In stepfamilies many things have happened and do happen to cause people to feel insecure. Marriages have broken up, children have been separated from a parent, sometimes siblings are separated, homes are different, the people in them are different and so on. (Previous chapters have looked at many reasons why stepfamily members might feel insecure.)

Jealousy reduces self-worth or self-esteem, and the lower the self-esteem of a person, the more likely it is that the person will not cope well with the experience. Some people feel jealousy so intensely that homicide or suicide is the only way they can let go of this deadly emotion.

People of high self-esteem also experience jealousy, but are more likely to be able to pull on their inner resources to help them get through it.

Jealousy can also involve comparison. It's as though a person says to himself or herself, "I'm less important, clever, attractive, capable, talented, loved than..."

This is really testing one's position in some sort of hierarchy and is linked to the psychological game of "I'm better than you." This is said to be the most common and powerful game people play in life. It is a game whereby some people, in order to affirm themselves and bolster their self-esteem, try to prove to themselves that they are better than other people. When something happens to them to make them feel they are inferior or inadequate or less important, they often experience jealousy of the people or person who has the desired qualities or possessions that would supposedly increase self-esteem.

Many people allow their lives to be governed according to how they see themselves in comparison with others. This can happen in stepfamilies between family members who are seeking security and affirmation of their self-worth.

Jealousy is a beast that often lies in relationships and families waiting to strike! It can take people unaware. When someone is jealous, it is not always that obvious to other people—although many little behaviors are clues.

Stepsibling jealousy

Stepsiblings are often jealous of each other for many different reasons. Jealousy is often felt acutely by children whose parent is living away from them, in a stepfamily household with other children. Just the knowledge that a parent lives with other children is enough to arouse hostile and jealous feelings.

Intense jealousy between stepsiblings may prevent positive relationships between them from ever being formed. Visit days may be very difficult because of this underlying jealousy, which may lead to conflict, aggression and other behaviors.

Jealousy can also make a child not want to visit the stepfamily home, but instead to keep distant. This way, the parent's love does not have to be tested (in competition with stepsiblings) and this feels safer. (This distancing was talked about in Chapter 5.)

(Note: The type of jealousy felt here is probably "normal." It is likely the parent still loves his or her own child as before, but to the child there is both a loss experience and the fear of losing what seems to be a competition with stepsiblings for the parent's love.)

When the child lives in the same house as a stepsibling, these rivalries exist too. Any attention given to a stepsibling by a child's natural parent can present a threatening situation. This is because the child sees himself or herself as losing the parent's love. (Remember fear of rejection.)

(Note: In this case the jealousy is probably delusional. There is no actual loss, although the child perceives it.)

Sibling rivalry is a normal occurrence in first-time families but can be far more intense between stepsiblings.

Stepsiblings who come to visit can arouse jealous feelings in their stepsiblings who live there. The house may be turned over to these visitors, who may be treated specially and who invade the personal space (physical and psychological) of the children who live there. The focus of attention of the step-couple (or the natural parent) at these visits may be seen by the resident children to shift from them to the other children.

Some children are jealous of their stepsiblings because they perceive them as having more privileges than they do. For example, they may have a bigger house, go for overseas vacations, be spoiled or generally be seen to have a better lifestyle. They might also be jealous because they think they are better looking, smarter, more popular.

When two sets of children come into a stepfamily and live together, one set of siblings may go away to visit the absent parent, while the other set might not have another parent to visit. This might mean that they miss out on extra vacations, special treats, presents and much more. The unfairness that they perceive can make them jealous of their stepsiblings.

Some children whose natural parent has died are jealous of their stepsiblings, who may have two parents.

Stepsibling rivalry can be so intense that it often puts stress on the marriage of the step-couple, which may then be placed at risk.

The unspoken or unconscious contracts of jealous children are often such that *the destruction of this union is the goal*. Family therapists see many couples in stepfamilies whose children seem determined to break up the marriage.

How to help children who are jealous of stepsiblings

- Natural parents and stepparents need to realize that children can harbor deep anxieties, which they may or may not talk about or even show.

- Children feel more secure when they believe that they are loved, wanted, respected and valued. Parents, stepparents, grandparents, relatives, friends and teachers can all contribute to a child's sense of security in the world.

- Some ways that a parent can reassure his or her child are to spend time talking, playing, being interested in the things that the child does; going to open school days, sports days, etc.; making phone calls, sending letters or cards (not only on birthdays); just being together in silence; holding, touching, saying, "I love you very much"; putting the child's artwork on display in the home; last thing before the child goes to bed, having a special time together; building a one-to-one relationship with the child.

- See if you can create ways for stepsiblings to get to know each other. Remember, as long as each child feels valued and loved, it is possible for a good friendship to develop eventually between them. Strong bonding between stepsiblings is quite common.

- If you feel guilty about what you have done to your child by breaking up the first family, acknowledge this. Know that when people live with guilt they are living in the past. It is far more constructive for all of you if you start to live in the present and work toward helping your child adjust and feel more secure.

- Children benefit by perceiving their parent to be confident about a positive outcome in their stepfamily. If you show signs of anxiety and are unsure of yourself, this anxiety is transmitted to the child. Believe that it will all work out and it is more likely to!

- Be patient with jealous children. Never say, "Don't be jealous." It's better to say something like, "I know it must be hard for you to have to share me with...but I just want you to know that you are very precious and important to me." (Remember, your actions must match your words!)

- Realize that jealousy shows in many different ways: aggression, tears, withdrawal, clinging, indifference and more. Suspect it is there when these behaviors show and do all you can to help your child and stepchild feel loved and valued.

- As much as possible, allow stepsiblings to "fight their own battles." If you must intervene, treat each child equally—never take sides.

Stepparent's jealousy of a stepchild

There are many reasons why a stepparent may be jealous of his or her stepchild. Some of these situations are:

- When a parent pays a lot of attention to his or her own child in a stepfamily, to the exclusion (or what may seem to be the exclusion) of a partner, it is possible that the partner will become jealous of that child. Thoughts such as, "He/she loves the child more than me" can begin to surface.

- Sometimes a stepchild resembles the partner's ex-wife/ex-husband and jealous feelings about that person are displaced onto the child.

- A stepchild might be seen by the stepparent to be "better than" his or her own children (more attractive, clever, capable, etc.) and this might bring forth jealous feelings.

- A parent might be seen by the stepparent to spoil his or her own child more than the stepparent. Thoughts such as, "What about me!" can surface.

- The stepchild may be allowed privileges given by his or her natural parent that are not given to either the stepparent or his or her children.

- A parent may put the needs of his or her child before those of his or her partner.

- A stepparent may be reliving old sibling rivalry issues of his or her own.

What to do when a stepparent is jealous of a stepchild or stepchildren

Whatever the reason (or whatever appears to be the reason) for jealousy of a stepchild by a stepparent, there are two people who can work together to get rid of it. If that doesn't work, a third person may be needed.

The *first* person is the jealous stepparent, who must try to find out exactly what he or she is jealous about. Having done that, the stepparent and parent need to have a good, long talk. Honest self-disclosure is needed. Good communication skills have to be used.

Many people find that in just talking about their jealousies and fears, they feel much better. Say something like, "It probably sounds ridiculous, but I am really jealous of your son/daughter. I'm trying to figure out what this is all about and I'd like to talk to you about it in the hope that you'll be able to help me."

The *second* person is the stepparent's partner—the parent of the stepchild. He or she needs to support the jealous partner and understand that jealousy involves insecurity. This person can help a lot by being affectionate, taking time, talking, doing more things together—anything—to help a sense of security develop and strengthen. (Children are not the only ones who can have a deep sense of insecurity.)

A *third* person may have to help if the above two suggestions don't work. This person will need to be a professional who is skilled at working with relationship issues.

Child's jealousy of a stepparent

If a child feels left out because his or her stepparent seems to have taken over the affection of his or her parent, jealous feelings are often aroused. The thought, "He/she loves him/her more than me," creates insecurity which may result in jealousy.

Jealousy can be very intense and is often described as hate. Some children have nothing to do with their stepparent and this often means that they reject the natural parent too (by not visiting and so on).

What to do when a stepchild is jealous of a stepparent

1. The parent and the stepparent need to acknowledge that the child is jealous.

2. Follow suggestions made above for dealing with stepsibling jealousy.

3. Stepparents who experience their stepchild's jealousy will also help to reduce this tension if they do all they can to foster a positive relationship with the child. The major rule here is to go slowly. In the final chapter the importance of taking time and proceeding slowly is dealt with.

New partner's jealousy of an ex-wife or ex-husband

Many second and subsequent marriages are destroyed because of jealousy of a partner's "ex." This can be instigated by a belief that the partner still cares about (or even loves) his ex-partner. This belief may be because of many different reasons.

- It can be because the new partner knows that the ex-partner is given money, privileges that she or he does not have, for example: she or he is perceived to live in a better house, or be provided with a better car. (This is often interpreted as, "She/He is better than me.")

- Self-defeating thoughts such as, "Was he/she a better lover?" "Did you do this with him/her?" "Were you happier with him/her before he/she left you than you are with me?" "Did you love him/her more than you love me?" all serve to arouse jealousy.

- Sometimes a partner spends time with an ex-wife or ex-husband—either just as friends, or in a joint parent role with their natural children. This can arouse jealousy because it can be interpreted as, "See! He/She really does still love her/him!"

What can be done when a partner is jealous of a husband or wife's ex-partner? See the guidelines under "What to do when a stepparent is jealous of stepchild or stepchildren" and substitute ex-partner for stepchild and partner for stepchild.

Ex-partners who are jealous of the new partner

Whether or not children live with or are seen to enjoy being with a stepparent, or even to be forming a good relationship, an ex-partner may feel jealous. This jealousy will be aroused as the result of thoughts such as, "Perhaps my children love (or will grow to love) him/her more than they love me."

If parents see themselves as having to compete with their ex-partner's new husband or wife for the affection of their children, intense feelings of jealousy toward this stepparent may arise.

Some suggestions for resolving this jealousy are:

1. Identify the thoughts that arouse the jealousy.

2. Be careful not to use children as a weapon (this always backfires and is very damaging to the well-being of children).

3. Do all that is possible to help the "letting go" process. Read books or attend groups that help people do this.

4. Rather than talk to family and friends (who are rarely objective), seek professional counseling.

5. If you are the person who feels jealous, realize that in the long run it is *you* who has to change.

Remember that jealousy comes out of insecurity connected with thoughts and beliefs (which are often unrealistic) about not being loved or valued as much as someone else is. You can plan your own strategy for working on it within yourself or others. The guidelines above will, collectively, give you direction.

(*Note*: There are people who are jealous of the television set or the softball team or work, again because they see these things getting more attention than they do. (Sometimes this can be true!) Good talking and more time together is the way to resolve issues such as these.)

Different signs of jealousy

- Aggression (verbal, nonverbal, passive, displaced. See Chapter 17).

- Anger, which either is open and obvious or is kept within.

- Manipulation.

- Psychological games.

- Scapegoating.

- Feeling rejected.

- Refusing to do things for others (this is a form of aggression).

- Demanding justice—saying/thinking: "It's not fair."

- Demanding love.

- Withdrawal.

- Reprisal.

And more...

Some general suggestions for dealing with jealousy

- Acknowledge it, own it, say to yourself, "I am jealous."

- Link it with your fear and identify this fear.

- Talk about it with someone with whom you feel safe.

- If you do not feel jealous yourself but know jealousy is being directed toward you, do all you can to help that person feel safe and secure with you.

- Realize that when you are jealous you are actually putting yourself down.

- Know that your own personal self-worth does not depend on you being "better" than someone else.

- Involve yourself in self-esteem enhancement—read books, take courses, listen to cassette tapes.

- Do not pressure another person to love you.

- Realize that love is letting go of fear.

- Realize that love is not finite. Just because someone else is loved does not mean that there is less for you.

- Know that your emotional life does not have to depend on the actions of others.

- Be in touch with the fact that you are you, there is no one like you. You are independent with your own goals, strengths and potential to develop.

- Never try to sabotage a relationship that threatens you.

- Monitor the thoughts that lead to jealousy and try to change them. Ask yourself, "Are my thoughts rational?"

Jealousy and hidden agendas

Human behavior is very complex and all is not always as it seems. The hidden part of us, our unconscious self, can drive us to behave in ways that camouflage what is really going on inside.

Our built-in (unconscious) defense mechanisms are always there to protect our fragile inner self—sometimes successfully, sometimes not. In many different and creative ways, people live their lives and manage their relationships so as to maximize their belief in themselves, and in doing so, to feel safer, more secure.

Here are some hidden agendas:

- Jealousy can be experienced in a person when really (unbeknown to this person) he or she has an inability to love. In this case the person does not have to face the fact that she or he lacks the capacity to really love. To face that would be too threatening. When this happens, jealousy acts as a defense mechanism to mask the reality of this inadequacy.

- A person might behave in a way that arouses jealousy in her or his partner. This is a game that could be called "I'll make you jealous of me and then I'll know you love me." This is a manipulative psychological game, where the player aims to prove to himself or herself that he or she is valuable.

- Some people discover that one way to get attention is to play the "Poor me, I'm a victim" game. They might (unconsciously) embark on the destruction of their relationship by being jealous, with the payoff being the sympathy and attention of friends and relatives. This is also a manipulative psychological game—the aim of which is to prove, "I'm really worth something! See how my friends are rallying around!"

- Another hidden and unconscious goal can be to break the relationship so as to rejoin the first-time family or be single.

- Finally, a person might become jealous of his or her partner and not realize that this is an unconscious strategy designed to get constant reassurance and attention from that partner.

Be encouraged

In this chapter the subject of jealousy has been explored. While it is true that intense jealousy is the exception rather than the rule, it nevertheless does exist far more than is realized. Often, however, jealousy is a passing thing and stepfamilies overcome the difficulties that cause it and are caused by it.

Many stepfamily members, over time, develop strong, loving and lasting relationships. If you believe this and are not defeated by current difficulties and, as well, use the knowledge, awareness and skills suggested in this chapter, you will almost certainly eradicate the "monster of jealousy" from your family environment!

Summary

This chapter on jealousy has looked at:

Three types of jealousy
Stepsibling jealousy
How to help children who are jealous of stepsiblings
Stepparent's jealousy of a stepchild
What to do when a stepparent is jealous of a stepchild or step-
    children
Child's jealousy of a stepparent
What to do when a stepchild is jealous of a stepparent
New partner's jealousy of an ex-wife or ex-husband
Ex-partners who are jealous of the new partner
Different signs of jealousy
Some general suggestions for dealing with jealousy
Jealousy and hidden agendas

10

I'm not the oldest anymore

Birth-order characteristics and sibling displacement

Birth-order characteristics

In this chapter we'll look at stepfamilies in which each partner has children and they all live together permanently. We will also consider stepfamilies in which there are two sets of children who, while not living together, spend quite a bit of time with each other.

Wherever children are living, their life experiences contribute to the development of their personality. The nature-nurture controversy that prevailed for so long has now come to terms with the fact that both genetic and environmental factors contribute to what a child is and will become.

One of the environmental factors that contributes to personality is the child's position in his or her family of origin. This is referred to as "birth order" (and includes adopted children).

Oldest children, for example, tend to develop a certain set of "oldest child" characteristics. These may differ slightly depending on whether the oldest is the oldest sister or brother of an all-girl family, all-boy family or a family of brothers and sisters.

Middle children have characteristics specific to them, as do third children in families of four children, or youngest children. Children in same-sex families have particular characteristics, and the family experience of "only" children contributes to only-child characteristics.

Age difference between siblings is also a factor in the personality development of each child. A brother who is 7 years younger than an older brother has a different sibling relationship and experience in the family than if he were only 14 months younger.

People sometimes say, "I can't understand how all those children from the one family can be so different!" The fact is, however, that even though each child is born into the *same* family with the *same* parents, each child is actually born into a *different* family!

With each succeeding birth (or addition to the family through fostering or adoption) the family changes, so that, for example, a first child is born into a no-child family, a second child is born into a one-child family, and a fifth child is born into a four-child family.

Each of these new children is faced with different family circumstances. Some of these are more children who are at different ages and stages of growth, older parents who probably have less time (and energy) for them, perhaps a tighter financial situation, and usually less space in the family home.

With all these differences (and many more not mentioned here), it's probably more surprising when children are similar, rather than dissimilar.

Children become accustomed to their position in the family. When something happens to change that, for example, when a new baby comes home or a sibling dies, the position of at least some of the children in the family changes.

When a new baby is born into a two-child family, for example, the previous youngest child is no longer the youngest and becomes a middle child. Or a middle child of three becomes the second oldest when a fourth child is born.

When the oldest child of a three-child family dies, the middle child becomes the oldest. If one child of a two-child family dies, the other child becomes an only child.

When changes like this occur, the younger the child is, the more likely it is that he or she, over time, will adopt the birth-order characteristics of his or her new position. Children who are five years of age or older when such changes occur tend, on the other hand, to retain most of the individual personality traits that are associated with their original position in the family. We will now look at some birth-order characteristics.

(*Note*: Birth-order characteristics are to be considered in a *general* sense, and not taken absolutely literally. However, similar personality characteristics that are consistent with respect to birth order have been found in adults and children and do help us understand why we are the way we are. These characteristics are highly resistant to change and are usually with us *for life*.)

Oldest children are likely to be responsible, nurturing, leaders, critical, serious, bossy, overcommitted, independent, controlling, achievers, self-disciplined.

Middle children tend to be confused about their identity, lower achievers, followers, competitive, lacking in confidence, quiet, shy, good negotiators, under the impression that they are treated unfairly.

Youngest children are likely to be playful, irresponsible, undiscipline, dependent, troubled by feelings of inadequacy, adventurous, friendly, creative.

Only children tend to be self-sufficient, independent, loners, achievers, selfish, intolerant, serious.

Sibling displacement

When two families (two parents and their respective children) merge to form a stepfamily, there are inevitable changes in sibling position for many of these children.

If two sets of siblings live together permanently, the children are more likely to experience emotional distress as a result of changes in sibling position (their own and even that of their siblings) than if they spend time with their stepsiblings on a part-time basis.

Some of these children may feel confused, anxious, resentful, hostile, uncertain and/or jealous as a result of the inevitable sibling birth-order displacement.

Before we talk about this more, let's look at sibling relationships in first-time families.

Sibling bonds

Whether or not siblings relate well to each other, a strong and familiar bond, or *emotional connection*, develops between them that is with them for the rest of their lives—and even beyond (when one predeceases another).

The personality and psychological development of each child *creates* and *is influenced by* this emotional bond which is the result of the many interactions siblings have and of how they perceive each other.

It's impossible to say who influences whom—it's just that *all* siblings are influenced by *all* other siblings. This is especially so when they are close in age to each other. It is also likely to be stronger if siblings spend a lot of time with each other and experience little parental influence.

Siblings use each other as reference points for the development of their own identities. Thus, siblings become a *major* influence in the development of each other's personalities.

Siblings and family breakup

When a marriage breaks up, the family breaks up—whether or not the parents separate and live in different homes. In either event, the parents' broken relationship represents, for the children, the loss of what has held the family together.

In these situations siblings often seek (and find) a degree of emotional security in their relationships with each other. They may enjoy one another or fight constantly, but in both cases the familiar emotional bond helps them feel better. (Remember the coming-close and distancing behaviors that reduce fear of rejection.)

Sometimes children split off and distance themselves to protect themselves from the deep fear inside. They may do this emotionally (by ceasing to connect or by being silent) and/or physically (by withdrawing or even, in the case of older children, leaving home).

Changed relationships among siblings in the Renston stepfamily

When children become part of a stepfamily and they live permanently with their stepsiblings, the coming together of these two sets of children can be quite traumatic for them. (Parents often fantasize that it will be great fun!)

> Amy, age 10, Brett, age 8, and Will, age 6, had lived with their mother, Justine, in a single-parent family for three and a half years. After their mother's marriage to Peter Renston, they moved into a new home with their stepfather and his two children, Helen, age 11, and Nathan, age 7.

It was not long before troubles started. Here is what each one had to say:

> *Amy:*   Helen keeps trying to boss me around and tell me what to do. She thinks she's so smart, I can't stand her. Just because she's the oldest she thinks she can boss all of us. I wish Mom would leave Peter so we could go back to the way it was. Back then, I was the

oldest and Mom and I used to have good times together. Now that doesn't happen. I used to help Mom make biscuits and now Helen butts in.

Brett: It's not that bad, I suppose, except when Nathan and Will gang up and laugh at me. They take my things, my soccer ball, and think it's funny. I liked it better before, though—just being with Mom.

Will: Me and Nathan have lots of fun—'specially when we're mean to Brett.

Helen: I try to get all the kids to behave because Dad doesn't like fights. It's hard at times. Amy is a pain and so is Will. Brett's okay.

Nathan: Only thing I don't like is Dad doesn't bring home toys and things. Helen and Amy fight all the time. Helen yells at me.

There's a great deal of stress among the children (and adults) in this stepfamily. It's not working out the way the parents had imagined. Before they married they had thought, "How nice it will be for Amy and Helen—they'll each have a sister," and "The boys will have a really good time since they're about the same age." How mistaken they were!

Let's now take a look at what is happening with these children with respect to birth-order characteristics and sibling bonds (see Figure 4).

Amy has had to relinquish her oldest-child position to Helen, who has entered into it with increased vigor because there are now four younger children under her. Her oldest-child characteristics of being responsible, bossy, critical and controlling are clashing with those of Amy, who has similar traits. Little wonder there is a struggle between these two children.

Furthermore, there are now two girls in the family and each one has lost the status of being the only girl. So for Amy, who valued this special status, there is a double blow: loss of the oldest-child position and loss of the only-girl status.

Brett is still the middle child but is now the middle of five rather than three children. Because his family position has not changed, there is a degree of familiarity for him, and his middle-child characteristics fit the position in which he finds himself. He remains the oldest boy, so in this respect there is familiarity, too. He has, however, lost his one-to-one relationship with Will (the boys) and that, for him, is a great loss.

Will is still the youngest and is therefore comfortable with his unchanged position in his new stepfamily. The youngest-child characteristics of Will and Nathan give them a lot in common: they both enjoy playing,

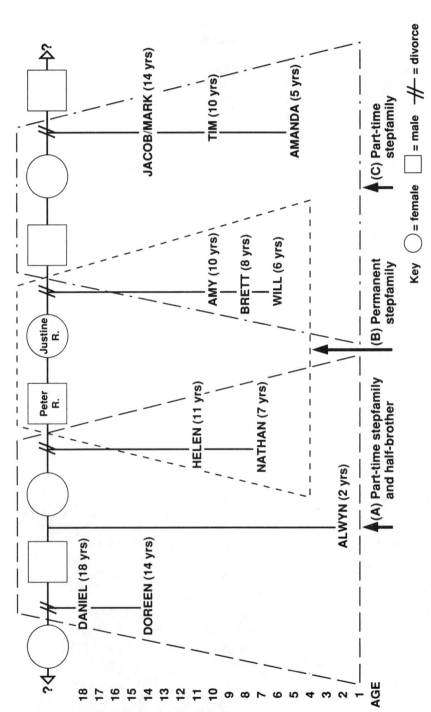

Fig. 4 Birth order and sibling displacement in three connected stepfamilies

exploring and being somewhat irresponsible. In fact they tend to lead each other into mischief and that's fun for them!

Helen has retained her oldest-child position, and her birth-order characteristics therefore fit her role in her new family. Her responsibilities are greater, and she has to prove to everyone that she can be relied on to do the right thing. She tries to make sure that the others do the right thing, too. She is therefore not very popular and finds herself alone in the family. At times she feels threatened by Amy, but being that extra year older, she feels confident in her leadership role.

Nathan has lost his youngest-child position, is now the middle boy (of three boys) and is not the only boy. He has, however, gained a playmate in Will, and their relationship is cemented, in part, by teasing and "attacking" Brett. While he is aware that his dad doesn't spoil him as he used to, the gain of a playmate seems to compensate. His youngest-child traits, or personality, make him an ideal friend for Will.

Changed relationships between siblings and stepsiblings

When two families come together to live as one stepfamily, they are still really two families living under one roof.

Initially they are kept separate by the (unconscious) separateness force that operates within each family to retain its boundaries. Over time, however, each of these family boundaries usually weakens as another boundary is forming—one that encompasses the new stepfamily unit. Once this boundary is formed people can say, "Now we are *one* family!"

The ways that siblings relate often change, too, as stepfamily life gets under way. While it is true that the nature of sibling relationships changes in the normal course of children growing up (developmental changes and so on), it is the presence of stepsiblings in the family home that interferes and affects the familiar ways that siblings relate to each other.

The other stepfamilies that are connected with the Renston stepfamily

We have, so far, looked at one stepfamily life for these two sets of children. In many cases, however, children belong to two stepfamilies and may also have half-siblings.

> The father of Amy, Brett and Will has remarried and lives with his new wife and her four children. This, too, is a stepfamily to which Amy, Brett and Will belong. They have four step-

siblings in this stepfamily: twins Jacob and Mark, age 14, Tim, age 10, and Amanda, age 5. When they go to stay with their father, as visiting children, they have this sibling group to relate with, get used to and be displaced by. (You will notice the age structure and the accompanying displacement with respect to position in this stepfamily in Figure 4.)

Sometimes when they visit their father, their stepsiblings are away visiting their own father. He has also remarried and has a stepfamily to which Jacob, Mark, Tim and Amanda also belong. The family links can go on and on.

Helen and Nathan, too, have other stepsiblings. Their mother has remarried and her stepchildren are Daniel, age 18, and Doreen, age 14. Helen and Nathan share with Daniel and Doreen a baby half-brother, Alwyn, age 2.

All of these children have had their lives turned upside down. All of them have had their perception of the world shattered and have had to make many changes and adaptations. That so many children do such a good job of it is astounding, given the obstacles they face!

Some children benefit from their changed sibling position and new relationships. "Only" children, for example, experience great change when they become part of a stepfamily and have stepsiblings. This can teach them valuable lessons about family life, which they would not otherwise have.

How to help children adjust to sibling displacement and changed relationships

- Give siblings the opportunity to be together, alone. They may also be helped if they can spend time with their natural parent with whom they live, away from their stepparent or stepsiblings, the way it was prior to stepfamily life.

- Do not intervene and try to force siblings to be loyal to each other. It's best to give them the freedom to maintain their sibling relationships in their own way.

- Give them time and (psychological) space to develop relationships with their stepsiblings in their own way.

- Do not take sides: allow children to sort out their own problems. (If you interfere, you are triangling.)

- Occasional outings involving two stepsiblings with each parent can help them feel more connected, and break down rigid sibling boundaries. Make sure that they all get their turn.

- Arrange for each child to spent time *alone* with *each* of his or her natural parent(s).

- If possible, arrange for stepchildren to spend time alone with their stepparent.

- Make time to talk with each child. If a child seems unhappy, encourage him or her to talk about it, and acknowledge what the child is saying. For example, Amy's mother or stepfather could say to her, "It must be hard for you, not being the oldest in the family anymore. Is that why you fight with Helen? What can we do that will help you feel better, do you think?" If Amy replies, "Make Helen be nice to me," gently explain that you can't do that. There are, however, other ways that you can help these two children relate comfortably. Amy and other children like her can be helped to feel more secure by being recognized in a positive way for *what they do and who they are.*

Take time

If you live in a stepfamily with two sets of children, what difficulties have they had learning to live together? What have you done (if anything) about this? What positive things have come out of having two sets of siblings live together in your stepfamily?

Be encouraged

When two sets of siblings come together to live in a stepfamily, there is displacement with respect to age and changes in the ways siblings relate to each other. Over time, however, and especially if the step-couple are patient and skillful, things usually settle down and a new familiarity takes over.

In many stepfamilies, new and positive relationships are formed. It is quite common for stepsiblings to become very good friends. If they have been together from a young age, a relationship more akin to a sibling relationship, with a stronger emotional bonding, is likely to develop.

There are some stepfamilies in which all-girl families benefit from having stepbrothers (and vice versa); where a girl is delighted about having a stepsister or a boy finds a special relationship with a stepbrother; or where an only child gets all the benefits of being one of a larger family. The combinations are many and varied.

If your stepfamily is struggling right now, and stepsiblings are not getting along, try to understand that stepfamily life is a process which is forever changing. If you are patient and relate to the children in your stepfamily by following the suggestions given here, it is likely you will find, in the years to come, that the joy of your stepfamily is reflected in strong and positive stepsibling relationships.

Summary

In this chapter you have read about:

    Birth-order characteristics
    Sibling displacement
    Sibling bonds
    Siblings and family breakup
    Changed relationships among siblings in the Renston stepfamily
    Changed relationships between siblings and stepsiblings
    The other stepfamilies that are connected with the Renston
        stepfamily
    How to help children adjust to sibling displacement and changed
        relationships

11

You're not my father

Discipline in stepfamilies

Stepparents are not instant parents

Many parents and stepparents report that the major difficulty they encounter in their stepfamily life has to do with the issue of discipline. Questions such as: "Who will discipline whom?" "What will they be disciplined for?" "How will they be disciplined?" can remain unanswered and unresolved. Many a stepfamily has floundered over the confusion and emotion that arises out of this issue.

Parents in first-time families often experience these same problems. There is, however, one significant difference in these families: the children are the offspring of *both* parents (biological or adopted children) and this gives each parent the "right" to guide and set standards for his or her own children.

This role of disciplinarian is just one role that parents assume. They are also nurturers, caregivers, friends, providers, teachers and mentors.

One of the traps that many stepparents fall into is the belief that they become instant parents to their stepchildren once they start living with them.

This belief frequently leads to conflict when stepparents try to discipline their stepchildren—especially early in stepfamily life—only to find that it doesn't go over very well. Children, and sometimes their parent, often challenge this intrusion into their psychological space.

Nevertheless, children of all ages need guidance, correction and setting of limits for them to grow up into well-adjusted human beings. This involves discipline and it is only natural for a stepparent to want to be a part of this process.

Given time, patience and skill, many stepparents do play an important part in the lives of their stepchildren, including disciplining them. Before stepparents can effectively do this, however, they need to build a base of influence.

Building a base of influence

This term refers to the establishment of trust. It is used in counseling to describe the trust that clients must have in their therapist before the therapist can help them make changes and solve their own problems.

Establishing a base of influence is the primary task of a good therapist who gets a sense of when it has developed. It may happen in the first counseling session or it may take many months. It is by following the rule, "go slow to go fast," that the therapist does this.

In stepfamilies the same principle and rule need to be applied. Stepparents need to develop a base of influence with their stepchildren *before* they get involved in the disciplinary process, and they need to *go slowly, slowly, slowly* in order to do this.

Even if stepparents know their stepchildren before they live with them, they still need to follow this rule once they start to live together. *Building a base of influence takes time!* This means that stepparents need to wait until they sense a degree of comfort and trust between them and their stepchildren before they try to discipline them.

When this happens they need, even then, to test this relationship carefully as they engage in disciplining. This doesn't mean that they need to be nervous and tentative, but it does mean that they need to discipline in a way that does not destroy the base of influence they believe has been established. If this is destroyed, it may never be built again.

We shall now look at discipline, what it is and how it can have negative or positive outcomes with respect to a child's development and stepfamily relationships.

Different forms of discipline

Discipline is training—especially of the mind and character. Children need to be disciplined by others, as part of the process of becoming *self*-disciplined.

When parents discipline children, they do so with respect to their own life philosophies, values, attitudes, rules and standards. It is actually a form of love (if it is genuinely done for the benefit of the child) and that is why some parents say, "If I didn't love you, I wouldn't care what you do!"

Discipline is given (and received) in different ways: verbally and nonverbally. Each of these can involve punishment. Depending on the way these methods are used, they can have negative or positive effects on a child's development.

Positive verbal discipline

Short statements and requests. Some examples are: "I don't want you to stay out late." "This is the way I asked you to clean the kitchen." "Come on, pick up your toys." "That is not how you talk to your grandmother." "Sit down and write a thank-you letter to your aunt." "You told me a lie—never do that again." "Say, 'thank you.'"

Explanations and reasons. This involves talking at greater length with children about an issue or disciplinary measure. For example, parents may talk with their children about behavior that is displeasing to them, and explain why this is so, and how, if it continues, it may adversely affect the life of the children or someone else.

Children of all ages benefit from this disciplinary mode. It helps them to think and to develop an awareness about the effects of their behaviors—on themselves and others—whether or not they have actually engaged in the behavior. It teaches them to appreciate another person's point of view and this, in turn, helps in the development of relational skills.

When a child is given reasons calmly and rationally, emotions don't get in the way. When a parent is angry and a child is upset and frightened, as so often is the case in disciplinary situations, the "right" behavior is taught in an emotional environment. It is preferable to aim for intellectual comprehension. This way a child learns to be governed by thoughts rather than emotions.

Setting limits and establishing rules. This is also part of the disciplinary process. Sometimes rules are written down. Some parents place a list of dos and don't's on the refrigerator or family bulletin board. For example, a washing-up schedule may be posted up, or rules about coming-home times.

(*Note:* Each of these methods shows respect for children because they are not being put down (as long as the tone of voice and facial gestures are not critical or threatening). This means that relationships are likely to be more positive because children don't feel frightened or angry. They are also more likely to develop high self-esteem when they are disciplined this way.)

Negative verbal discipline

In many families a destructive form of verbal discipline is used. This includes criticism, ridicule, discounting and sarcasm. Examples are: "You idiot, you're so clumsy. Can't you ever hold your glass without spilling your milk?" "Hah! Look at him—he'll never get anywhere, he's so stupid." "I knew I couldn't trust you—you deceitful brat!" "You'll never have any friends." "Now that's really brilliant." "What a joke. Look everyone." "One more time you fool, and you'll really get it from me!"

This type of verbal discipline is a form of punishment (its aim is to inflict psychological pain and discomfort) and is devastating to the development of children's self-esteem because it conveys a lack of respect and value for them. Children's self-esteem is derived from the way they perceive other people valuing them, and children who are repeatedly spoken to in this way eventually *believe* they are not valuable.

This adversely affects their relationship with the disciplinarian—and other relationships as well. If you want to have a child living with you who is pleasant and agreeable, this is *not* the way to discipline.

There is a before and after element to the disciplinary process. Limits to children's behavior can be established *before* they have done wrong. Other times, children are disciplined *after* they have violated a preferred code of behavior.

Positive nonverbal discipline

Sometimes parents send a message, without any words, that says "no." This is especially common in disciplining small children whose parents, for example, may shake their head when the children are about to reach for a china treasure from the shelf. This sort of discipline is not likely to damage the child's self-esteem.

Nonverbal discipline also involves punishment. Let's take a look at some of the ways in which children are punished and the effects of this.

Different forms of punishment

Punishment is often involved in disciplinary action. It is given *after* something wrong is done, in contrast to disciplinary measures which can be taken either before *or* after some wrong behavior.

There is another difference. Discipline involves teaching or training. Punishment involves giving discomfort or pain to someone, *so as to teach or train* that person not to engage in certain behavior again. It aims to teach a lesson, which is, "This is what happens if you engage in this behavior."

Adults, as well as children, can be punished. They may, for example, receive a speeding ticket if they have exceeded the speed limit or a parking ticket if they have parked in a no parking zone.

This form of punishment is based on withdrawal—in this case the withdrawal of money. This form of punishment is one of many we will now consider.

Verbal criticisms

This is mentioned in Negative verbal discipline above, and, because of its effect, can be a punishment rather than a discipline.

Withdrawal of privileges

Sometimes privileges are withdrawn: "No, you can't go to Melissa's party—you've been very naughty." "Television is banned for the next week." "No pocket money for two weeks—that'll teach you." "You might as well go right now and phone your friends and tell them that you can't go camping with them this weekend." "I told you I'd buy you an ice cream—well, I'm not going to now."

Withdrawal of objects

Favorite objects can be taken away also. "Give me your bicycle—I'm going to lock it up for a week until you learn how to behave." "No more crayons until you learn not to write on the walls." "Just to teach you a lesson you're not going to play your music for two weeks—give me your cassette player."

When children are frequently disciplined with this form of punishment, they are disempowered and are likely to become resentful toward the person who punishes them this way. Even though, in some instances these strategies may be the most effective to "teach and train," if used often they result in bad relationships and a buildup of anger and fear. These emotions create a barrier between parent and child, whose relationship might never be a positive and happy one, even when the child becomes an adult.

Withdrawal of love

Perhaps the *most damaging* form of punishment is the withdrawal of love, attention or recognition. Some parents use this form of punishment and may not speak to a child for days on end, or may cease to look after them. This is very damaging to the well-being of the child and should be avoided at all costs.

(*Note*: Adults who feel compelled to use this form of punishment need to work on their own unresolved issues. Professional help may be needed.

Sometimes parents withdraw completely following the breakup of a family. This is because of the internal pain of separation and not because of a desire to punish children for something they have done that is wrong. In a situation such as this, it is important to explain the reason for the withdrawal to children.)

Isolation

Another form of punishment is isolation. (This is the basis of our prison system.) In a family, children can be sent to a room: "Go to your room and don't come out until I tell you." Sometimes parents separate squabbling siblings by sending each one in a different direction, with the instructions that they do not have anything to do with each other until given the go ahead.

This strategy for dealing with conflict between children does have some advantages (if not used too often). One of these is that the danger of triangling is avoided. (Chapter 2 talks about triangling.) It also has an advantage of giving the opportunity for emotions to settle down.

On the other hand, it has disadvantages in that it teaches children that when there is conflict, they must distance themselves from it. (We have already talked in this book about the danger of avoiding conflict.)

Physical punishment

Physical punishment is thought by many parents to be a necessary disciplinary tool. The old dictum—spare the rod (or smack) and spoil the child—still has its place in some families (and schools).

Different situations need to be taken into account where physical punishment is concerned. On the one hand, a smack on the hand of a toddler who persists in poking things into the light socket is probably the most appropriate way to teach him or her not to do that anymore.

On the other hand, extreme forms of physical punishment are very destructive to the psychological well-being of children.

Some children who are punished this way grow up to take out their rage and anger on others. They become delinquents and criminals in society or go through life physically and verbally abusing those around them.

They may be exploitative, users of people, never happy, never developing their self-esteem and never really knowing why they are this way. Sometimes people seek therapy to help them resolve the anger rage and sense of powerlessness that has its origin in the punitive experiences of childhood.

It is interesting to note that when children are punished with these extreme methods, they are often not the only ones who suffer. The giver of the punishment pays a price, too, for disciplining in this way.

> Natalie, a mother of three, was examining through therapy why it was she always felt strained and bitter toward her mother. She could not understand it because her mother seemed to be loving and always wanting to help. She came to realize that she had a deep and awful fear of her mother, who had, on countless occasions in her childhood, punished her by hitting and yelling. This helped explain why Natalie did not like being close to her mother. It also explained the anger she felt toward her. Her mother, on the other hand, was always complaining that her daughter did not love her, or want to be close to her.

You can see in this story that the mother suffered, too, as a result of the punishment she used years earlier to discipline her daughter. How much better it would have been for the two of them if the mother had learned some constructive ways to discipline her child.

Punishment is one of many strategies used to discipline children and is actually aversive conditioning of undesired behavior. Initially it is specific to a situation. Over time, however, this conditioning serves to control situations not yet encountered, by posing the threat of being a consequence of other behaviors.

It leaves children with a choice between engaging in miscreant behavior and receiving punishment (or at least having the risk of punishment) and not engaging in the behavior and therefore not receiving the punishment.

Conscience and concepts of right and wrong

> Lina really wanted to raid the cookie jar when her mother was out shopping. Inside were her favorite cookies and she was so hungry. Should she, or shouldn't she? She was tempted but decided against it. Why? Because she knew she would be doing the wrong thing. She also decided against it because she knew that if she did and was found out (and it seemed that her mother always had a way of finding out), she would not be allowed to watch her favorite television program.

In the story above we can see that Lina resisted temptation because she feared punishment. She was also wrestling between what was right and wrong.

Overall, the aim of disciplining children is to contribute to the development of conscience, which is an inner voice that evaluates whether something is right, good or desirable, or wrong, bad or undesirable. It is with their conscience that children learn to discipline themselves.

When children learn to resist temptation, or feel guilty after they have done something they know to be wrong, or confess if they have, they are *developing their conscience*. Adult guidance plays a crucial role in this.

It is according to the values, attitudes and life philosophy of parents, stepparents, relatives, school teachers, religious teachers, scout leaders and so on that children learn about the concepts of right and wrong. Part of this learning process involves discipline (sometimes by way of punishment).

Children who are disciplined by frequent physical punishment or by having privileges, objects and love and recognition taken from them are *less* likely to develop normally with respect to their conscience than are children who are disciplined in constructive ways. This means that they are less likely to develop a concept of what is right or wrong. It is often said that these people "lack a conscience." Partly this is because these forms of punishment are usually administered with a lack of rationale, understanding or reasoning. The child is not given information which he or she can use for future decisions about behavior.

Pleasant and unpleasant experiences all play a part in shaping the personality of children. One way parents can better understand children is to better understand *themselves* and their *own* childhood experiences.

An exercise that you can do follows. The aim of this is to help you develop an awareness about your own experiences with discipline as a child. This awareness will probably help you better understand your children and stepchildren and how you can constructively engage in disciplining them.

How to understand children (and yourself) better

1. Close your eyes and go back down the path of your life to childhood. Take your time—as though you are turning back the pages of a big diary.

2. Think of the worst experience you had in childhood with your father or mother (or someone else) with respect to discipline of you.

3. Think about how you felt and thought *during* and *after* that event. Put words to your feelings and thoughts.

4. Now ask yourself this question: "On the basis of this experience, what decision did I make?" (This could have been about your relationship with that person, it could have been about how you would raise your children one day, it could have been about a change in your behavior ... just think.)

5. Now ask yourself another question: "What do I wish had happened in that situation?"

6. After answering the question above, ask yourself: "Have I been influenced in my life by either of the above? How have I treated my own children as a result of the above?"

Here is an example of how Marguerite used this exercise.

> Marguerite closed her eyes and went back in her memory to a scene in her kitchen where her mother was going to the pantry to get the long cane to whip her legs. Marguerite could not remember what it was she had done wrong. The words that came to her mind were "terror, powerless." She realized that the decision she made at that moment was, "I'll never let myself get close to my mother."

She wished her mother had sat down and explained why she had done wrong and asked her not to do it again. Her life had been influenced because of two decisions she made. The first was never to be close to her mother and the second was never to treat her own children this way.

Take time

Do the above exercise. Perhaps you and your partner could each do it and share with each other what you discover.

It is by exploring our own lives that we can be enriched and helped in the way we parent our own children. We were all children once, and to reflect on experiences in our own youth can give us insight into what is happening in the world of our offspring—or the offspring of others.

Role models

Parents are role models for children, whether they intend to be or not. The most positive way for children to learn how to behave is by observing desirable behaviors of their parents, stepparents and other people in their lives.

Children who witness lack of self-control in a parent or stepparent are not being helped to become self-controlled themselves. Sometimes, though, they adopt opposite behaviors.

In the story above about Marguerite, she chose to be different from her mother. She chose the opposite path on the basis of what she wished her mother had done. Unfortunately, many children who are at the hands of a negative form of discipline will grow up to use those same techniques with their own children. Do you?

Take time

Reflect upon your childhood and the way you were disciplined. Do you use the same methods with your children (or the children of others)? How do you feel when you do this? If you use other methods, what are they? How effective do these methods seem to be? How do you know this? Are there any changes you'd like to make to the way you discipline your children and stepchildren? What are they?

Now that we have looked at discipline and punishment, and you've had the opportunity to do some personal growth work, we will address the discipline issues that plague many stepfamilies.

Who will discipline whom?

Around the issue of discipline in stepfamilies, this is usually the biggest question. Various solutions are tried—some work and some don't. If a solution works for all concerned, however, irrespective of what it is, it's probably a good idea to stay with it.

Here are some different ways that parents and stepparents have resolved the discipline issue of "Who does it?"

Parent and stepparent discipline

In some stepfamilies it is decided that the children will be disciplined by parent and stepparent, regardless of the age of the children.

While a united front might seem to be the best approach, this strategy can present many problems. For example, when stepparents attempt to discipline their teenage stepchildren, they usually find the going tough. Teenagers are inclined to resent a stepparent telling them what to do or not do. (At that age they usually resent anyone telling them what to do!) The retort—"You're not my father/mother, you can't tell me what to do"—is a common one, especially if the stepfamily is recently formed.

Past hurts, resentment and grief at the loss of the natural absent parent and the original family can make children unable to accept or respect a stepparent. When this happens disciplinary measures are likely to be ineffective and may, in fact, make things worse. This is a time when a wise stepparent holds back and focuses on becoming a friend to the child, rather than a parent. (Remember how it is important to establish a base of influence.)

When a parent and stepparent want to jointly discipline children in their stepfamily, they have more chances of success if the children are younger. Even if one set of children lives with another parent, they are more likely to adapt to joint disciplining at a younger age.

Whatever the ages of the children, communication skills are needed to make sure that parent and stepparent are on the right track—together!

When two families merge, difficult times can lie ahead. This was the experience of Derrick and Lisa.

> Derrick's son and daughter were allowed to come home from school and eat whatever they liked. They were then expected to go and do their homework before dinner. On the other hand, Lisa's three children were allowed one piece of fruit for an afternoon snack and were encouraged to go outside and play until dinner time.
>
> Whose set of rules were the ones to follow in this merged family? Lisa's children began to challenge their mother about afternoon snacks and Derrick's children wanted to play instead of doing their homework.
>
> Because Derrick and Lisa had opted for joint disciplining in their stepfamily, they were committed to resolving this issue. They used the communication skills they had learned (fortunately) and arrived at a mutually satisfactory decision: all of the children could eat whatever they liked for an afternoon snack (within reason) and all of them could have half an hour of relaxation time before doing their homework.

In this case the parents of each set of siblings made the disciplinary decision together and enforced these new limits. They were united and the children could not play one against the other. This is a common game in stepfamilies, and one of the advantages of joint disciplining is that this game fails and children soon give up on it.

Parents and stepparents who wish to jointly discipline need to have many long talks about their individual values and attitudes concerning discipline. Compromise is often needed while a strong and confident management or leadership team is being built.

Joint discipline by divorced natural parents

Many divorced parents, irrespective of whether they have remarried, continue to jointly discipline their children. This is especially common where older children are concerned and "big" issues arise (such as dating rules, learning-to-drive rules, educational considerations, money rules, etc.).

This can have negative effects on stepfamily life, as it can leave stepparents feeling like outsiders. They may never develop a sense of connectedness with their stepchildren and their stepchildren may fail to acknowledge that their stepparent is (or can be) an important person in their lives.

Other stepparents are quite comfortable with this arrangement—especially if they have children living elsewhere and are involved in their upbringing. They are more likely to want to develop a friendship with their stepchildren and leave the disciplining to their partner and his or her ex-partner.

One parent as sole disciplinarian

There are stepfamilies in which the natural parent is the sole disciplinarian. Neither the current partner nor the ex-partner joins forces with this parent to discipline the children.

Sometimes this is by way of agreement between parent and stepparent and others times not. When the parent and stepparent have not even discussed this important issue, serious relationship difficulties are evident.

> Karen and Norm had been married for two years and lived with Karen's two children, age nine and six, from her previous marriage. From the very start Norm got the message that he had better keep out of the lives of Karen's children. In many different ways she conveyed her intention to raise her children by herself.
>
> Karen had been a single parent for five years prior to her marriage to Norm and was quite accustomed to disciplining her children herself. Her ex-husband had made occasional contact after the marriage breakup but she had not heard from him for four years.
>
> Karen's children knew that their mother was the only one who disciplined them. Norm was "just there." Several times he had asked that the children do this or that and the response from Karen was startling: "Don't you tell my children what to do!" Norm learned to back off and keep to himself.

Karen had entered marriage with an unspoken (or even unconscious) contract: "I will be the only one who disciplines my children." Any attempt on Norm's part to challenge that aroused great anxiety in her, which resulted in aggression.

Even though some parents and their new partners agree that only the natural parent will discipline, there are disadvantages associated with this decision. Apart from older children who, as we have seen, usually respond more favorably to a stepparent as a friend rather than a parent, younger children do miss the opportunity to learn how parents can work together in raising children. This provides a valuable role model which helps equip children for their own adulthood and parenthood.

Another disadvantage is that there are times when the natural parent may be absent. What happens then? In this event an agreement is often reached whereby authority is temporarily delegated to the stepparent.

There is yet another disadvantage. If stepparents become aware that a stepchild needs to be disciplined, they have either to keep it to themselves or tell the parent and suggest—or even request—that disciplinary action be taken. The parent can then be in a difficult situation for two reasons. First, if she or he does not agree that discipline is needed, this can be interpreted by the partner as lack of caring and support in their married relationship. Second, if he or she does discipline, as requested, there is an element of triangling. The natural parent is coming in on an issue that is really between the stepparent and stepchild.

Sometimes, of course, it might be that the parent agrees that discipline is needed, and appreciates the suggestion.

One way for a stepparent to discipline indirectly is to say something like, "I just want you to know that I'm not at all happy about the way you speak to your sister," or "When you speak to your sister that way, I'm glad it's not me on the receiving end." Honest self-disclosures such as these are not attempting to discipline, nor enforce, certain behaviors. They do, however, give feedback which might influence a child.

Whether or not stepparents take on a parental role, they need to be able to relate assertively to their stepchildren. Open and honest communication gives the opportunity for a healthy and lasting relationship to develop.

Disciplining with a family conference

In some families a very democratic process is used to sort out disciplinary issues. This is known as a family conference and, believe it or not, can work.

Here are the guidelines for this procedure:

- Tell everyone in the family there is to be a meeting to discuss disciplinary issues. All family members attend—even the little ones.

- Make a time and place for this meeting.

- Nominate a chairperson—you could draw a name from a dish if you want to be truly democratic. Or a parent or stepparent could fill this role.

- The chairperson asks each person to speak, one at a time, stating his or her thoughts about any issue they want to discuss.

- Then comes the discussion time.

- Someone can write down all the suggestions and as they are talked through, a solution will most likely emerge.

- A general agreement must be arrived at. This might depend on a majority vote.

- Everyone needs to know at the outset that compromise will be necessary.

- Emotional outbursts are not allowed, and result in the offender being dismissed from the meeting. (This is a disciplinary action in itself and probably should be agreed upon by all present before the meeting commences.)

To some of you this will probably seem very strange, if not risky. "What if the decision is not what I want?" some of you may be thinking. Just remember, in a stepfamily in particular, compromise is absolutely essential if happiness is to be achieved.

(*Note*: When an issue is calmly discussed, resolution is usually reached.)

If a parent and stepparent cannot agree who is to discipline children in their stepfamily, they can have an issue of their own. The assertive communication skills in Chapters 17 and 18 are the key to the resolution of this issue.

Now that we have explored different decisons as to who does the disciplining in stepfamilies, let's take a look at what it is that needs to be disciplined.

What needs to be disciplined?

Our values, attitudes and rules about codes of behavior have been learned and shaped by our experiences in our families of origin, our school, our scout group, religious educators or wherever. Many of the lessons were taught to us and other lessons were learned just by observation, or as the result of some experiences which might have been good or bad.

Parents usually want to teach their own children according to their own values, attitudes and rules. In first-time families, natural parents (usually) bond to their children and establish a relationship with them while they are babies, before disciplinary measures need to be taken.

Because of this, natural parents also have time to sort out what is important to the two of them, so that they are more likely to agree on what needs to be disciplined.

Agreement, however, with respect to many discipline issues does not always occur in these first-time families. A mother might allow her child a cookie before dinner and her husband may oppose this; a father might give his daughter permission to take the car and the mother might not; a mother agrees that her son can join the football team, to be met with great opposition from the boy's father; a father does not fuss about a neat bedroom and his wife insists that their son clean it. There is an endless list of disciplinary issues over which parents can disagree.

In some instances parents overdiscipline because this gives them a sense of power. They do it for the sake of having control—although they probably are not aware that this is why they do it. They make a rod for their own backs if they are indiscriminate about what they discipline.

A good rule is to save discipline for what really matters—in first-time families *and* in stepfamilies. Parents and stepparents need to tell each other what is important to them and, if there is disagreement, they need to use communication skills to resolve their differences.

When children become teenagers it is even more necessary to restrict discipline to what really is important (usually in terms of safety and moral development). Limits may be set, for instance, around coming-home time, or always letting parents know where they are.

On the other hand, an untidy bedroom or messy hair could be over-looked.

Adolescence is the stage in life concerned with the (psychological) search for identity. At this age children test parental values and limits, as part of discovering who they are as their own separate people.

For parents and teenagers it can be a bewildering time, and relationships that were previously tranquil and enjoyable can become stormy and unpleasant.

This is why *wise* parents and stepparents back off a little, give teenagers their space and only discipline behaviors that top the list in order of importance. (This is actually a good rule of thumb for children of all ages.)

Take time

1. Write a list of discipline issues in your stepfamily.

2. Make a mark next to what is really important and a different mark next to what really is not so important.

3. If you share the discipline role, discuss your lists with each other.

4. If you are sole disciplinarian, it is still helpful to discuss your list with your partner. Are there any changes that you plan to make with respect to what you discipline?

Discipline differences for children

When children visit a parent (perhaps in their second stepfamily), they are often disciplined in a different way from the home where they live. There may be different rules, such as: "When you are inside, take your shoes off." "Please ask if you want any food—don't just help yourself." "In this house, I'd like you to make your bed when you get up in the morning."

It is quite all right for children to have different rules in different places—just as long as they clearly know what the rules are. After all, life involves learning different rules for different places and situations, so this can be a beneficial learning experience for children.

Positive and negative reinforcement

We have seen how discipline involves teaching or training children how to behave. We have also seen how this teaching or training can be either constructive or destructive. You have had the opportunity to reflect upon your disciplinary methods and also upon your own childhood experiences.

One way to teach acceptable behaviors is to reward them when they occur—rather than punish them when they don't. This is called positive reinforcement, whereas punishment is called negative reinforcement. Here are two stories to illustrate this:

> Wilma looked out of her kitchen window and saw little Sam playing in the sandpit with his sister Alice. As she looked, she saw him pick up some sand and throw it into Alice's face. Alice cried. Wilma raced out and smacked Sam for what he had done, saying, "Bad, you shouldn't do that. Don't do that again or you'll get a harder smack!"

Here is another possible scenario:

> Wilma looked out of her kitchen window and saw little Sam playing in the sandpit with his sister Alice. She went out and joined them, saying, "You two are having great fun, aren't you? Sam, I noticed you helping Alice with her sandcastle—that was a good boy."

The first situation illustrates negative reinforcement (or punishment). Because every child has an innate need to be recognized, many children learn that negative attention is better than none, and so they misbehave again and again. If Sam gets his mother's attention only when he is naughty, he will almost certainly continue this behavior. Needless to say this is not going to help their relationship.

On the other hand, in the second situation Sam learned that his good behavior was rewarded by his mother's attention and praise. He felt valued and accepted. Sam and his mother are well on the way to developing a strong and loving relationship.

Take time

Think about your use of positive reinforcement in raising your children and stepchildren. Do you only comment when something is wrong? Become aware of ways that you can give praise and recognition to your children and stepchildren (and spouse).

The dictum "reward good behavior and ignore the bad" has much merit. A child whose efforts to clean a bedroom are complimented (or rewarded) is more likely to want to keep a neat room than a child who is reprimanded for messiness. There is a reward for the parent or stepparent, too: the reward of a more positive and enjoyable relationship.

Disciplinary issues in stepfamilies

That disciplinary issues exist in stepfamilies has already been acknowledged and discussed. Some of the reasons are:

- Stepparents having different attitudes about discipline.

- Stepparents having different values that determine their attitudes about discipline.

- Children in a stepfamily having experienced certain disciplinary methods and standards that are familiar to them, and resisting new rules and methods.

- Resentment toward "intruders" (stepparents) who try to discipline them.

- Different rules for different sets of children.

- Contracts (unspoken or unconscious) that determine certain behaviors, for example, the unspoken contract, "I'm going to teach these kids how to behave."

- A power struggle between divorced parents or between parent and stepparent.

- Inability to compromise—inflexibility.

- Inadequate time spent with a child or children so that a base of influence does not develop. This especially applies to visiting children.

- Unfinished business in a parent, stepparent or child that results in a high degree of emotionality.

- The forces of separateness and togetherness, which make parents and their own children want to adhere to the old rules and the old ways (and therefore retain their togetherness), and resist any attempts to change discipline practices that a stepparent wants to introduce (they want to remain separate).

- Divided loyalties on the part of the children who think (probably unconsciously in many instances), "If I do as he/she asks me to, or take any notice of what he/she says, that means I'm acknowledging that he/she is a part of my life—and I refuse to accept that."

- Aggressiveness that comes from children and aims to punish a stepparent for what has happened to them.

- The power of the absent parent who, in many ways, still lives in the stepfamily home. Just because a parent does not live with children, or even see them, does not mean that he or she fails to have influence. This presence can prevent a stepparent and stepchild relationship from growing.

- An "I'll do it my way" attitude on the part of the natural parent. There is a need to control the way the family operates (or at least to try).

- Lack of communication skills, which is a *major cause* of discipline problems in stepfamilies. These skills are needed between parent and stepparent, parent and ex-partner, between parent and children and between stepparent and stepchildren.

- Lack of consistent disciplinary actions or guidelines.

- Children may be exposed to at least two sets of rules with different parents. Given that each parent may have remarried, there can even be additional and new influences with which the children have to contend.

- Protective behavior by some parents of their children, which excludes the stepparent from relating honestly or being involved in disciplinary action.

- Stepparents whose children live elsewhere often experience a deep sense of loss, guilt and anger, and this contaminates their relationship with their stepchildren.

- Failure to acknowledge that children have rights: namely, the right to be respected and treated with dignity. Children also have the right to talk and say how a situation is for them. This is often denied and the child's resentment affects the disciplinary process.

- Some people overdiscipline, and fail to select what really matters.

- A rigid approach to the discipline of children is just as likely to fail as is a slack and chaotic approach full of inconsistencies.

- Lack of support from a partner in forming a positive relationship with his or her children.

- Failure to admit mistakes (we all make them).

- Rushing—not taking time to develop a base of influence.

How to get the discipline issues sorted out in stepfamilies

While the previous list might have left you feeling somewhat daunted and discouraged, there is hope. There are many changes you can make and much you can learn. Here are some guidelines:

- Read this chapter and gain a thorough understanding of the issues surrounding discipline.

- Parents and stepparents need to have long talks about everything that is included in this chapter (and other chapters as well).

- Decide on who will discipline whom, what the child will be disciplined for and how it will be done. Make provisions for unexpected situations where instant decisions have to be made.

- Learn communications skills (see Chapters 17 and 18).

- Get other books about child raising, attend classes and learn all you can about parenting.

- Remember that the relationship between parent and stepparent is a significant key to sorting out discipline issues.

- Where possible, maintain contact and relate comfortably with ex-partners. The children will be the beneficiaries.

Summary

This chapter has concerned itself with disciplinary issues, namely:

Stepparents are not instant parents
Building a base of influence
Different forms of discipline
Different forms of punishment
Conscience and concepts of right and wrong
How to understand children (and yourself) better
Role models
Who will discipline whom?
Disciplining with a family conference
What needs to be disciplined?
Discipline differences for children
Positive and negative reinforcement
Disciplinary issues in stepfamilies
How to got the discipline issues sorted out in stepfamilies

12

I'm walking a tightrope

Balancing acts in stepfamilies

In this chapter we will take a look at individual and group behaviors in stepfamilies that aim to achieve a state of balance between various family members. All of these strategies, mostly driven by unconscious forces, are designed to reduce anxiety.

When there is tension (or anticipation of it) between various step-family members, these people or other people in the stepfamily may feel tense and anxious. This often results in behaviors that aim to reduce or eliminate this tension. These behaviors may be those of the people involved in the tension-producing situations, or they may be those of family members who witness or fear it.

In order to understand this we will first take a look at the idea of a comfort zone and how it influences behavior.

The comfort zone

The concept of a comfort zone is applied to many areas of life. It refers to a range of conditions and behaviors with which we are comfortable. When these are not present, or there are changes and we feel discomfort because of this, we are then outside our comfort zones.

Whenever we experience ourselves entering these external parameters, we experience anxiety or discomfort and strive to return to what gives us comfort and security.

Most people, for instance, become accustomed to having a certain bank balance with which they feel secure—or at least comfortable. If, however, the bank balance drops below a certain figure, this produces anxiety: "Help! I've spent too much—I must save and get my bank balance up again." Most of us know this experience.

At the other end of the comfort zone is the experience of having a bank balance that goes beyond what we are used to. Perhaps we get a bonus, or a legacy or a lump sum paid into our account. When this happens, what do many people do? They go and spend it and without consciously realizing it, they bring their balance back to familiar territory: back to their comfort zone.

Maintaining a comfortable body temperature often requires us to reach for the heater or a jacket or, if the temperature is too warm, to seek a cool place or shed some clothes. For each of us, temperature needs are unique and we strive to stay within a range that is comfortable for us.

Let's look at another example. For many people, becoming an assertive communicator is very difficult. The skills themselves are not hard to learn, but it is using these skills that challenges people to go outside their comfort zones and behave in a way that is quite unfamiliar.

It is this new territory that produces their anxiety and, unless they resolve to control this anxiety rather than have it control them, they are unlikely to progress and become assertive communicators. They remain stuck forever—captive to their own emotions!

You will recall how (in Chapter 2) Rachel learned and practiced these skills and her family put pressure on her to stop. In this case, *her* new behavior took them outside *their* comfort zones!

People always endeavor to live within their own individual comfort zone. This drive is instinctive and driven by unconscious forces. (Remember how our unconscious self is like the submerged part of an iceberg and is really what controls us.)

Now that we have looked at the idea of the comfort zone, let's look at some situations in stepfamily life that involve balancing behaviors to keep people within their own comfortable territory. Some of these situations are specific to stepfamilies and others are experienced in other families.

Keeping a balance by keeping the peace

Conflict, or even the thought of it, arouses anxiety in many people even though they may engage in and create it themselves. Most people probably wish to avoid conflict and prefer peace and harmony. Why is conflict so threatening to so many people?

It is because we all have a need to feel secure and loved so as to reduce our instinctual fear of being abandoned or rejected. We also have a need to feel valued by others, as this helps us value ourselves. Conflict threatens both these needs.

When there is a lack of harmony or a pervading tension in the air many people, therefore, try to reduce it. They desire peace in their relationships and in the relationships of others around them. Sometimes they are open in their efforts to bring about this peace, other times they do it behind people's backs. They may or may not be aware of what they are doing. Sometimes peacemakers maneuver (often unbeknown to others) interactions between members of the family so that friction is avoided or reduced—or, if it has occurred, they openly get involved and try to restore a balanced state of peace.

Here are examples of this:

> Betty did not like it when her second husband, Alex, became entangled in arguments with her 12-year-old son. She learned to recognize the danger signals and embarked on a "prevention of confrontation" program. Whenever there was the slightest hint that discussion between her husband and son would turn into confrontation, she intervened and changed the subject.

> Robert always felt anxious when his second wife told his children what to do. As soon as she left the room, he did all he could to make his children happy.

> Gloria, age 10, always tried to make peace between her parents when they disagreed by telling a funny story to make them laugh.

> David was uncomfortable with the tension he felt was happening between his daughter and her stepmother (his wife). If he discovered that his daughter had done something wrong, he did all he could to stop his wife from finding out.

In all of these instances, the peacemaker was really acting in the interests of himself or herself, rather than in the interests of the other people. By intervening and preventing conflict between other people, or by trying to help others feel better, this person is really making himself or herself feel better.

David, Gloria, Robert and Betty have triangled in on other people's issues, and in so doing, are actually preventing those people from forming honest and open relationships with each other.

(*Note*: When people triangle in on interactions between other people with the aim of achieving a state of balance between them, all that happens is that the state of balance becomes more precarious. This is a good example of a solution to a problem becoming the problem.)

Take time

What do you do when other people do not seem to be getting along with each other? Do you feel tense? Do you intervene to try to sort things out? How do you do this? What do you think would happen if you kept out of it and left others to sort out their own relationships?

Exercise

Here is one way you can challenge yourself to move outside your comfort zone.

Next time you find yourself in a situation in which there is conflict, try to keep quiet or go away. Be aware of the feelings you have and what you are thinking.

You may find yourself thinking, "If I don't intervene, it will be a disaster." It will be a real challenge to you, in this case, to keep out of the interaction that involves other people.

Interestingly though, *if stepfamily members are left alone to struggle with their individual relationships, they usually sort them out.*

It may take a long time, and it may be difficult waiting for it to happen, but in the long run it is worth it—for everyone.

(*Note*: If conflict persists between stepfamily members, it is better to seek professional help than to have a family member continually intervene.)

Keeping a balance by having a fight

Believe it or not, this is what some people do! These are people who feel more comfortable when there is tension in the air—if not all of the time, at least some of the time. They might have grown up in families where conflict was usual and part of a range of experiences to which they were accustomed. Their zone of comfort is threatened if life becomes too peaceful or too bland, and there is an urge to create an argument or fight.

They may have been raised in a family in which people did not connect emotionally unless they were engaged in conflict. Hence, conflict had an important role in the family.

> Vera came to counseling to seek help in her marriage. Tempers flared as Vera and Tim fought about almost anything. The smallest issues seemed to result in major warfare.
>
> In therapy Vera began to understand that conflict in her marriage actually kept it together. It helped maintain a balance

of connectedness between her and her husband. She realized that when they fought it was the only time they ever looked at each other, talked to each other and related to each other. She said, "At least something happens then."

Fortunately for Vera and Tim and their children, they were greatly helped by counseling, and learned how to communicate with each other, spend time with each other and even look into each other's eyes. They learned to connect in a different way—but to do that they had to break through the boundaries of their individual comfort zones. They learned how to balance their relationship in a different way.

Keeping the balance by approaching/avoiding

In Chapter 5 we looked at the concept of personal space and boundaries and how this relates to the appropriate closeness and distance that people seek between each other.

We are now going to look at a strategy used by people to help them maintain, or balance, these psychological space needs. This is referred to as the approach/avoidance force and aims to balance emotional space between two people. (Remember, it operates out of the unconscious part of us.)

> Penny and Rick married and commenced stepfamily life after having known each other for 18 months. Penny had one seven-year-old boy who lived with them, and Rick's children lived with their mother. These children came to stay every second weekend.
>
> As with all stepfamilies, there was much adjustment to be made as everyone became used to their new lifestyle. The greatest problem (and surprise) for Penny and Rick was that they seemed to have lost that "something special" that they had always shared.
>
> A pattern began to emerge. Many times when Rick wanted to talk intimately with Penny and go off to the bedroom to be together, she became silent and remote. He felt pushed aside and tense and anxious, thinking that she didn't love him the way she used to.
>
> He tried again and again to get her to talk to him and be with him. He tried to be close physically by touching her and even sent her some flowers. (He did this so *he'd* feel better.) The more he tried to get close, the more Penny pulled away by not talking much, and spending more time with her son and going to bed early.

After a month of this Rick became angry and stopped approaching Penny. Instead, he avoided her by working late at the office for the next few days. Then something interesting happened: Penny phoned him at work and asked him to come home early because she wanted to spend an evening alone with him, having arranged for her ex-husband to have her son for the night.

The next few weeks were like old times. It was not long, how ever, before Penny again began to distance (avoid) Rick and he then began to pursue (approach) her. When he tired of this he pulled away, she pursued him to bring them together again.

This approach/avoidance behavior between Rick and Penny is a delicate balancing act between them that allows each to stay within their comfort zone of closeness or distance from each other. Like a yo-yo coming close and then distancing, unconscious forces in both partners contribute to this interaction.

Needless to say this pattern of interaction does not usually contribute to a blending marriage and stepfamily. While all of us do this *to some degree*, with Penny and Rick it was extreme. If you experience this in your relationship, here are four suggestions:

1. Develop self-awareness about what happens when you find yourself engaging in avoiding or approaching behaviors. (See Chapters 2 and 18 on self-awareness.)

2. Think about this and see if you can gain some insight as to why you do this and where the pattern might have originated.

3. Use assertive communication skills to talk about this with your partner. This is very important.

4. If the patterns continue and disrupt your relationship, seek professional help.

(*Note*: It is important to realize that all couples unconsciously maintain a state of balance in their relationship. The approach/avoidance phenomenon is natural and if a relationship maintains a comfortable balance because of these behaviors, then let it be.)

Trying to please everybody

Because of the need some people have to see everyone happy, they continually try to please everyone. In stepfamilies, even more than in first-time families, this is a formidable task!

If a family member expects a perpetual state of happiness to exist, this unrealistic expectation will certainly lead to disappointment and disillusionment.

Patricia and Brian had been in their stepfamily life for three and a half years. Between them they had seven children. It had, from the outset, been Patricia's hope that she would be a good wife to her new partner and a good stepmother to her stepchildren. She wanted to be appreciated and loved by them all. She had visions of one happy family, with lots of laughter and good times together.

She had tried her best. She prepared foods she thought they all liked, often preparing different dishes for one meal to please them all. When her own children complained to her about their stepfather or stepbrother or stepsister, Patricia either tried to make them feel happy or tried to negotiate between them all to resolve any conflict.

When Brian's children challenged her along the way, she tried to please them and often gave in to their requests—even though she didn't want to. When her husband wanted to borrow her car (because he had lent his to his son) she said yes, even though this meant she had to postpone her shopping trip. And so on ...

This stepfamily did not grow, relationships were strained and eventually the marriage broke up. Why? Because Patricia had tried so hard to achieve the impossible. She had maneuvered back and forth between herself and family members in an attempt to balance their satisfaction and needs.

Her lack of assertiveness and her high level of anxiety surrounding anyone's unhappiness contributed to the failure of this stepfamily unit. She was left feeling embittered and resentful and, of course, blamed everyone but herself.

Patricia (and her family) would have been much better off if she had learned assertive communication skills and made her own needs known, set limits and allowed every person in her stepfamily to sort out their own relationships.

(Note: People tend to treat us as we behave. We pull from others what we are willing to take. When people behave as doormats they are usually treated as such.)

The role of the "problem child" in creating balance

Many parents, stepparents, teachers and family members know about the problem child. These children exist in many families and are often taken to a therapist to "get fixed up."

What some people don't know is that a problem child often fulfills an important function in the family—keeping it together. When a child of a stepfamily develops problematic behaviors, this may be a way of keeping the stepfamily together by giving them all something to talk about, focus on and take the spotlight away from other problems. This helps maintain a balance by masking the *real* trouble spots.

Problem children can even unite, or bring together—at least temporarily—both natural parents, who now live apart. In doing this, children experience being with the two of them again—by giving them a common goal which unites them. This helps these children feel more secure. (Remember coming-close behaviors to reduce feelings of rejection.)

Even if both parents went their separate ways long ago, and have since established themselves in new relationships and new families, unconscious forces can work to lead children to seek security by being with them, together—even if it is because of being problem children.

The problems these children have give them attention and recognition and this usually reduces their anxiety, too. It's as though these children think, "If I'm a problem to them, and they pay attention to me, that means they care about me, value me, and won't reject me."

These children might also have an unconscious agenda or contract which is, "If I become a problem, they will all have to focus on me, and that will unite them—then I'll feel more secure." (A state of balance is restored or achieved.)

Yet another hidden agenda might be, "If I'm a problem in this stepfamily, my mother might leave my stepfather and go back to my father."

(*Note*: This behavior is not deliberately planned by children, When they become a problem, they are really hurting inside, and giving reassurance, attention and love is one way to help them. Professional help is often needed as well.)

Familiarity and balance

Marriages in stepfamilies can be just as troubled as those in first-time families—in fact, the higher divorce rate of second and subsequent marriages suggests that they are more delicately balanced. Not only do partners have to contend with all the elements of a couple relationship, they have all the additional complications that go with stepfamily life.

We have already looked at the way a family (or stepfamily system) unconsciously maintains a balance or homeostasis (see Chapter 2). We talked about interpersonal dynamics and how, whether or not the family functions healthily, it always finds a way to maintain a sameness. It is from this sameness that the sense of familiarity is derived.

Adults and children who face the challenge of adapting to stepfamily life usually become accustomed as time goes by to the way this group of people functions together,

If something happens to change the way the stepfamily functions, a new balance is sought. For example, a child who has lived elsewhere may move into the family home. Or a child might be born into the stepfamily. Illness or death may strike. A parent may lose a job. Constantly a stepfamily is in a state of "process"—constantly, like any family, it has to change to achieve a new balance.

This change evolves unconsciously and is the result of changes in individual members. It takes time and often considerable pain—but always the goal is to live once again in a state of balance that becomes familiar and compatible.

Take time

Think about your stepfamily. What was it like for you at the beginning of stepfamily life? What seemed different and out of balance for you? How has this changed?

Reentry time and balance

Almost every day, in different ways, family members have to adjust to reentry time. This refers to those times and occasions when, for example, someone comes home after a day at work, after being away for a holiday, or away on a visit day with the other parent.

When people reenter the family environment, the state of balance that has existed while they were away is temporarily thrown out of balance. That is why, when people barge into a room, or arrive home and take over, other people may be irritated and uncomfortable. The sudden change in the internal dynamics of the family home is jarring.

The people who have been away also have to adjust to being home again. For them, too, reentry time can be a period of delicate adjustment if tempers and nerves are not to be stretched to the limit.

It is a good idea to go slowly—even tentatively—when you reenter your family environment, or experience a family member reentering. This is especially important with children who have been away for visiting times or have come for visiting times.

For them the changes of going from one home to another, and one person to another, can be quite disturbing. They need time and (psychological) space to settle down and reestablish an emotional connection with where they find themselves. In reentering relationships or places, they go through a process of getting back on balance.

Parents, too, whose children come and go, have to make these adjustments. Often they are thrown off balance after time with their children. After a while, however, maybe a day or so, their emotional equilibrium is regained.

Children in stepfamilies are especially vulnerable to having their "nose put out of joint" when stepsiblings come to visit. This can result in individual tension and friction between children. Many a parent and stepparent know about these topsy-turvy times as children get together and have to seek and find balance of stepfamily functioning.

The role of the scapegoat in maintaining family balance

The term scapegoat comes from Old Testament times when, once a year, a priest would lay upon the head of a goat all the sins of the people. The goat bore their guilt and then was sent into the wilderness, leaving the people free of the burden of guilt.

In families a child often becomes the scapegoat for all the hangups, inadequacies and sins of family members. Statements such as: "It's his fault," "She can't do anything right," "Trust him to get it wrong," "Don't ever rely on her," are heaped upon the sacrificial scapegoat, who is always the weakest member of the family with respect to self-esteem, confidence and assertiveness. Of course it doesn't help a child, assaulted in this way, to develop these qualities!

Children readily take out their frustrations on the scapegoat child by excluding him or her from play, and by taunting, criticizing, ridiculing, nagging and teasing. It puffs up their own (pseudo) self-esteem and makes them feel better.

Some adults derive much sadistic pleasure from this practice, too, and were often scapegoats themselves when they were children. In a way they are "getting their own back."

A stepparent sometimes becomes a scapegoat—especially in a stepfamily where he or she lives with a partner and the partner's children. In an effort to keep the original family united, this partner and children may blame, ridicule and put down the new stepparent in an "us-versus-him or her" situation. Togetherness and family boundary issues operate here.

By keeping the new stepparent outside the original family unit, the balance of the family relationships (prior to stepfamily life) is more likely to be maintained.

Another reason why a scapegoat is created in a family is that tension between other family members can be reduced. We see this, for example, where parent and stepparent are not coping well with their relationship. Instead of looking at themselves and their interactions, a child is blamed for their unhappiness. "If it weren't for him, we'd be happy."

Children balancing themselves between two families

Children in stepfamilies have two or more families. Even if one parent does not remarry, or has died, there are usually relatives that belong to the side of the family with whom the children do not live. Often it is hard keeping in touch with that other side.

Adults often reject their ex-relatives, who may also reject them. This means that it can be difficult for children and these relatives to keep in touch. Many children are caught up in this web of bitterness and rejection against their will.

Sometimes they, or their ex-relatives, try to maintain contact with each other. This can be difficult for them to arrange and it can also be a difficult situation for the parent who does not want to have anything to do with these ex-relatives or they with him or her.

In cases such as these a delicate balancing act on the part of the children often evolves. They do not want to upset their parents nor their relatives from whom the parent is now estranged. They usually learn (if they are wise) not to gossip about one to the other and to pursue both relationships quietly, thus maintaining a sensitive state of balance between them. It's as though they think, "I love my parent and I love my relatives. I'll be careful not to upset either."

If all this becomes too difficult and stressful, they may try to restore their own emotional balance by ceasing to maintain any contact with relatives. When this happens, however, a huge part of the child's life is lost.

(*Note*: After divorce it is almost always in the best interests of the children that they maintain contact with relatives on both sides of the family. Parents who do not encourage this are punishing their children for their own shortcomings.)

Go-betweens who try to balance relationships

In some stepfamilies there is a go-between person, working behind the scenes as well as openly, trying to keep a state of equilibrium and balance between family members.

A mother is the go-between for her husband and her children

This is very common and creates many problems. Countless women, for example, know the experience in their stepfamilies of trying to keep the peace between her husband and their own children. Let's now take a brief look at some of the ways this may happen, as well as some of the causes.

A mother often feels very protective of her children once they have entered stepfamily life. Because of this the mother may try to keep things as they were beforehand. This means that she tries to keep the relationship with her children separate from the relationship with her husband. In doing this, the mother becomes the buffer between the two sets of relationships.

The mother, for example, protects the children from their stepfather's anger, complaints and irritating habits. This may be done by encouraging the husband to come home late, after the children have gone to bed. Or if the husband is angry with the children, the mother may take the children's side.

Sometimes the mother is pressured to spend more time with the children—or with her husband. She may feel guilty if she doesn't. Sometimes a mother gets hints that her husband and children are jealous of each other. Her husband says, "You care about your children more than you care about me." The children say, "Why are you always with him? ... " The mother really begins to feel as though she is walking a tightrope!

Deep down she usually wants her children and husband to like— even love—each other. She tells her husband not to shout because she knows her children don't like that; she tells her children to remember their stepfather's birthday; she tells her children to wipe their feet before they come in the door because she does not want her husband upset; she works on the side to sort out conflict between them; she does all the talking at the dinner table to ease the silence; she tells her husband things about her children she thinks he will appreciate; she tells her children things about her husband she thinks they will appreciate; she is always trying to get them to *love each other.*

(*Note*: A mother such as this truly believes that if it weren't for her, her children and husband would never get along with each other. The truth is: *because* of the way she behaves, they will (probably) never get along with each other.)

A father is the go-between for his wife and his children

A father engages in similar strategies as shown above. Although this is probably not as common, the results are still the same.

A wife wants her parents and family to like her second husband

She arranges outings together; she asks her mother to cook her husband's favorite meal; she asks her husband to wear the clothes her mother likes on him; she asks her husband to buy her mother a present for her birthday; she asks her mother to buy a present for her husband's birthday; she is always trying to get them to *love each other* (or at least *like* each other).

A husband wants his parents to like his second wife

This is done the same way as above, for the same reasons.

A child keeps a balance between time spent with parents who no longer live together

If he or she lives with one parent, there is often an effort to have equal time with the other. This balancing by being "fair" reduces (in the mind of the child) the risk of being rejected by either one, or causing a conflict between them.

A child (often the oldest) takes on the role of keeping things running smoothly between parent and stepparent

He or she acts as counselor; tries to solve problems; and keeps the rest of the family happy or busy.

Take time

Do you fulfill a balancing role in your stepfamily? If you do, how do you do this? What is the payoff for you? What is the payoff for the others?

A natural child balances between stepsiblings

A natural child of the step-couple might learn at an early age to relate fairly and equitably between two sets of siblings.

He or she doesn't want to be seen to favor anyone or be the cause of any friction.

Balancing by keeping busy

Some families maintain an emotional balance by keeping busy—very busy! They are always on the run—here, there, everywhere. They manage to make contact along the way but it is superficial and swift. This way they avoid conflict and thereby keep their anxiety levels within their comfort zones.

There is no time to discuss issues—there is only time, at best, to tell each other what they are doing in their lives. Intimacy does not exist in these families.

When a stepfamily is formed and some members come from a busy family and others come from a not-so-busy family, there might be troubled times ahead before a new balance is achieved that is comfortable for everyone.

Many partners get caught up in the business (busy-ness) trap. They work long hours, failing to come home for family dinner time and even work overtime during the weekend. They may be helping to balance the budget, but are they helping their family life have a healthy balance?

Being fair to all the children

Many parents in stepfamilies work hard to treat their stepchildren and their own children fairly. This way, they believe, they will eliminate any risk of stepsibling rivalry. Sometimes this balancing act works. Sometimes it doesn't.

Children have uncanny ways of declaring something unfair. A parent is often caught in the middle and, if he or she is one of those people who wants to make everyone happy, then it becomes more difficult to set limits and to discipline confidently.

We have already seen in the chapter on discipline how some parents do not want their own children disciplined by their partner. If two sets of siblings live together and continue to experience different disciplinary standards and methods, this makes it more difficult for stepsiblings to experience a sense of fairness between them.

Parents and stepparents fare better if all the children who live together have to abide by the same rules. This certainly helps contribute to an emotionally balanced family life.

(*Note*: When put to the test, most parents (at least secretly) favor their own children. This is natural. There are, however, some parents who are harsher on their own children than they are on stepchildren. This may be a strategy (conscious or unconscious) to win the approval or love of their stepchildren, it may be in accordance with their disciplinary values or it may involve unfinished business from the parents' past.)

Balancing time

Perhaps the most common complaint heard by counselors from step-couples is, "We can never find time to be alone together."

From the first day of their stepfamily life, these couples have had at least one other person involved in their relationship. Sometimes this child is grown and lives far away, sometimes the child lives elsewhere and comes to stay occasionally, and sometimes the child lives with them permanently.

It can often be very difficult for partners to find time to be together alone—and yet this is absolutely necessary for their relationship to develop and grow.

Sometimes, when relationships are stressed and a couple is not getting along too well, they find a way to retreat. They may do this while at home, for example, by going to bed early or arranging for the children to go out so they can be alone. Even a night out together presents an opportunity for them to renew their relationship.

It is also necessary for parents to find time to spend alone with their own children—preferably *one-to-one* on different occasions. Many parents make a point of spending time alone with each of their children. This may be by taking them shopping, going for a walk, to a movie or whatever.

Children appreciate this special time with a parent—it gives them a chance to get to know their mother or father in a more personal and intimate way. It also gives parents the opportunity to get to know and relate more closely to their child.

Relationships between stepparent and stepchild benefit greatly if they, too, spend time together alone. They can get to know each other in a way that is not possible when other people are around. This helps them as well as their stepfamily life. Many stepparents grab the opportunity to drive a stepchild to tennis, or football or ballet—just so that they can be alone together.

Grandparents in particular need to be considered by parents and children when time is being planned. These relationships are (usually) of prime importance to children, who need to be able to maintain a balance between all the relationships in their various families.

With the pace of daily life involving work, school, housework, outside activities and so on, balancing time or budgeting time to meet the various needs of stepfamily members is often given a low priority. Before people realize it, a year has gone, then another year ... and stepfamily life is often struggling to stay afloat.

When the time budget is managed well, stepfamily life is more likely to be healthy and balanced. This means that members of it are more likely to be happy in themselves and in their relationships.

A top priority needs to be given to making time for different stepfamily members to be together as twosomes, or together as a family. This is the way that strong relationships are forged (not forced) as a stepfamily history is made.

Balancing money

Stepfamilies often experience financial stress as a result of past marriages that have required financial settlement and ongoing expenses. Many stepparents are contributing financially to two families and this puts a strain on current family life.

In many of these families, as with other families, both partners work and contribute to family expenditure. Conflict often surrounds the issue of how money is spent and who will spend it.

Some step-couples choose to have separate bank accounts, others decide to open a joint account. Decisions have to be made with respect to expenses for his children, her children, their children. Differences emerge with respect to different attitudes about money. All of these things have to be resolved if the stepfamily is to merge comfortably.

A balance has to be maintained between her values and attitudes and his. New ways to deal with the situation may be initiated. The key to this is communication. (See Chapter 16 on money issues in stepfamilies.)

Lifestyle balance

It's easy to become serious and intent on getting all the work done, all the jobs up-to-date. A balance is needed, however, between work, play and other activities. Stepfamilies are more likely to blend when they make time to have fun, to relax, to listen to music, go to church, watch a video, go camping, have friends for dinner, go on a picnic, to a playground, to the beach, for a walk or whatever.

Take time

Think about all of the above. Talk about these things with your stepfamily members and find out what everybody is thinking, feeling and wanting with respect to their lifestyles.

Lifestyle pie exercise

1. Look at Figure 5 and you'll see a lifestyle pie. You will notice that this pie represents the total time available in Marianne's life. In pie "A" Marianne has indicated how she perceives each activity in her life filling her time. In pie "B" she indicates how she would like to be spending her time. This helps her to identify where her lifestyle is out of balance. With this information she can start to make changes to meet her needs.

2. Now list all the activities in your life right now.

3. Then use these items to do your pie A.

4. Then do pie B, indicating how you would like to spend your time (you might want to delete or add activities).

5. Notice whether or not there are differences between the two pies and think about what this means for you.

6. If you wish, talk about your findings with family members. You could suggest that they do this exercise also and then talk together.

(*Note*: The aim of this exercise is to bring about a better balance in your lifestyle—as well as that of your stepfamily.)

Getting out of balance by trying to stay in balance

This often happens when a *self-fulfilling prophesy* is involved, unbeknown to anyone.

> Nigel entered his third marriage with two wives and two sets of children behind him. In each case, his wife had left him and taken his children away. While he was happy to be remarried, there was, lurking in his mind, the belief that this marriage would also end the same way.
>
> This made him feel quite tense when his wife was not loving and attentive to him. To him, these were signs that things were going downhill. He became very needy of her, resented her going out and leaving him and wanted constant reassurance that she loved him. His fear, which accompanied his belief: "One day she will leave me as the others did," made him behave this way.
>
> He kept trying to restore the balance he experienced in their courting days. In doing this, however, he contributed to the failure of the marriage. This wife, too, could take his be-

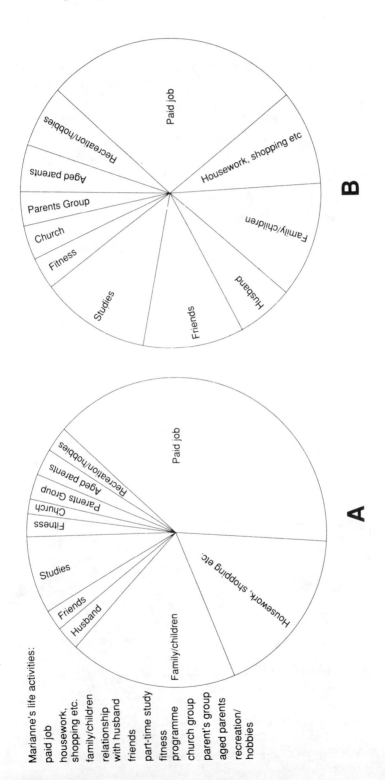

Marianne's life activities:

paid job
housework,
shopping etc.
family/children
relationship
with husband
friends
part-time study
fitness
programme
church group
parent's group
aged parents
recreation/
hobbies

**Fig. 5   Lifestyle pie showing (A) proportion of time Marianne actually spends on each life activity
(B) proportion of time Marianne *would like* to spend on each life activity**

havior no longer and left him. He was then able to say to himself, "You see, I was right all along. She has left me."

Many of us live with self-fulfilling prophesies. Some of them lead us down painful paths in life. In Nigel's case, the more he tried to balance his third marriage relationship, the more it got off balance.

Take time

Develop you self-awareness about what is happening in your family. What patterns do you notice? What do you think they mean? How openly are you able to communicate with your family members about your relationship with each of them?

(*Note*: Sometimes it is better to leave things alone by being patient and discreet. Too much talking and probing can be threatening to people. Once again, a balance is needed—in this instance with respect to self-disclosure. Too little or too much can destroy a relationship.)

Be encouraged

In this chapter we have looked at many areas of stepfamily life that need to be kept in balance and how this balance is related to people's comfort zones.

You may become aware of other areas that require balance, as well as other ways that it is obtained or maintained. As you continue to learn about yourself and your stepfamily, you are certain to gain new insights which will greatly help you grow and help your family members do the same.

Summary

The sections you have read about in this chapter were:

The comfort zone
Keeping the balance by keeping the peace
Keeping the balance by having a fight
Keeping the balance by approaching/avoiding
Trying to please everybody
The role of the "problem child" in creating balance
Familiarity and balance
Reentry time and balance
The role of the scapegoat in maintaining family balance
Children balancing themselves between two families
Go-betweens who try to balance relationships
A natural child balances between stepsiblings

Balancing by keeping busy
Being fair to all the children
Balancing time
Balancing money
Lifestyle balance
Lifestyle pie exercise
Getting out of balance by trying to stay in balance

13

Why don't I see Granny now?

The changed nature of relationships in stepfamilies

Before we look at the way some relationships can change once a stepfamily is formed, we will briefly consider again some of the emotional effects on adults and children of separation, divorce and death—any of which precedes stepfamily life.

Emotional effects of separation, divorce and death

For most *parents* the experience after separating from their children is one of excruciating sadness, anger, fear and sometimes guilt. Sometimes it seems too much to bear. An underlying anxiety that their children will cease to love, need or respect them affects these parents' confidence and self-esteem. Many fear losing parental influence.

For *children*, fear that they won't be loved anymore, or accepted by the parent, affect the way they relate to others. Many children feel anxious, guilty, angry and sad as well.

Young children often blame themselves for the family breakup. They might think that because they were naughty, a parent left.

Children between ages *four and eight* (approximately) may believe that a parent has left because he or she does not love them anymore. They might think, for example: "I don't think my mother really loves me—if she did, she would have stayed." To protect themselves from this threatening thought they often (unconsciously) use the defense mechanism of blaming others. Instead of admitting that they believe they are unloved, they may accuse the parent who stayed of driving the other parent away. Children in this age group are likely to be very supportive of the absent parent, and do not like to hear anything said against him or her.

Both parents need to reassure their child that he or she is loved by each of them. Actions that give this message credibility are, of course, necessary. Remember the saying: "actions speak louder than words."

(*Note*: Never bad-mouth the other parent (estranged or ex-partner) to a child. Whatever the feelings are between two parents they need always to remember that they are both parents of their child. Trying to get a child to side with one parent against the other is very damaging to children. This is triangling of the worst kind.)

Children from about the ages of *nine to twelve* are more likely to act as though the separation of parents has not affected them at all. Sometimes they use denial and declare, for example, that Dad has gone overseas to work, instead of facing the reality that Dad has left home and lives in the next suburb. Sometimes they rationalize, saying things like: "It's good that Dad has left because now I have two families."

In this case, the defense mechanisms of denial and rationalization help the child to feel better by offering protection against the awesome reality that child and parent are now separated forever.

Adolescents are inclined to deal with separation of parents in a different way. They usually have more understanding about why their parents cannot live together anymore—although when parents have kept their differences under cover and then suddenly separate, it is more difficult for adolescents to grasp the situation. In spite of some rational comprehension of the situation, children in this age group do, however, usually feel deserted and angry, sad and fearful.

Sometimes separation and divorce of parents comes into the lives of *adult children*. They may be in their twenties, thirties or older. They, too, go through a period of adjustment and wrestle with many of the emotions experienced by younger offspring. Sometimes these older children cease to have contact with the parent who has left. They blame and judge and any attempts by this parent to reconcile are to no avail. Note that here, again, defense mechanisms are at work.

A word needs to be said about parents who continue to live with their children after the departure of their former partner. To some people it seems that these parents are the ones who suffer least—after all, they still have their children!

For these parents, however, there is the pain of a broken relationship to come to terms with (irrespective of who ended it), added responsibilities and constant reminders of how their children have been affected. They are left with the task of pulling all of them through the emotional upheaval and rebalancing the family unit. This is no mean feat and many a custodial parent breaks under the strain.

Often parents who are left with the children are reluctant to ask for help and battle on bravely. Support systems of family and one-time relatives may fall away, and a sense of aloneness in the world is common. Relationships between them and their children can become very strained—especially when, as so often happens, children misbehave or rebel at home, at school or in society. To these parents comes most of the responsibility of dealing with the daily issues of raising a family—all alone.

Where a parent is widowed, help is usually more forthcoming as family and friends rally around. These parents, too, however, have much to deal with, including coming to terms with their loss and helping their children go through their own grieving process as well. This can take considerable time. Some people never recover from the death of a loved partner or parent. If this is your experience, professional help may be of great assistance.

Adjusting to life and finding a balance once a stepfamily is formed presents another challenge to those people who have already been through much emotional trauma following the breakup of a previous family. Here are new faces, new behaviors, new relationships. We need to note here that some adults and children are in their third or fourth stepfamilies. Part of the new challenge is to become accustomed to having these new people in their lives, but an added stress is that relationships between members of the previous family (or families) may change.

The same people may still be there but the way they interact is now different. Limited access between parent and child, for example, means that those involved in this time together have to spend it in a new and different way. In addition, individuals themselves may seem to some family members to have changed and, in some instances, they actually have.

Let's now look at some different relationships and the changes they encounter.

Relationship between access parent and child

The way a child relates to his or her natural parent changes dramatically when that parent does not live with the child anymore. Now, times spent together are likely to be over an entire weekend, a full day or on vacation. Other times a phone call or letter is the way to keep in touch. In many ways this creates, especially at the beginning, an artificiality in the way parent and child relate.

Children are usually taken out for the day or weekend, or away for a vacation, and then returned home. Sometimes they stay with their step-family—the family in which the access parent lives. Young children, as we have seen, are often very distressed at "goodbye" time and this, in turn, can be very distressing to parents.

(*Note*: Some fathers and mothers decide not to see their children at all when this happens, thinking that this is better for the child. This is a great mistake. All children benefit from regular contact with the access parent, unless that person is brutal and damaging to the child. If a parent is troubled as a result of access visits and is thinking of terminating them, consultation with a professional therapist is recommended.)

Given time, however, children eventually become much more accus-tomed to this coming and going. They may never like it but they do be-come used to it and are able to learn that they will be seeing their parent again—it is not goodbye forever!

When a parent has short periods of time with a child in this way, the relationship is quite different from when they lived together perma-nently in the same home. In some ways, parent and child have to learn to relate differently. This emphasis is usually on having a good time—or, at least, relating in a happy and relaxed way.

Many parents spoil their children on these access visits or allow them to get away with behavior they would not normally tolerate. It is not unusual for a child to return home with gifts and a tummy full of ice cream, potato chips or chocolate. This, however, usually tapers off as time goes by and gradually a more balanced and normal parent-child re-lationship develops.

When children visit new stepfamilies, they usually have a lot of ad-justing to do.

> Melanie was seven when her parents divorced. At first she used to see her father every Sunday, and on school holidays he took her camping with some friends of his. Three years later her father remarried and now she had to share him with her new stepmother, stepbrother and stepsister. She hated the way her stepsister interrupted when she was playing with her father and she began to think she would rather not visit any-more. Her special relationship with her father had changed. He seemed different and did not spend as much time with her as he used to.

Her father, too, noticed changes in Melanie. She seemed less spontaneous and often withdrew when he took her to his home. Even when they were alone in the car she seemed quiet. He felt quite uncomfortable with her a lot of the time and didn't know what to do about it.

Fortunately, he was able to talk to his wife about it and they agreed that sometimes he would take Melanie out for the day so that they could just be alone together. He started to do this and gradually he and his daughter relaxed and enjoyed each other's company again. He also talked to her about his new family, reassuring her that she was the most important little girl to him, and after a while she was happy to go and stay and play with her new stepbrother and stepsister. He also started to phone her in the middle of the week just to say "Hi."

This is a good example of how a parent can help a child feel more secure in a new stepfamily. Melanie's father used the self-awareness skills described in Chapter 18 (to notice the change in his daughter), communication skills (to talk to his wife and Melanie), patience (he did not rush things) and creativity (he thought of a way to sort out the problem).

Whatever the ages of the children and whatever the living situation of the absent parent, sensitivity, awareness, communication, time, patience and creativity go a long way toward establishing positive and loving relationships between them.

Sometimes parents and children get caught up in their own lives and keeping in touch becomes a low priority. Other times, a parent and child just don't get along with each other. If this is the case, there's no point in trying to force a relationship just because there is one. Better for the contact to be less frequent and more positive than more frequent and less positive. Birthday cards are one way to acknowledge the presence of each other and can provide a link over the years that may ultimately lead to reconciliation.

If these relationships slip away and contact is lost altogether, parent and child usually have much sadness, anger or guilt. This can affect their lives and their relationships. Often people do not realize that problems they encounter later on in their lives are the result of the trauma of a broken family or the loss of a parent.

Take time

If you are an access parent, think about how you keep in touch with your children. Do you feel relaxed about this relationship? Is it important to you? If so, in what way? If not, why do you think this is so?

(*Note*: Many parents and children cease to maintain contact because they think the other person does not want to see them. Always check out this dangerous assumption—you may well be wrong.)

If you are a permanent parent, how do you assist your child or children to have an ongoing relationship with their absent parent? Is it by saying nothing and leaving it to them? Or is it by encouraging them to go and telephone mother or father and say hello? How do you encourage, if you do?

Parents and their new partners are giving children a real gift when they make it easy for them to keep in touch with the absent parent and relatives. If they discourage or even make it impossible, they are punishing children for something they have not been responsible for, namely, the breakup of the original family.

If you are a child of divorce and have a parent with whom you have not kept in touch—either because of your own actions or his or hers—think about what this means for you. Do you ever think of him or her? Have you tried to make contact or thought about it? How could you do this if you decided to? What would you like to say to this parent?

(*Note*: In cases such as these, many children (young or not-so-young) carry a lot of anger toward the parent who has rejected them. There are different moves children can make to help them resolve this pain. First, they can actually make contact by letter, phone or in person and express to the parent (using assertive communication skills covered in Chapters 17 and 18) what is on their mind and how they are feeling about this. Second, they can write a long, spontaneous letter, saying anything at all, and then, after reading it and rereading it many times, throw it in the wastebasket. It can be quite amazing how therapeutic this can be. Third, they can seek professional help. They might try to talk about it to friends or family, too, but usually professional therapists are better able to help.)

Relationships between grandparents and grandchildren

Grandparents are another group of people who are often deeply affected by separation and divorce. There are many instances where, out of spite and revenge, parents prevent their children from maintaining contact with the parents of their ex-partners.

It is usual for grandparents to grieve deeply when this happens. There are stories cf them waiting outside schools just to get a glimpse of their own grandchildren. How tragic!

Most grandparents experience great joy through having grandchildren. At this later stage of their lives, they are able to relax and enjoy many rewarding experiences with them. When grandchildren are kept away from them, the emotional toll can be devastating for them, and when an angry parent punishes parents-in-law by alienating them from their grandchildren, there is often little they can do.

This situation is regrettably all too common. When anger is used to interfere with relationships between innocent family members, the person who behaves in this vindictive way is also suffering, and is dealing with hurt and anger in a self-destructive way as well as hurting others.

For the children who are not allowed or given the opportunity to keep in touch with grandparents, the separation from the loved (or even not-so-loved) "old folks" has a lasting effect. A part of their lives has been wrenched away. Many people do not realize how valuable the grandparent-grandchild relationship is in the development of their children.

In therapy it is often disclosed by clients that the most important person in their childhood was their grandmother or grandfather. They will often weep at the memory of precious times spent together. Often it seems to them as though their grandparent was the only person who made them feel really loved and special.

Whether or not this is the case, separation, divorce or a new stepfamily can very easily sever the connectedness between grandparent and grandchild. Sometimes a parent deliberately brings this about, sometimes a move to a far away place makes contact difficult (but what about the phone and letters?) and sometimes they just drift apart.

Then again, there is another aspect to the end of a grandparent-grandchild relationship. This involves self-defeating behavior on the part of the grandparents themselves. Sometimes they sever their relationships with their son-in-law or daughter-in-law at the time the marriage breaks up or perhaps at the time the new stepfamily is formed. They may act coldly, be critical or aggressive or withdraw altogether, and then wonder why the son-in-law or daughter-in-law does not keep the children in touch with them.

Sometimes these grandparents believe that their own child (the mother or father of the grandchildren) will be the link between them and the grandchildren. This is often a mistaken belief.

Grandparents are like everyone else when a stepfamily is formed. They, too, have to go through a period of adjustment as they become accustomed to new faces and changed family interactions. The emotional hurdles that grandparents face are often not acknowledged—or even recognized—by their children, relatives and friends.

Sometimes grandparents, through their own actions, create a situation in which contact with their grandchildren is made very difficult.

Helen and Ted had lived through the shock and grief of their son's separation and subsequent divorce. Their grandchildren lived with their ex-daughter-in-law and because of their anger at her for leaving their son, they had decided they wanted nothing to do with her. Their hostility to her only served to alienate her from them.

Tom, the father of the children, subsequently remarried (forming a stepfamily) and found it difficult to find the time to keep his children and his parents in touch with each other. Gradually, the grandparent-grandchild links weakened. Many times Helen and Ted wanted to ask their grandchildren to stay over. They did not do this, however, because this meant having to talk with their ex-daughter-in-law, which made them angry and uncomfortable. The children, too, wanted to see their grandparents but were met with a terse reply when they asked their mother to arrange it.

There are many families in which grandchildren and grandparents lose contact because of unfinished and unresolved issues between people who were once part of one extended family. The sad part is that children are so often caught in the middle of these conflicts, and, through no fault of their own, miss out on a very important part of life: a relationship with their grandparents.

Sometimes grandparents are rejecting of their own child's remariage, and this distances them from their grandchildren.

Vi and Jack loved their three grandchildren and spent as much time with them as they could—especially after their son-in-law left their daughter. Often they babysat while their daughter went to work or had an occasional weekend away for a much needed break.

When their daughter married a man who had two children of his own, Vi and Jack found they did not like their new son-in-law and they liked his children even less. They resented these newcomers, who seemed to take their daughter and grandchildren away from them. They also resented the fact that they were expected to be loving grandparents to their step-grandchildren. It wasn't long before the newcomers in the family got the message and gradually these grandparents and their grandchildren were seeing less and less of each other as their daughter and her new stepfamily withdrew. They did this to avoid the tension that existed when they were all together.

Difficult though it may be, grandparents need to be careful to build positive relationships with their grown-up children, ex-daughters-in-law and sons-in-law, and their grandchildren. This means being patient and tolerant, compromising and relating in a way that does not destroy relationships. A good rule is to "keep the door open."

Of course, sometimes grandparents do all these things and still they lose contact with their grandchildren. There are many different ways in which grandchildren and grandparents lose contact. Sometimes the parents of the children feel guilty or embarrassed about keeping in touch with their ex-parents-in-law, or are angry at them for something they have done in the past. These parents, too, need to try to overcome these obstacles so that their children may continue to build and enjoy a relationship with their grandparents.

Take time

If you are a grandparent, reflect on your relationships with your grandchildren. Do you keep in touch as much as you want to? If so, how? If not, what stops this from happening? How could you begin to build a relationship again with them?

(*Note*: Here again, barriers can be knocked down and relationships rebuilt. A friendly letter, a birthday card, a phone call can do much to renew contact. It is often helpful to get in touch with your ex-daughter-in-law or son-in-law and say you are sorry things turned out as they did but now you want to get on with living and would very much like to be in touch with your grandchildren. Assertive communication skills are crucial. Use your self-awareness wheel (Chapter 18) to say what you want to say.)

If you are a parent of children who have lost contact with grandparents, bear in mind that almost always everyone benefits if this relationship is renewed. What can you do to help this happen? If you do not feel like doing this, what do you think is stopping you? Do you have resentment and anger toward your ex-mother-in-law or ex-father-in-law? Do you feel guilty? How can you deal with this?

(*Note*: Forgiveness is often difficult—but it is possible. Many people find it in their hearts to forgive past hurts and get on with living. As long as they hold onto their resentment, they are living in the past. Is that a good way to live? If your anger or guilt seems insurmountable, remember that there are professional therapists who can help you.)

Relationships between children and other relatives

As well as having a continuing relationship with parents and grandparents, children benefit and usually enjoy keeping in touch with cousins, aunts and uncles and other family members. Contact with extended family members is known to be important in children's lives. It helps give them a sense of their psychological roots and this contributes to the development of self-identity and self-esteem.

As with grandparents, parents can help their children build ongoing relationships with their relatives—on both sides of their family of origin. Sometimes an adult has to swallow pride to do this and may find the experience quite challenging. Usually, though, when parents realize that they are helping their children adapt to changed living arrangements and stepfamily life, they are willing (and able) to do this.

Be encouraged

However difficult a relationship may seem, whether it be between a child and his or her parent or an adult and his or her ex-relatives, there are always ways to improve it or, at least, to negotiate so that other in-nocent people do not suffer. The key is that you have the self-awareness to look at the situation objectively (that is, without becoming entangled in your emotions) and then to trust your own awareness about what is really happening.

With practice and the use of assertive communication skills, many relationships can be rebuilt and grow into lasting and rewarding experien-ces or can, at least, be maintained in a way that is constructive for every-one involved.

Summary

In this chapter we have looked at:

Emotional effects of separation, divorce and death
Relationship between access parent and child
Relationships between grandparents and grandchildren
Relationships between children and other relatives

14

Now we have one of our own

The biological child in the stepfamily

The initial impact of the biological child

So far in this book we have not considered the child who is the biological child of the step-couple and whose arrival heralds a whole set of changes for everyone in the stepfamily.

Sometimes these children are born into households where their half-brothers or half-sisters live. Other times some of their half-siblings live with them and others don't. Yet again, they may not have any half-siblings living with them. However it is, when the parents of a stepfamily have their own child the nature of the stepfamily system changes.

The arrival of a baby who is the biological child of the stepparents is a unifying force for some stepfamilies. In many ways this child serves to pull the family members together, giving them a common bond and often resulting in their feeling more like a family. Not only the parents, but their respective children can form an instant attachment to this cute little person who is a powerful agent of togetherness, being biologically related to all of them.

In other stepfamilies the arrival of the natural child may create greater disunity among family members than already exists. Here is a threat to the love that may be seen already as being sparsely spread between stepsiblings, here is a "toy" over which they can all fight, here is a reminder that this (step) family is for real: the parents intend to stay together and the child symbolizes this state of permanence.

Here are two examples of the variety of stepfamilies into which children can be born.

A second family for father

In some cases a man leaves his first wife and children, marries his second wife, who may be a younger woman, and has another set of children with her. When this happens the man has two complete sets of children to whom he is father. Each child in his first set may accept (and even love) each of the new half-siblings in the second set, but often they do not. Quite frequently an "us versus them" situation develops which persists throughout adulthood.

The father in this situation often tries to balance himself delicately between the two families. He is often seen by the first set of children as having rejected them: "If he had loved us, he would not have left" "He loves his other children more than he loves us." It is common for his financial resources to be stretched, as well as his available time.

The normal stresses of living with a young family (sleepless nights and so on) place additional burdens on him, and so it's not surprising that his first children are, in some ways, going to miss out.

This, in turn, causes their resentment and jealousy. On the other hand, his second wife may resent the time and money he spends on his first family and this puts a stress on his relationship with her.

In situations such as these it is important for the father to do all he can to continue being a father to his first set of children. He and his first wife need to bury (or, better still, resolve) their differences for the benefit of their children. The more that children believe, in a very real way, that they are still loved by the nonresident parent, the fewer emotional problems they have then and will have in future years.

The first wife helps her children if she gives them "emotional" permission to continue their relationship with their father. This means that she does not talk against him or his second wife, does not ask for inside information about what happens in the other family and is supportive and encouraging of her children having contact with their father and his new wife. This is often very difficult to do, and presents a real challenge for personal growth. The important reason for doing it, however, is for the children's emotional health.

The second wife in a stepfamily such as this does well if she goes slowly in building her relationship with her stepchildren. This means she gets to know them by spending time with them, by restraining herself from being mother to them (until she has built a base of influence) and by realizing that they and her children are biologically related and therefore have a right to develop a sibling relationship with each other.

Needless to say, good communication between this man and his first and second wife goes a long way toward making this potentially stressful and emotional situation easier for everyone.

Two original families plus the biological child all living together

Another very different stepfamily is one in which two people have married and brought with them their two respective sets of children. They then, either early or later on in the life of the family, have their own child.

Many unforeseen struggles and challenges can lie ahead for these parents.

> Bernie and Zoe came into their marriage with two children each. Bernie's wife had left him and disappeared, leaving him to care for two daughters, ages ten and eight. Zoe had a daughter, age eight, and a son of six.
>
> Four years after they married they had their own child, Damien, to the great joy of all members of the family. This child really pulled them together—especially the four children, who felt much closer to each other now that they shared a baby brother.
>
> And so the next six years rolled by. Bernie and Zoe educated themselves by reading all they could about how to build a happy stepfamily and they also learned (and used) communication skills, thus enabling the skillful resolution of family issues and creating a climate of intimacy between themselves and the children.
>
> It was not until the three older children got to the ages of 18 and 20 that the troubles started. It was at this time that they left home, one to travel abroad and the other two to attend college in a country area. This was also the time when the 16-year-old, who still lived at home, was totally occupied with sporting commitments, extra studies and being a teenager.
>
> The first indication that Bernie and Zoe had that anything was wrong with Damien was when his class teacher asked to see them. They learned that Damien cried a lot in the school playground, would not play with the other children and was disruptive in class.
>
> He began to behave differently at home, too. He stayed in his room a lot, lost his appetite and refused to go to school in the mornings. Several times he ran away.

His parents were mystified—what had gone wrong? What had happened to change this happy, outgoing little boy into such a troubled and unhappy little fellow?

The most significant factor in this stepfamily that contributed to Damien's disillusionment and frustration was the age difference between him and the other children.

Biological children in stepfamilies are often much younger than their half-siblings. This is one of many factors operating in stepfamilies in which stepcouples have their own child. And if they have only *one* child (as Bernie and Zoe did), these factors are likely to have a more pronounced effect than if they have two or more. Let's take a look at these.

Factors that affect the biological child in a stepfamily

- Parents are so taken up with the older children and all that has to be done for them that the emotional energy and availability that they might otherwise have for their own child is greatly diminished.

- Older children become like parents and discipline, nurture play with and often spoil their young brother or sister. This can mean that the child is being raised with many different standards, rules and expectations from all these "parents." Often, the older children place unrealistic demands on the younger child, expecting or asking for behaviors that are beyond the capabilities of the child.

- The younger child is often the center of everyone's attention and considered to be something of a plaything. This can teach the child that he or she is "the center of the universe." The child might learn to think of himself or herself only and be unable to think of others (either in childhood or adulthood).

- Demands of older children often seem more urgent to parents than do those of younger ones: "Quick Mom, I'm late already!" "You don't understand, I need a new notebook tonight!" An "urgent" instead of an "important" set of guidelines for parental action can develop, which often leaves the small child last in the scheme of things.

- In some families the reverse is true and the needs of the youngest are considered to be the most important. This can lead to resentment and anger in older children which might then be displaced onto their young sister or brother.

- The youngest child can also (usually without realizing it) divide the family, with jealousies arising between half-siblings because he or she seems to favor one or more of them.

- The younger child may be disciplined less harshly by parents than were the older children, and this can lead to resentment.

- Close attachments can exist between a much younger biological only child and older half-siblings, leaving the child feeling abandoned when the older ones grow up and leave home, or become busy with their own lives. When this happens it can seem to the young child as though the family has disintegrated. This is what happened to Damien in the story above.

- The identity of much younger biological only children is often closely tied up with their older siblings. For example, they identify with teenagers, being familiar with the music, activities and conversation of these older children. Their peers often seem very boring and childish by comparison. This also was Damien's experience.

- Because the parents of the much younger child are older, they often do not have friends with young children. This can leave them and their young child without the opportunity to socialize with other families who are at a similar stage of family life.

Take time

If you have a biological child in your stepfamily, think about the points above. What factors listed do you think are relevant for this child? Which are relevant for you? Which are relevant for other family members? Can you think of any factors that have not been mentioned here? What are they? What changes might you make now that you understand these influences more clearly?

Step-couple decision to have or not to have their own child

The biological drive to procreate is innate and natural. When two people have decided they want to spend their lives together and that couple form a stepfamily, it is just as natural for them, as it is for couples the first time around, to think about having a child that is theirs.

What makes the decision more difficult, however, is the existence of other children, especially if both partners have a child or children of their own. In spite of this, with many warning signs illuminated by lack of money, time, energy, housing space, family conflict and so on, many couples still decide to go ahead with it.

Sometimes (and this is quite common) issues arise because a partner who does not already have a child wants one, whereas his or her partner has had enough of parenting and is either adamant that there be no children, or at least lukewarm about the idea.

The opposite situation can also occur: a partner with children who live, or don't live, with the couple may want more children and the other partner may not.

(*Note*: Whatever the situation, skillful communication is needed between partners to resolve this major issue—ideally before they decided to live their lives together. (See Chapter 8 on spoken contracts.))

If parents want to have their own child, they usually benefit by deciding when: right away; in two years time; in four years? There will be many considerations: age and stage of life, health, finances, available time, space, the other children, family lifestyle and—often ignored—plans for the future.

The trap of the biological child

Unfortunately, many couples in stepfamilies believe that a child of their own will help strengthen their marriage and enhance relationships between family members. Nothing could be further from the truth. If a marriage needs a child to hold it together, it is experiencing some very serious difficulties which need to be addressed.

It is easy for people to fantasize a cute baby, all smiles, with everyone happy and united because of it, rather than the realities of life with this baby in the household. Certainly there are many wonderful times made possible because of babies, toddlers, infants, primary-school children and even adolescents. These times, however, are interspersed with sleepless nights and exhaustion, demands on time and patience, anxious times when illness strikes and a total commitment toward the parenting role often to the exclusion of the parents' and other children's desires and needs.

The trap for the biological child

If the biological child of the step-couple begins to realize that he or she is the glue that holds the family together, life for him or her can become a balancing act demanding great skill.

This takes its emotional toll on the growing child whose role in life becomes one of keeping everyone happy. This is the ultimate trap for the child (rather than for the parents and other children), who was brought into this family to keep it together.

The love child

For many people whose first marriage fails, there is a longing to have a child with someone they really love. This might seem a strange statement to some people who say, "Surely their first child, at least, was the result of a love union."

Many people disclose, often quite ashamedly, that they never had deep feelings for their first spouse. Marriage therapists often hear the words, "I should never have married him/her."

These loveless unions, however, rarely affect the love these parents feel for their children. In fact they often feel more affection for them to compensate for the lack of feeling they have for their partner.

The reasons for marriage are many—some positive and some negative. Countless numbers of people find that down the road marriage falls apart.

If and when they eventually find themselves in a marriage that is filled with shared joy, love and promise, the arrival of a child conceived out of this depth of feeling and passion is, to them, a very romantic and special experience. This "love" child symbolizes their special relationship in an almost spiritual way.

For many couples and these children, life continues to be rosy as the years unfold. However, sincere commitment and work is almost always needed to make the stepfamily experience a happy one for everyone in it, including the love child and his or her parents.

Rejection of the biological child by family members

When children, grandparents and relatives hear that a baby is on the way in the stepfamily, jealousies and resentment are often aroused. Because stepfamilies are born out of loss, so often with accompanying bitterness and resentment, unresolved issues (unfinished business) come back to haunt those who feel these emotions, as well as those who are the target of them.

Ex-spouses often report feeling angry, displaced and more betrayed than ever when they learn that their ex-partner is to parent a child with another person. Children of the step-couple may also experience emotional distress—and are often not able to identify just what it is they feel. Grandparents and other relatives, too, may have a mixture of emotions with which they have to come to terms.

It's often hard to understand why such intensity of emotion can be aroused over one little baby. The reasons can be many and varied but always have to do with some perceived threat, which may or may not be in conscious awareness.

Deep anxieties relating to rejection—"She won't have as much time for me now"—and loss of acceptance and being valued—"He will love the new baby more than he loves me"—are at the core of much personal distress. Then there is the togetherness factor which is being challenged— "How dare they bring an 'outside' child into our family!"

Family values and attitudes may have been violated—"It was bad enough when he started living with this woman! Now do we have to accept their baby?" Genuine concerns, too, may be expressed and felt— "How will you ever manage? You have so many stresses already, why add to them?"

(*Note:* The best way to deal with these reactions is to acknowledge them by letting these people know that you are aware of what they are thinking and how they are feeling. This involves using empathy skills so that you really try to see things from the other person's point of view. Be patient and positive (especially with children), and encourage them to gradually get used to the idea of the new child. If they see you being positive and not defensive, they will very likely come to share your joy.

Mostly, in spite of initial emotional reactions, family members settle down and gradually accept the new child. Time can work wonders and people's attitudes do change!)

Take time

Think about the role of a biological child in a stepfamily. What experience have you had with respect to this, either as parent, ex-spouse, half-sibling, grandparent or relative? What emotions did you feel? Do you still feel them? How have you dealt with your own emotions?

Guidelines for integrating the biological child into a stepfamily

- Be positive when you announce the pregnancy by saying that this baby is on the way and you are happy about it.

- If you are not happy about it, be honest to family members and ask for their emotional support.

- If one parent is happy about the child and the other is not, professional help may be needed. Marriage difficulties may be the reason for this conflict or may, on the other hand, be caused by it. Either way, resolution should be the goal.

- Help the children who will be half-siblings to this child get used to the idea. You could read stories to younger children about babies coming into families. With older children you could just talk about it (don't overdo it!).

- When older children reject parents because of this issue they are feeling very threatened but usually mask this with anger, disgust, resentment and so on. Try not to become defeated by this and understand that they are using defense mechanisms to deal with their inner plan. Given time, healing will probably occur. Keep in touch, be positive not defensive, and always be loving, letting your children know that they are still very special to you and the new child will not change this in any way.

- Many mothers encourage children to place their hands on their abdomen and feel the baby inside. This can help children feel bonded to their baby brother or sister before birth. In stepfamilies this may present problems, however, especially if the mother has no children of her own. She and her stepchildren may not feel comfortable engaged in such an intimate time together. If the stepmother also has her own children, she may want only them to have this experience. If this is the case, these times could be private and not talked about too much in front of the other children in the stepfamily. Ideally, though, it will help stepfamily life if all of the children share equally in the growth of their baby half-brother or half-sister.

- When the baby is born, allow each child to hold the infant. Give them the opportunity to be there during feeding time and to help with bath time. A peek into the bassinet is all right, too!

- On the other hand, do not allow children to treat their new baby as a plaything. The baby has rights to be treated with respect and dignity.

- As much as possible, try to arrange for equal time that half-siblings spend with the baby. Jealousies may be aroused if one child is seen as being favored to fill a surrogate mother or father role.

- As the child grows, be aware of your child-raising methods. If you have older children, ask yourself, "Am I treating this newcomer fairly? Am I too soft? Am I too strict? Will my older children feel jealous or envious of this child because of what I am doing?" Some parents report that they are either more lenient or more strict with the child or children born of their second marriage.

- If you have older children, be sure they are not neglected because of this newcomer. If they live apart from you, they need special reassurance that they are loved and the new baby has not taken you away from them. You could keep in touch by seeing them, phoning, writing.

- Give biological children the opportunity to get to know all of their half-siblings—even if they live far away or are much older.

Be encouraged

Biological children in stepfamilies can be a source of joy to everyone—parents, half-siblings, grandparents, relatives and friends. When parents, in particular, develop awareness and skills to take them through the hurdles they will inevitably encounter, their rewards can be many.

In a stepfamily there may be three sets of children: hers, his and theirs. The lives of all these children are greatly enriched when they learn to relate positively to each other, get to know each other and learn about themselves and life from each other. The fact that a biological child of the step-couple creates a biological bond between the two previous sets of children gives them a unique place in stepfamily life.

For step-couples who share in parenthood together, their biological child symbolizes their union and can give it a deeper meaning, love and commitment. As long as expectations are realistic and personal growth is encouraged in each and every family member, a stepfamily can be richer because of natural or biological children.

Summary

In this chapter we have talked about:

The initial impact of the biological child
A second family for father
Two original families plus the biological child all living together
Factors that affect the biological child in a stepfamily
Step-couple decision to have or not to have their own child
The trap of the biological child
The trap for the biological child
The love child
Rejection of the biological child by family members
Guidelines for integrating the biological child into a stepfamily

15

Mom, can't you leave him alone?

Sexuality in stepfamilies

We are very sexual beings. Whether we feel comfortable with this thought or not, it is a fact. When a stepfamily is formed, the sexuality of different members is expressed in many conscious and unconscious ways—some of which seem natural and comfortable and others that do not.

In this chapter we'll consider some different sexual relationships. The first is that of the step-couple and addresses some of the issues that they encounter.

The other sexual relationships are ones that *can* exist in stepfamilies, and they are aberrant. Since they are realities in some stepfamilies, acknowledgment, better understanding and guidelines are needed for those people or their family members who are involved in them.

Sexuality and the step-couple

While there are many reasons for marriage a second time around, the sexual desires of each partner are usually a powerful force. The sexual drive is natural and instinctual, and is one of many factors (unconscious and conscious) that lead people into marriage.

When partners embark on stepfamily life together, they usually hope to enjoy loving sexual times together as a part of their relationship. Partners who have been sexually dissatisfied in their first marriage may seek to have this part of their lives fulfilled.

They may, or may not, have experienced a period of celibacy between the end of the first marriage and the beginning of this new relationship. They may, or may not, have had time vacationing with, or even living with, each other prior to stepfamily life.

Many couples who embark on stepfamily life have only a weekend for a honeymoon. Financial restrictions and difficulties with childcare often mean that, once married, children are around all the time.

This frequently places great strain on a new relationship. Unlike marriage the first time around, step-couples are often denied the opportunity to get to know each other freely, and to establish and enjoy the sexual part of their relationship.

This situation is damaging to any relationship and often leads to conflict. One of the most common complaints therapists (and friends) hear is, "We can never find time to be alone!" If the dwelling is small and if children are around, the opportunity for quiet, private times together is almost impossible.

Many step-couples feel inhibited and embarrassed when they know children are in the house, in the next bedroom, or they think they may be heard or the children know what they are doing. When, where and how they have their times of lovemaking is restricted and they often end up saying, "Let's wait until the children aren't here." Even when this happens, other activities often take priority.

It is not uncommon for a partner, whose stepchildren live in the house and are therefore seen as the cause of the infrequency of lovemaking times, to become angry about this.

With children around it is not unusual for step-couples also to feel inhibited and embarrassed at *openly* displaying their affection. They may feel awkward at being loving with each other in front of the children.

This is especially common with partners when they are with their own children. As they try to balance their stepfamily relationships between their children and their new partner, they often try to protect their children from feeling uncomfortable. They believe that their children don't like seeing them being affectionate with the new stepparent and so conceal their love for their new partner by not touching, or not using terms of endearment.

Partners in stepfamilies often experience conflict because of these issues. Unlike a first marriage, which usually offers freedom for the physical expression of love and sexuality until the first child is born and even for some time after, stepfamily life often presents time, space and energy restrictions from the start.

On the other hand, some people who were coy about this in their first marriage decide that things will be different in the second one. Sometimes they make this decision for themselves, but other times they make it so as to be more honest in family life and to show their children what love *can* be between two people.

When partners show their love for each other in front of their own or each other's children, they become role models for a loving marriage. As long as their behavior does not involve explicit sexual behavior, their children are receiving valuable lessons for their own lives as to how to "be" in a relationship.

Loving sexual times together are an important part of any married relationship. These are the times that couples share privately.

Inevitably, however, couples find in second marriages (as they usually do in the first marriages) that passion cools over time. This does not mean that love cools—only the intense urgency of it. Sexual feelings and desires between two people who love each other are natural and can extend into old age. As they enjoy each other sexually, they are truly *love*-making (enjoying love) and *making* love (creating love)!

Sometimes a partner is plagued by thoughts such as, "I wonder if I am as good a lover as his first wife?" or "I wonder if she got more pleasure in lovemaking in her first marriage?" Thoughts such as these are undermining to a relationship and need to be talked about.

(*Note*: The thoughts need to be talked about, rather than the questions answered. These questions are evidence of insecurity and partners need to reassure the partner who asks them that he or she is loved—and enjoyed. Making comparisons with a previous partner is destructive to a relationship and attempts to seek such answers are dangerous. If the questions and self-doubts persist, it is advisable to seek professional help.)

Needless to say, if a person does have a secret belief that the first marriage partner was a better lover, this must never be disclosed—unless the destruction of the marriage is sought. Few people react well to being told that they compare unfavorably with a previous partner—especially in this way!

Sometimes people say such things to their partners in a moment of anger and wonder why such lack of tact destroys their marriage. In doing this they drop an atomic bomb and the fallout lasts forever!

On the other hand, couples do need to be able to talk about issues in their relationship and this includes their sexual relationship. Many couples are inhibited and awkward in talking about these things. Frequently couples fail to let each other know what they want—or don't want—from each other.

If your relationship is this way, there are books you can read and trained professionals who can help you to discover new ways to enrich your relationship and enjoy being together.

Assertive communication skills are very necessary skills for couples to use with respect to *every* aspect of their marriage and family life. This includes the many issues concerning sexuality.

Take time

How do you and your partner show your affection for each other in front of the children? What difficulties have you encountered with respect to maintaining and enjoying the sexual part of your relationship? Are you able to talk with each other about your sexual life?

Children's reactions to their parent and stepparent's sexual relationship

When children first become aware that a parent has a sexual relationship with someone who is not their other parent, it can be, for them, a time of emotional confusion. Feelings of joy may be mingled with anger, anxiety, sadness, guilt and hate as they try to make sense of what is happening. One of the reasons for this is that children have often, up until then, been blind to the sexuality of their parents.

This is because many parents have long ago given up cuddling on the sofa, kissing in the hallway or exchanging seductive glances. At best, they have few times alone together to express their love for each other in a sexual and intimate way. Mostly, this is only in the privacy of their bedroom or when they're on vacation.

Because of the lack of open affection between them they often seem sexless to their children, who commonly say or think (if they are old enough to know about such things), "I can't imagine them doing it—not my parents!"

Some children are in stepfamilies in which their parent and stepparent openly touch, show affection and even engage in more explicit sexual contact. These children often witness a sexual aliveness which was not present in the parent's former marriage (or at least not for some time).

Whether or not children "see anything happening" between their parent and stepparent, they usually know that something is happening. Older children may be angry about it—or just plain embarrassed. Younger children may snicker and say things like, "Gee, Mom, can't you leave each other alone? or "I can't stand it, here they go again."

When children have lost a parent through death, and the other parent has remarried, a time of adjustment follows. It may be very painful for a child to see affection between parent and stepparent—particularly if his or her own parents had related this way themselves. On the other hand, a child living in this situation may feel more secure now that he or she is living with loving parents.

Some children are very judgmental and parental about matters that concern the sexual behavior of their parents.

> Trent had developed a loving relationship with Jessie. Before he spent the night at her house, he decided to ask her two teenage daughters what they thought about it. The oldest one said, "It's okay by me," whereas the younger one asked, "Do you intend to marry my mother?" When he said they had not decided yet, she said, "Well, in that case, I don't want you sleeping here!"

The girl was setting limits that she perceived her mother unable or unwilling to do. Many children are like this, if not quite as parental! Strong family bonding and an unwillingness to let outsiders in can make children protective of parents. They do not willingly accept the new sexual relationship into which they know their parent has entered.

When this happens they are really protecting themselves from their own anxiety and discomfort. Unconscious forces lead them to behave in ways that reduce their anxiety and keep them within, or at least closer to, their comfort zone. (See Chapter 12.)

Guidelines for helping children come to terms with sexual behaviors between parent and stepparent

- Until children get to know their future stepparent (usually they meet this person prior to the marriage), be restrained and discreet with touching, cuddling and kissing in front of them.
- Gradually touch more and allow them to become accustomed to seeing you show affection for each other.
- Do not engage in sexual talk in front of children or where they can hear.
- Never talk about the ex-partner (their mother or father) with respect to sexual issues so that children can hear.
- Talk with the children and ask them what they feel comfortable with and what troubles them. Accept the feedback and respect their thoughts and feelings.
- Behave in ways that convey to children that you love each other, without engaging openly in sexual behavior.

Now that we have looked at some issues concerning the marriage relationship in stepfamilies, we shall look at some aberrant sexual relationships that sometimes exist in stepfamilies.

Sexual behavior between stepsiblings

Sexual taboos that exist in biological families are not always clearly defined in stepfamilies. Incestuous expressions of sexuality in some of these families are, however, a reality. This can range from playful seduction to actual intercourse. It can be between teenagers or older children who are attracted to each other and mutually seek contact in what could be called a "normal" way; between younger children who mutually consent to engage in sexual exploration which is an expression of childhood natural curiosity; or between two children of the same or differing ages, one of whom forces himself or herself onto another.

Sexual forces are very powerful and often compel a young person to do what he or she knows is "not right." In stepfamilies this can involve a variety of sexual encounters with a stepsibling and may be with the same or opposite sex.

Sometimes this happens when children feel deprived of love, affection and recognition, and in order to satisfy these needs they turn to the nearest, most available person. Because of the proximity and familiarity which exist between the stepsiblings (especially if they live together) and their mutual experience of family disintegration, they are vulnerable to having these needs met by way of sexual experimentation and experience with each other.

While this may be by mutual consent, it is frequently true that one child manipulates or forces another into a compromising situation to meet his or her own needs. This, of course, happens in first-time families, too, but it is no less serious in stepfamilies.

(*Note*: This is a boundary and personal space issue. The "invading" child has a poor sense of boundaries and invades the personal space of the other.)

Children who are exploited in this way often make attempts to let a parent know what is happening. Therapists often hear, years later when these children reach adulthood, how they tried to tell a parent at the time, only to be told, "Don't be silly, he wouldn't do that!" The refusal (or denial) on the part of the parent to acknowledge that the child might be telling the truth only serves to increase the child's sense of powerlessness, anger and isolation.

Other times children might be happy and secure, yet are driven by curiosity and the availability of each other to engage in sexual behaviors together. Many report in later years that they were influenced by the behavior of their parents, who were role models. "They got together, so why shouldn't we?"

Many children never fully recover from these sexual experiences. They carry with them into adulthood the shame of what they have done, anger at the violation of their bodies and overwhelming feelings of powerlessness. Many carry their secrets throughout life, never disclosing to anyone the pain of what happened in their childhood.

Others are so troubled by these memories that they seek psychotherapy to help them resolve the emotional turmoil that is still with them. In other cases, these memories are repressed (repression is a defense mechanism) and these adults have no awareness as to why they feel so awful, why their relationships don't work out and why life is a battle. Professional therapists often work with these people who may rediscover early experiences such as the above, the recollection of which becomes the key to resolving their inner pain and conflict.

Guidelines for parent and stepparent to minimize the risk of sexual encounters between stepsiblings

- Use what you are learning in this book to help build a happy, secure stepfamily—one in which all members know each other, can be honest with each other and feel loved.

- Create a balance in your thinking between trusting the children and being mindful of their natural curiosity and vulnerabilities.

- If a child seems withdrawn, unhappy or rebellious, give him or her the opportunity to talk with you. If you sense that the child is troubled by something, gently encourage him or her to talk about it. (Use the skills in Chapters 17 and 18.)

- Be alert to signs of sexual interactions between stepsiblings. If you suspect anything, talk to the children separately as well as keeping a watchful eye on them.

- If a child tells you, or seems to be trying to tell you, that something is happening, take it seriously.

- If you hear strange sounds in the night, investigate. (It is a fact that children often wait until the parents are asleep before embarking on their clandestine sexual activities.)

- Finally, if all else fails and you know that these things are happening between the children of the stepfamily and you are unable to resolve the situation, do not delay in seeking professional help.

Sexual behavior between stepparent and stepchild

Much of what has been said in the previous section about sexual behaviors between stepsiblings applies to sexual relationships between stepparent and stepchild. It is more likely to be true, however, that the stepparent forces himself or herself onto the child, rather than there being mutual consent. It is also true that this stepparent is more likely to be the stepfather who molests his stepdaughter, rather than a stepmother and stepson interaction, or a homosexual one between stepfather and stepson or stepmother and stepdaughter.

Considerable information has been gathered about these tragic circumstances and the long- and short-term effects of them on children. Articles, newspaper accounts, books, lectures, workshops and professionals have brought the incidence of such perverted behaviors into public scrutiny, discussion and action. Whenever these things happen in families, including stepfamilies, they are very damaging and are to be deplored.

One of the most alarming characteristics of the sexual encounters is that of the denial of the natural parent that anything is happening to his or her child. As with stepsibling sexual behaviors, the denial or refusal of a parent to accept that what he or she is being told is the truth is the final assault on a child's dignity, self-worth and trust.

It is even more astounding that in some instances a parent has the facts before his or her eyes and even then denies the reality. So great is the power of the defense mechanism of denial that this parent is not purposely pretending that nothing is happening but actually believes that nothing is! (Remember, defense mechanisms serve to protect us from a reality that is too painful to bear, too threatening to our innermost self.)

Phoebe was only seven when her mother married her stepfather, Dan. It was not long after they started living together that Dan began to go into Phoebe's room while her mother was doing the dishes and cleaning up after dinner. He would sit on the bed and read Phoebe a story. He then kissed her goodnight, turned out her light, slipped his hands under the sheets and fondled her body before leaving the room.

Phoebe did not know whether this was right or not. She only knew she felt funny about it and did not like it. She said to her mother, "Dan touches me after he turns the light off." Her mother's reply was, "Dan loves you, you know he does, he's a wonderful stepfather to you. Your own father never loved you as much."

Several times Phoebe tried to tell her mother she was confused, too, because Dan did seem to be nice to her and after a while she felt bad about saying things about him. Her mother made no attempt to check out what she was being told, choosing instead to believe in Dan's integrity and that Phoebe was fantasizing.

Dan's molestation of Phoebe continued into her teenage years, when she was subjected to full sexual encounters with her stepfather. She never told anyone. Why? Because deep down she did not believe that anyone would believe her and there was also a confusing sense of betrayal of Dan should she do so.

There are countless different stories that people tell about their sexual molestation at the hands of a stepparent (or parent or someone else). Such stepparents are very damaged people and need help, but they, too, usually deny the reality of their deviant behaviors.

What they are doing is unlawful, unjust and exploitative. They play on the trust (or the weakness) of their spouse, who is the parent of the child they violate, and they also play on the trust of the child.

Guidelines for protecting children from sexual advances of stepparents

- Always take seriously any comment a child (younger or older) makes that indicates a stepparent is making sexual advances.

- Be mindful of human weakness. Stepfathers and stepmothers may have hidden personality characteristics that cause deviant and aberrant behaviors involving your own children. Painful though it might be, listen to what you hear your children say, see and hear what is happening around you and always be prepared to do some checking.

- Time alone with stepchildren gives stepparents the opportunity to engage in these behaviors. Parents can do a lot to prevent this if they have reason to suspect anything deviant is going on.

- Realize that perverted sexual advances may range from seduction (with no "hands on" behaviors, for example, use of sexual language or covetous looks) to bodily contact of all different types. Watch for signs—remember, your child needs you to protect him or her.

- If you feel tempted to make sexual advances to your stepchild, treat these signs very seriously. Sometimes self-discipline is sufficient to prevent this from happening but other times it isn't. Before it is too late, seek professional help.

- If you are a stepchild and you have experienced (or still are experiencing) sexual assault at the hands of a stepparent, there are people who can help you. The important thing is to do something about it.

- Read through the guidelines above for stepsiblings. Many of these apply to this section, too.

This chapter has dealt with the sensitive subject of sexuality and looked at different ways in which it can be expressed in stepfamilies.

Some of these realities are unpleasant and concern children. From being embarrassed and angry about their partner's sexual behavior in the new relationship to willing or unwilling participation in their own sexual encounters, children can have many adverse experiences with respect to their own sexuality, as well as that of other family members.

Be encouraged

If any of the above experiences are yours, or have been yours, it is important to know that there are professional people who can help your family and the individuals in it. With the right help at the right time and with the passage of time, stepfamilies *can* get on the right track and settle down to the process of creating a positive and happy lifestyle—for each and everyone in it.

In the great majority of stepfamilies, sexuality is a source of joy and enrichment and stepparents can contribute very positively to healthy sexual attitudes in their stepchildren. This can happen in many different ways.

When stepparents respect their stepchildren, spend time with them and develop positive relationships with them, the self-esteem and sexual identity of the stepchildren are enhanced. Many children have wonderful times with their stepparents: they may go hiking, they may crawl under the car and fix the engine together, they may bake cakes, go to a sporting event or just sit together and chat.

The maleness of boys can be developed and affirmed because of their relationship with a stepfather *or* stepmother. The femaleness of girls is enhanced in this way, too. Whether or not children have a positive and ongoing relationship with their absent parent, they can reap many benefits from having a stepparent.

Together, with the parent of their stepchildren, stepparents can also teach their stepchildren valuable lessons about relationships between men and women as well as of parenthood. Parent and stepparent are role models for marital and parental relationships and, if their relationship is a good one, this is a positive thing for children to see, live with and learn from.

Stepsiblings can also learn much about life from each other. Sometimes a family of girls merges with a family of boys—or at least one boy, and this offers the girls an opportunity to know what boys are all about. (They might not always like what they see and hear!) Boys, too, can learn what it is like to have a sister, to learn about girls and what makes them tick.

In these situations there is usually some friction and statements such as, "Boys! I can't stand them! or "You girls are so stupid!" This is normal and common. This does not mean, however, that the experience of learning to live with each other is not a valuable life lesson.

Many children of stepfamilies are the beneficiaries of their bonus family and develop an appreciation and deep love for their stepsiblings and stepparents. These ties can be strong and can bind male and female children to each other as well as children to stepparents—and at no time have these relationships been anything but wholesome, healthy and happy.

Summary

In this chapter on sexuality we have looked at:

> Sexuality and the step-couple
> Children's reactions to their parent and stepparent's sexual
>> relationship
> Guidelines for helping children come to terms with sexual behaviors
>> between parent and stepparent
> Sexual behavior between stepsiblings
> Guidelines for parent and stepparent to minimize the risk of sexual
>> encounters between stepsiblings
> Sexual behavior between stepparent and stepchild
> Guidelines for protecting children from sexual advances of
>> stepparents

16

Why do we fight over money?

Money issues in stepfamilies

Money is often said to be one of the major causes of conflict in marriage and family life. What probably is not known by most people is *why* it is that money seems to be the catalyst for arguments, conflict and unhappiness.

In stepfamilies, issues surrounding money are especially common. In this chapter we'll look at money from the point of view of the psychological forces and concepts that cause these difficulties.

Values and attitudes about money

For most of us it was in our family of origin that we had our first lessons about money. Some of us may have received pocket money if we did some jobs around the house, and others of us may have been given it without having to earn it.

Some of us received more or less than our friends—or even our siblings. Some of us received it from our mothers and others from fathers. Some received none.

Punishment came, for many of us, in the form of "no pocket money." Others among us were able to earn more if we were good, and many of us received an increase on our birthday.

And then there was the saving of money—for some of us! Parents and schools may have encouraged or taught us to save, and perhaps we opened a savings bank account. Yet others among us couldn't save at all—as soon as we got it, it went.

Many of us had parents who talked about money, either to us or between themselves. From them we learned what they valued about money and their attitudes toward it.

Some money values are: having money; the right to earn money; the right to spend as you wish; generosity; integrity with money; being debt free; having some money for a rainy day; spoiling children once in a while; spending money on oneself once in a while; money earned through hard work ... and many more.

Some attitudes about money are: money is everything; money is not important; it's best to save for the future; spend it while you have it; spend a little, save a little; never gamble; a good father provides for his family; mothers can spend money on themselves; money is security; money must be earned and not won or inherited; honesty and money go hand in hand; never borrow and never lend; people who don't save are irresponsible; people who are mean with money aren't worth knowing; children need to learn how to look after their money; children become better citizens if they get a part-time job as soon as they are old enough; children should be given money to spend and enjoy—when they're adults they might not be able to do this ... and many more.

It's little wonder, with the diversity of attitudes about money, that stepfamilies wrestle with money issues. These issues also cause trouble in first marriages and first-time families—but in stepfamilies there are many more reasons why money is, or can be, such a potentially explosive issue.

Different money issues in stepfamilies and the *real* reasons for them

Maria and Sergio married after knowing each other for three and a half years. Both of them had children who remained with their respective ex-partners, except on school holidays when Maria's boys, ages 12 and 10, and Sergio's daughters, ages 12 and 9, came to stay.

It was during these times when the children were with them that conflict over money was the most intense. Maria did not believe in spoiling her boys. She had put aside what she considered to be adequate money for vacation expenses, plus some extra to buy them some clothes and gifts. Sergio, however, liked to spend "big" when he had his daughters with him.

They were each given a hundred dollars when they arrived, and on top of that he bought them expensive clothes and gifts. When he ran out of money, he used his credit card (in spite of the fact that he owed money all over the place).

These conflicting values and attitudes made vacation time terrible! Maria's boys were jealous of their stepsisters, who openly displayed and talked about their gifts and treats.

Maria became angry at Sergio and his daughters. Sergio was enjoying himself and soaking up the attention his daughters were giving him. It really made him feel good.

Let's look now at some of the *real* issues underlying the money issue.

For Sergio

- *Self-esteem:* Sergio's low self-esteem was given a boost by the attention he got from his daughters and the belief that he was being a good father.

- Sergio's *guilt* at leaving his wife and children six years earlier was assuaged when he spent lavishly on his daughters.

- Sergio felt more *powerful* with this display of spending. People noticed him in the shops and he felt as though he was *in control* of his life. (He did not usually feel this way.)

- Sergio wanted to show his ex-wife's husband that he was as successful as he. This thought also raised his *self-esteem*.

- Sergio saw his daughters for two weeks three times a year. He often became anxious when he thought of them and wondered if they still loved him. When he spent money on them and spoiled them, his *fear of rejection* by them was diminished and he felt a lot better.

- By spending the way he did, he had a sense of pulling closer to his girls. He felt as though they belonged to each other. The *force of togetherness* was at work.

- He also felt more *independent*. In many ways in his marriage he had to rely (for house payments in particular) on Maria's earnings, which were considerably greater than his. He hated this dependency—it did nothing for his self-esteem.

- His spending masked an *unspoken contract*: "If I spend money on you girls, you will love me."

For Maria

- She deplored Sergio's values and attitudes about money. The *values and attitudes* she had tried to teach her boys were threatened.

- Sergio's behavior was, to her, a *bad role* model for her children. This made her feel anxious and angry because she was afraid that her boys would learn to be like Sergio.

- Because of her boys' dissatisfaction and jealousy, she also experienced *fear of rejection* by them. Perhaps they would think her an inadequate and heartless mother.

- Maria had a lot of *unfinished business* about the way her mother had had to work so hard to compensate for her father's irresponsibility with money.

- Her own father's carelessness and extravagance with money taught her to be very careful and cautious with it. Her own *childhood experience* influenced the way she raised her children.

- She *displaced her anger* at her father onto Sergio.

- She had always hoped, when she married Sergio, that their two sets of children would get on well together. She longed for one happy family. Her *spoken contract* with Sergio, made at the time of their marriage, was that they would treat their children the same way when they came to stay. This had been broken.

- She was *jealous* of Sergio's daughters, who had more money spent on them than Sergio ever spent on her!

- She and Sergio were engaged in a *power struggle*, an "I'm better than you" struggle, as they tried to convince each other about the rightness of their attitudes.

You can see from the above that Maria and Sergio's issue over the way they spent money on their children was not as simple as it seemed. Many hidden and unrecognized factors contributed to *making* this an issue.

While your situation is probably not identical to this one, you may find yourselves identifying in some ways with it.

There are countless ways in which money becomes an issue in stepfamilies. The following account of Andrea and Ralph illustrates a different situation:

Ralph had been divorced for four years when he married Andrea. For her, this marriage was her first. Ralph had three young children who came to visit once a month. The rest of the time Ralph and Andrea led a busy life, working, socializing and engaging in sporting and other activities.

After three years they had a child of their own, which was followed two years later by another one. This was when money troubles started to disrupt their relationship.

Andrea had given up her well-paid job to stay at home and look after the children. She began to be dissatisfied and angry when she realized that Ralph spent more on the children of his first marriage than their own. In addition, he had just paid for a new car for his ex-wife. She was furious—especially as his ex-wife had remarried!

When she confronted him, he became very defensive and terrible fights ensued. However they tried to resolve this issue it would not go away. Day by day Andrea's resentment grew and day by day Ralph was determined not to give in to her.

Let's look at the *real* issues here:

For Andrea

- She began to believe that Ralph loved his first wife more than he loved her. She was jealous and *feared rejection* by him.

- She did not have a sense of *togetherness* in her family. This made her feel alone and anxious—and angry.

- Ralph's behavior took her outside her *comfort zone*.

- She hated being stuck at home and not having the *independence* of earning money. This affected her *self-esteem*.

- She began to realize that she had an *unconscious contract* in her marriage which was, "I'll love and look after you if you do the right thing by me."

- She feared not only that he didn't love her, but that she would stop loving him. This also triggered a deep *fear of abandonment* or aloneness, when she thought of the implications of this.

For Ralph

- He had always felt *guilty* about leaving his first family and felt better when he helped them financially.

- Ever since his first wife had remarried, he had felt threatened. He had thoughts running through his head such as, "What if her husband begins to control my children?" "What if he is a better provider and husband than I was?" *Catastrophic fantasies* and a likely *self-fulfilling prophesy* came into play.

- To prove to himself that he was "okay," he transgressed the *boundaries* of his wife's new marriage with gifts of money. This behavior raised his *self-esteem* and *reduced his fears.*

- His *unfinished business* of his first marriage (he had never really let go) and the *guilt* he felt about the way he had behaved resulted in the *defense mechanism of undoing* coming to the rescue. This means he thought that by doing nice things, he canceled out the bad things.

- His drive for *separateness* lead him to "do his own thing"—irrespective of what Andrea wanted him to do.

- His drive for *togetherness* pulled him back into his original family.

- He had a need to prove to his ex-wife's husband that he was a good guy. His *pseudo self* sought approval from her second husband.

These are some of the psychological issues that operated behind the scenes in the many fights that Ralph and Andrea found themselves having over money. It was only when they sought professional help that they began to understand what was *really* happening.

Money is a symbol of many things, including power, success, security, togetherness, individuality, independence and personal freedom.

Stanley and Ursula's issue over money seemed to be mostly because of the fact that she had it, and he didn't. But that was only the tip of the iceberg, as you shall now see.

Ursula had inherited her husband's estate upon his death. While she could not be considered rich, she nevertheless was comfortably off.

Stanley had a high paying job, and contributed to his two children from his first marriage by paying for their school expenses and giving them a fairly generous clothing and extra-tuition allowance.

When he and Ursula had a child of their own, he contributed equally to expenses for the child throughout her growing up years until she was 18. He had, however, not contributed to general household expenses from the time of marriage, and begrudgingly gave extra housekeeping money for the times his own children came to stay.

Overall, Ursula kept the household running, always paying for most of the expenses. Her resentment grew year by year until, after 25 years of marriage, she told Stanley she was leaving him—she was sick and tired of his meanness and lack of contribution to the expenses of the family. She felt totally unsupported by him and decided to get on with her own life—without Stanley.

What had happened in this marriage to create such conflict over the years about money? Here are some of the reasons:

For Ursula

- Her *childhood experiences* had taught her the *value* that "men are providers for their families." When her husband died and she remarried, she expected to contribute substantially for her own children. Her *unspoken contract* at the time of her marriage to Stanley was that she would share household expenses with him, but in the event of them having a child (or children) of their own, he would be the provider.

- Her *unassertiveness and lack of assertive communication skills* meant that she harbored deep resentment over the years and never really told her husband how she was feeling about his lack of financial support.

- She was a *conflict avoider* and just kept paying out to keep the peace.

- She had an *assumption* at the time of marriage which she failed to *check out*.

- She was playing the *psychological game* of "Poor Me." This got her attention from her friends, who always sympathized with her and supported her complaints.

- She had learned as a child to be independent so people would value her. In a way, she *unconsciously sought independence.*

- She (unconsciously) liked to be *in control* and this was part of her *unconscious contract*: "I'll always be the one in control of my family."

For Stanley

- He had never dealt with his *unfinished business* of grieving for the family he had lost and the anger at the way they had treated him.

- He took out his anger on his second wife and child by being *passively aggressive* (withholding money).

- He had always felt inferior—especially with women—and this, too, was behind his passive control of money issues in his marriage. He used money as a weapon to attain *power*.

- His first marriage had cost him money and he had a deep *fear* of being without money. To him "money was *security*."

- He was also scripted to be *dependent*, and so unconsciously he was living out this life script.

- His *unspoken contract* at the time of marriage was, "You have more money than I have, so you can support us."

There is one more very common scenario in stepfamilies which causes arguments over money. This is the scenario of separate bank accounts and attitudes of "my money is mine."

Many men and women who have been previously married and suffered financially as a result resolve *never* to get themselves into such a vulnerable position again. They sometimes find themselves, however, with partners to whom joint bank accounts and sharing of financial resources are symbols of marriage. Needless to say, much marital conflict is caused by these opposed and differing values, attitudes and life experiences.

These relationships are dealing mostly with issues of togetherness versus separateness, of boundaries ("This is *my* money—keep away!") and, greatest of all, of fear.

That money *is* security cannot be denied, and many people become fiercely independent and even uncompromising when faced with proposals of joint bank accounts and pooling of financial resources. They want to take sole responsibility for their *own* (and often their children's) financial security. This reduces their anxiety about losing their independence and being bereft of financial resources.

For their partners, there is anxiety, too. Their partners' financial boundary keeps them out and they often feel excluded, unloved, rejected and angry.

By now, you are probably realizing that money issues are many and varied and are *really* caused by a great diversity of beliefs, inner thoughts, emotions and unconscious forces. *Every conflict over money is unique and involves different personal issues.* That is why getting advice from friends as to what to do usually fails.

That is why *every solution must be unique.*

How to resolve your money issues

- Learn how to use the assertive communication skills for conflict resolution.

- Use these skills in *every* way: do an awareness wheel about your issue, set procedures, follow the conflict resolution format and use all other communication skills as you proceed.

- Remember, you *must* compromise and negotiate.

- Apart from using these skills there is something else you can do. Read this book thoroughly and do some *deep thinking* about *what makes you the way you are.*

- If you find some answers as to why your money issue *is* a issue, disclose and talk about your discovery with your partner.

- Never try to analyze your partner with respect to this issue.

- If you are still not able to resolve your money issue, seek professional help *rather than* going to friends and family for advice.

Be encouraged

It's probably realistic to say that most couples and stepfamilies wrestle with issues concerning money. There is nothing unusual about that.

It's also important to realize that *every* money issue is different. There may be common themes, but the reasons for them are as diverse as each of you.

If you accept this, and understand some of the hidden and underlying reasons for these conflictual situations, you are better equipped to deal constructively with them.

Ideally, before stepfamily life begins, couples should talk with each other about their money values and attitudes and how they want to manage money in the marriage and stepfamily. For couples already in stepfamilies, it is *never* too late for resolution of these issues.

If there are points of disagreement (and there probably are), that is not necessarily cause for despair. It is, instead, cause for a thorough discussion, using self-disclosure and the assertive communication skills taught in Chapters 17 and 18.

When these skills are used successfully (and *that* only comes with practice), many issues, including money issues, can be resolved. This is part of the blending process of stepfamily life.

Summary

In this chapter you have read about:

Values and attitudes about money
Different money issues in stepfamilies and the *real* reasons for them
How to resolve your money issues

17

I'll be honest with you

Assertive communication skills (Part 1)

Many times throughout this book you have read about the need to talk or use communication skills. The skills that you need in order to do this are a combination of assertive skills and communication skills.

In this chapter and the next, assertive communication skills, which are crucial for the enhancement (and success) of your stepfamily life, are set out for you to read about and learn.

First of all one thing needs to be stated: *talking is not necessarily communicating.* Many people talk endlessly and are very poor communicators. On the other hand, there are people who say little but are excellent communicators.

Assertive communication skills enable people to say clearly what they want to say, to listen and hear what other people are saying, and to discuss and resolve issues rationally.

Those of you who are really committed to working toward the goal of a cohesive and happy stepfamily will take these skills and practice and practice them until they are on automatic. This will take time, patience, perseverance and even courage!

First of all we will look at what assertive behavior really is and how it is the "umbrella" for all of the communications skills.

Assertive behavior

To be assertive is to say to people what you think, feel and want (or don't want). This needs to be expressed honestly, with integrity and lacking any intention to be hurtful.

Assertive communication involves a willingness to be vulnerable as you disclose your real self.

It means that you are true to yourself and believe that you have the *right* to say what you want to say. It also means that you accept that other people have a right to say what they want to say. In this way you respect yourself and you respect others. There is, in this regard, a sense of equality.

This sounds simple enough, doesn't it? The truth is, however, that very few people communicate this way—they are, instead, nonassertive or aggressive. (See Table 1.)

Nonassertive behavior: beliefs, payoffs, your harsh inner critic

If you are nonassertive, you are failing to express yourself in the way you have just read about. Instead you are *putting yourself last* in much of what you do and say.

You might, for instance:

- say "yes" when you would really like to say "no";

- say you agree when you don't;

- do something you don't want to do, because you don't want to say you don't want to do it;

- feel angry but never let anyone know (in an honest, self-disclosing way);

- want to make a request but be too scared to do it;

- love someone and feel discomfort at saying so.

Why is this? What stops you from honestly and assertively being yourself in your relationships?

The reasons for behaving in this way are many but, broadly speaking, they fall into three categories. You will probably identify with one or more of these.

1. Beliefs

While you have beliefs that embrace many areas of life, this refers to your beliefs about yourself. These beliefs are firmly entrenched in your psyche and are with you all the time.

They are beliefs that you have about your worthwhileness and about how you view yourself in comparison with other people. These beliefs had their origins in your childhood. Some of these might be:

- I'm inferior to other people.

- I'm not as smart, attractive, wealthy, artistic, nice, popular, worthy, capable, funny ... as other people.

- Because of the above: *I have no right* to say what I think, feel, want.

- I'm *only* young, single, a secretary, a laborer, a second wife, a second husband, a stepmother, a stepfather ... and therefore cannot say what I really want or need to say.

- I left school at 15, so therefore I'm inferior to people who've had more education than I have.

- I live in a poor neighborhood, so therefore I'm not as "good" as people who live in rich neighborhoods.

- I'm weak and frail and therefore less valuable than healthy and strong people.

- I'm not very attractive and therefore am inferior to beautiful people.

- If I say what I really think, feel or want, I'll be seen as someone who is not very nice.

And the list goes on and on ...

Take time

What beliefs do you have about yourself that are similar to these? Where did they come from? How long have you had them? How often do you think these thoughts? Do you think they are really true? What is your evidence? What power do these beliefs have over you?

2. Payoffs, or rewards

When you fail to say what you are thinking, feeling, wanting (or not wanting), you actually get a reward, or payoff.

Here are some of the payoffs you might experience:

- Peace; lack of conflict (this is the most commonly experienced payoff)

- I won't be rejected (if I always agree and do what people want me to do).

- I won't have to take responsibility (if I don't say what I think or want to do, I don't run the risk of having to take responsibility for others).

- I won't feel anxious and tense (because of what I think people will say to me).

- I won't be criticized.

- People won't think I'm stupid (if I keep quiet, they won't know the real me—the real "stupid" me).

- People will like (love) me because: "I always say I agree with them even if I really don't; I always do what they want me to do or what I think they want me to do; I always say "yes," even if I'd like to say "no."

- I'll know I'm not running the risk of hurting anyone (that makes me feel better).

- I won't upset anyone (if I keep my mouth shut).

- I won't be laughed at, yelled at, ridiculed, humiliated ... (that is safer).

- People won't get back at me (if I keep quiet).

And so on . . .

Take time

When was the last time you were nonassertive? Who were you with? What payoffs did you get for your behavior? Where and when did you learn to be this way?

Are there other rewards you get that are not listed above? What are they? What do you think it would be like for you to forego these payoffs and become assertive?

Are you nonassertive in your closest relationships? In your marriage? What do you think stops you from being assertive?

3. Your harsh inner critic

This is the resident critic that lives inside your head. It is that inner voice that engages in inner dialogue and can tell you that you

- are stupid, dumb, incompetent, ridiculous, inarticulate, unpopular, feeble, weak ... and so on;

- have no hope of ever succeeding at anything you try to do (or at least at some of the things you really would like to do);

- will make a fool of yourself if you say or do certain things;

- are a total failure in life;

- are unlovable and not a nice person;

- could never do what other people do (for example, succeed in a career, give a party, play tennis, be confident, stand up and talk in front of others, be a friend to your children, or become an assertive communicator).

Take time

How familiar is your harsh inner critic to you? How is your life controlled by this nagging and powerful little (or big) voice in your head? Where did it come from? Does it remind you of your mother? Your father? Your brothers or sisters? Your school teachers? Your school peers? Anyone else?

Now that you have begun to do some thinking about some of the reasons for your nonassertiveness, there is something else for you to know about this way of relating: it is dangerous!

The traps of nonassertiveness

- Nonassertiveness stops you from getting to know yourself.

- Nonassertiveness stops others from getting to know you.

- Your strategies for avoiding conflict actually create it.

- This way of relating aims to help you feel more secure, but in reality makes you feel less secure.

- It stops people from feeling confident.

- It contributes to low self-esteem.

- It is a major cause of aggressiveness.

- It involves "gunnysacking."

Your gunnysack

In World War I, gunners stored ammunition for their weapons in a bag, or sack. This gunner's sack is a good metaphor for the "ammunition" stored by nonassertive people which they often use to hurt others—or themselves.

You may not have realized it, but *you* have a gunnysack. It holds all the hurts, resentments, anger and maybe rage that you have stored up in your lifetime. This is the ammunition that may have been there for thirty years, two years, since last week or this morning.

Sometimes this ammunition is inwardly directed. People hold all or some of it inside themselves—forever. The inner tension and stress that this creates can cause ulcers, bad backs, migraines, digestive problems, skin rashes and other forms of *physical* ill health.

It can also cause people to suffer from depression, high states of anxiety, insomnia, irritability, low self-esteem and other forms of *psychological* ill health.

(*Note*: These health problems may have other causes too, but failure to deal with issues in life (by gunnysacking) is known to contribute to ill health more than most people realize.)

Sometimes the tension (that comes from gunnysacking) gets too much to hold in. The metaphor of the gunnysack is truly appropriate as people aim their ammunition at other people, in the form of aggressiveness.

They usually are quite unaware, however, that their own *nonassertiveness is often the cause of their tension and aggressiveness.*

(*Note*: Assertive people have gunnysacks, too, but because of the way they communicate, they are mostly kept empty.)

Aggressive behavior

Another way people relate to others is by being aggressive. This behavior is the opposite to nonassertiveness, in that, instead of putting self last, it involves *putting self first*. There is an agenda (conscious or unconscious) that *aims to hurt people*.

This way of relating, often unconsciously and artificially, restores a person's (pseudo) self-esteem: "I'm sick of always being put last, of never having my say, of not being noticed or respected—so I'll take out my anger on you! Then I'll feel better." Do you see how nonassertiveness can lead to aggressiveness?

Different types of aggressive behavior: verbal, nonverbal, passive, displaced

Verbal aggression

This includes:

- criticizing
- blaming
- threatening
- discounting
- swearing
- accusing
- withholding
- being sarcastic
- yelling
- ridiculing
- putting down

It also includes many statements that begin with the word "you," for example:

"You *should* know that's not how I like it."
"You *ought* to grow up and stop being so silly."
"You *never* phone me when you're going to be late."
"You *always* forget our anniversary."
"You *make me* absolutely furious."

The words in italics create trouble and are very common in relationships. Statements beginning this way frequently pull an aggressive response from the recipient. Then there is likely to be warfare.

On the other hand, some people recoil when they are spoken to this way, holding their anger in and putting their anger and resentment into their gunnysack.

Take time

Do your family members speak this way? What is your reaction? Do you communicate this way?

(*Note*: It is usually not legitimate to say, "You make me furious!" What is really happening is that you become emotional because of your own life experiences. *You* actually make *yourself furious*. (See Chapter 7.))

Nonverbal aggression

This ranges from a punch in the nose or a physical fight to a cold stare of silence. Some people give the silent treatment and this can go on for hours, days or weeks.

Sometimes a look of disdain, disgust or impatience is delivered. Words are not needed, so explicit is the nonverbal message.

Nonverbal behaviors such as these are very aggressive and do *not* contribute to the blending of a stepfamily.

Passive aggression

This is very common and frequently masquerades as something else. Here are some examples:

Susanne was very angry at Jason who had come home late for the past three nights. She decided to teach him a lesson. She did this by keeping him waiting for her the following day when they had to go out. She also "got at him" another way. As they had an arrangement that he pay the telephone bill, she decided to phone her sister who was abroad and have a long, long talk. She'd make him pay (literally) for staying out late.

Mike was upset at Marianne because he thought she had ignored him at the dinner party they went to on Saturday night. On Sunday he got up early and turned the television on loud (because he knew that Marianne wanted to sleep in).

Take time

Be honest: how often do you do this sort of thing? Why do you do it? What stops you from assertively saying what you are feeling, thinking or wanting instead of behaving this way? How do you feel when someone behaves this way toward you? In your stepfamily how much of this goes on?

Displaced aggression

Sometimes you might feel tense and uptight and without knowing why, you take it out on someone or something. Perhaps it is your partner, your child, your stepchild, the cat, the door!

Your anger, however, has come from somewhere else, yet you act as though these people or things were the cause of it.

Take time

Do you displace your anger from time to time? Think carefully about yourself and the way you behave toward your partner, your children, your stepchildren, your family members. Is there any possibility that they often unjustly receive your anger in this way? Do you ever talk about this after it happens? If not, why not?

Dealing with aggressive emotional outbursts

Sometimes people need to let off steam. Unfortunately, this is usually done aggressively, so that other people are hurt (emotionally or physically) in the process. Here are several suggestions for dealing with this:

- Learn to tune in to yourself, so that you know when the temperature is rising, or about to rise.

- Try to determine what your anger is about. You will know from what you have read in this book, especially in Chapter 7, that it may come out of your past.

- If you do know what it's about, see if you can talk about it *before* the eruption.

- If you "let it out" in an aggressive way, wait until you have cooled down and then *communicate assertively about what you think caused your anger.*

- If you can think of a way that you can be helped in the future so you won't get so angry, assertively tell the people what it is. We call this "making a request for change."

- Some couples have an agreement: to give each other the personal space and freedom to let off steam. There is a rule, however: the other person does not join in.

- If you repeatedly have to let off steam, professional psychotherapy may be able to help you, and your family.

Now that we have looked at nonassertive and aggressive communication and the way that this contributes to the curdling of stepfamilies, we will look at why it is that assertiveness contributes to the blending process.

The power of assertiveness

- When assertiveness is used along with specific communication skills, it is far more positive and powerful than nonassertive or aggressive behaviors. *It is the key to good relationships.*

- It *prevents invisible walls* from going up between people and helps break them down if they are already there.

- It enables people to *know each other's real selves*, instead of their pseudo selves.

- Assertive communication skills are used to resolve conflict. Issues that exist in stepfamilies (and elsewhere) can be resolved rationally and with dignity. Everyone can come out of difficult and contentious situations with self-respect and the enhancement of their relationships.

(*Note*: Sometimes people think they are being assertive when they are really being aggressive, for example, by always "standing up for themselves" or putting their own needs first. *This is not what it is to be assertive.*)

Table 1: Three different ways of relating

NONASSERTIVE BEHAVIOR	ASSERTIVE BEHAVIOR	AGGRESSIVE BEHAVIOR
Some causes: 1. Limiting *beliefs* about self that come from childhood 2. *Payoffs* or rewards that provide some comfort 3. Critical self-talk: the *Harsh Inner Critic* 4. Nonassertive role models GUNNYSACKING (keeping hurts. resentments, etc. inside) • *Allows domination of self by others* Confidence is usually lacking Self-esteem is low Self-respect is lacking **Communication:** Nonassertive behavior usually involves use of "you," or "people" when talking about self	Expresses: Self-awareness, especially thoughts, feelings or emotions, wants/don't wants Resolves issues Does *not* gunnysack (or keep hurts, resentments, etc. inside) Involves CHOICE to be assertive or not Involves having the RIGHT in any particular situation to be assertive • *Does not try to dominate others or allow others to dominate self* Confidence is usually present Self-esteem is usually high Respects self and others **Communication:** Asserive behavior involves *speaking for self* by using "I, me, my or mine"	Some causes: 1. Nonassertiveness/gunnysacking 2. Low self-esteem (aggressiveness often boosts feeling of self-worth) 3. Aggressive role models There are four types of aggressive behavior: 1. *Verbal:* statements such as: • you should... • you never... • you make me... • you ought... • you always... • criticism... • blaming... • threatening... • ridiculing... • discounting... • putting down... • withholding... • sarcasm... 2. *Nonverbal:* ranges from a silent stare, a raised eyebrow, to hitting 3. *Passive:* deliberate acts that aim to punish or hurt others but are often camouflaged 4. *Displaced:* putting aggression onto someone or something else, when it does not belong there • *Aims to dominate others* Confidence (genuine) is usually lacking Self-esteem is low Respect for self and others is lacking
CONTRIBUTES TO *CURDLING* OF RELATIONSHIPS	CONTRIBUTES TO *BLENDING* OF RELATIONSHIPS	CONTRIBUTES TO CURDLING OF RELATIONSHIPS

How anger and fear prevent people from being assertive

Many people believe it is wrong or bad to feel angry. They hide their feelings of annoyance, irritation, resentment and anger so that no one knows about it. They feel safer this way. They deny it in themselves: "Me? Angry? Never!" (The defense mechanism of denial comes to the rescue.)

They even go so far as to judge people who get angry as being in some way unbalanced or inferior.

> Christina had been married for 12 years and had never been angry with her husband or children. She even told her friends that she never felt angry.
>
> Several years later Christina's emotions came to the front and ultimately resulted in far more conflict and turmoil than she ever set out to avoid. An underlying resentment began to make itself felt and one day she announced that she was leaving.

Why do you think she behaved this way? What stopped her from being honest with herself and her family?

Here are some of the reasons:

- She believed that if she let her husband and children know she was angry with them, they wouldn't love her.

- She believed that if she expressed her anger, her husband and children would think she didn't love them.

- She was fearful that if she became angry, she might not be able to control it.

- She didn't like other people being angry with her and this was one way to control her husband's and children's anger—by not being angry herself.

- As a child, when her mother was angry with her, she felt very unloved. Christina learned to equate anger with absence of love.

- She was taught that nice girls don't get angry.

(Note: *A good relationship is one in which you feel safe enough to express your anger when you feel it*. When you can do this, in a constructive and assertive way, you are well on the road to building strong, honest, and loving relationships.

You also need to give others the freedom to tell you if they are angry with you. Remember, they too have a right to be assertive.)

Be encouraged

If you are now realizing that you, and other family members, relate nonassertively or aggressively, don't despair. The first step is always to recognize how you do communicate.

The next step is to decide that you want to make some changes in communication patterns in your marriage and stepfamily. It's comforting to know that these skills *can* be learned and only require the commitment to practice and practice and practice!

Be content to learn slowly. Habits of a lifetime are tenacious, but will eventually go. Start by becoming more and more aware of the times that you aren't being assertive and ask yourself what stops you from communicating assertively.

Allow other people to have their personal space and make their own decisions about learning to be assertive. If you experience resistance from family members because you are changing, give them time to get used to the new you—but don't fall back into old ways just to keep them in their comfort zones.

In becoming assertive you will be a positive role model for other family members and help them relate honestly and without fear. This will encourage them to change the way they communicate.

Summary

In this, the first of two chapters on assertive communication skills, you have read about:

Assertive behavior
Nonassertive behavior: beliefs, payoffs, your harsh inner critic
The traps of nonassertiveness
Your gunnysack
Aggressive behavior
Different types of aggressive behavior: verbal, nonverbal, passive, displaced
Dealing with aggressive emotional outbursts
The power of assertiveness
How anger and fear prevent people from being assertive

18

Let's talk

Assertive communication skills (Part 2)

Now that you understand what is meant by assertiveness, you need to learn specific communication skills. These will enable you to self-disclose and get to know each other, as well as to successfully sort out and *resolve the many issues* that arise in your marriage, with your children and step-children, with your ex-partner (if you have one), your ex-parents-in-law and other members of your expanded family.

Speaking for yourself

This communication skill goes hand in hand with assertiveness. When you want to express your thoughts, feelings, wants and other dimensions of your *self*-awareness, it is important to speak for yourself.

It has become very common for people to fail to speak for themselves. They use the word "you" when they should be saying "I." Here is a dialogue illustrating this:

> *Tom:* For goodness' sake, tell me what's wrong!
> *Therese:* Well, you can't go on forever taking those insults.
> *Tom:* Who can't? I can't?
> *Therese:* No. I can't!
> *Tom:* Well, why didn't you say that—you said "you."
> *Therese:* Well, I can't go on forever taking those insults.

Here's another example:

Ann: How was your day with the kids?
John: Disappointing. When you take a whole day to take your kids out and they don't even thank you at the end, you think you might as well not have bothered. You just should stop seeing them—they don't appreciate you at all.

Now let's hear what John says when he speaks for himself:

John: Disappointing. When I take a whole day to take my kids out and they don't even thank me at the end, I think I might as well not have bothered! I just should stop seeing them—they don't appreciate me at all.

This second way of communicating is much more powerful because John *speaks for himself* by using the words "I" and "me." The conversation now relates to him and is a direct expression of his own experience.

Other words to use when you speak for yourself are "my" and "mine." Speaking for yourself is an important assertive communication skill and you need to practice it and practice it ... until it becomes the natural way for you to talk.

There is an added bonus. Most people discover, after learning to use this skill, that they feel more confident and have a better sense of who they are.

(*Note*: Sometimes people use the words "one" and "people" instead of speaking for themselves. This, also, is to be avoided.)

Take time

Start to listen to the people around you, at home, on the bus, in the train, on the radio, etc., and begin to notice whether or not they speak for themselves. This will help you develop a keen ear and make it easier for you to catch yourself when you fail to use this skill.

Apart from everyday communication, such as in the examples above, this skill is *absolutely necessary* if you are to resolve the issues in your marriage and stepfamily. This is because you then own what you say about yourself.

Defining an issue

Every marriage and relationship encounters issues, and stepfamilies usually have plenty of them. *Unresolved issues are the reason for the curdling process in stepfamily life.*

Issues arise when two or more people have differences in values, attitudes, opinions, wants—or other areas of life experience.

Although people are usually able to recognize when something is not right between themselves and one (or more) people, they often have difficulty identifying the *real* issue and then being able to resolve it.

In order to resolve an issue it must first be defined.

Milton and Annalisa frequently argued over Annalisa's children's bedtime. Milton didn't like the way they were allowed to stay up late, interfering with his evening. Annalisa could see no reason why they should have to stop doing what they always had done, which was to go to bed when they wanted to.

What was the issue between Milton and Annalisa?

Milton defined it as, "Annalisa's children's bedtime." Annalisa defined it as, "Milton's inflexibility." Who is right? Which definition did they need to use as the basis for their discussion and use of communication skills?

Because Milton raised the issue, they decided to use his definition as the basis for their discussion.

If one person has an issue with another person, it is an issue for the two of them and needs to be resolved. It is never valid to say: "That's your problem."

Take time

Think about your life and any issues you have. Are they in your marriage? With your children? With your stepchildren? With your ex-spouse? How are these issues affecting the quality of your marriage and stepfamily? Do you want to resolve them?

(*Note*: If you have a long list of issues to resolve, always start with the simplest one. This gives you the opportunity to practice your new skills and gives you more chance of a successful resolution.

Once you have defined your issue, the next step is to use the self-awareness wheel.)

The self-awareness wheel and how to use it

The self-awareness wheel provides a framework for resolving issues. It is your guide for saying what you need to say.

In Figure 6 you will notice the six segments of the awareness wheel which represent dimensions of awareness, each one of which relates to *you*! When you have an issue, every part of your awareness is involved.

Here is a brief description of each dimension of awareness:

- *Your senses:* What do you actually see, hear, smell, taste or touch (with respect to this issue)?

- *Your feelings or emotions:* Do you feel angry, sad, scared, loving, happy, irritated, resentful, excited, etc. (about this issue)?

- *Your thoughts:* What are your ideas, opinions, beliefs, values, attitudes, expectations, presumptions or assumptions?

- *Your wants* (as the outcome of your issue):
  a. For yourself?
  b. For the other person?
  c. For the two of you?

- *Your body sensations:* Do you feel tense, or have a knot in your stomach or a headache? Are you tired? Is your heart pounding? Etc. (Sometimes you might not have any awareness of a body

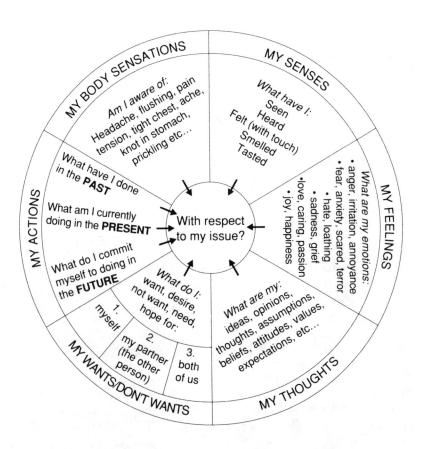

Fig. 6 SELF-AWARENESS WHEEL showing the six dimensions of self-awareness and how to use them to resolve an issue

sensation. In this case just leave this segment blank. It is, however, the only segment that can be left blank.)

- *Your actions* (with respect to this issue):
  a. What have you done in the past or up until now?
  b. What are you doing now?
  c. What action do you intend to take (not what you "think" you will take, but actually will take)?

Figures 7 and 8 show how Milton and Annalisa used the awareness wheel to prepare for discussion to resolve their issue.

Take time

Draw an awareness wheel and write your issue on this page. Think carefully and in each section write down your awareness with respect to the issue. Use Milton's and Annalisa's awareness wheels as your guide.

This is the second step in resolving an issue. (The first is to define the issue.) Now you need to learn how to go about discussing this with the other person.

Self-disclosure and inviting disclosure

When you self-disclose, you tell someone what is in your awareness wheel. You do this by speaking for yourself.

Some people find it difficult to open up and share themselves with others and other people feel comfortable doing this. Yet, even for these people, there may be times when it becomes difficult. We will now look at some of the factors that help or hinder self-disclosure.

What helps and hinders self-disclosure?

Some people are helped to self-disclose when:

- they have the full attention of the other person
- there is eye contact
- they trust the other person
- there is privacy
- there is a code of confidentiality
- the physical surroundings are comfortable
- there is adequate time for a full discussion

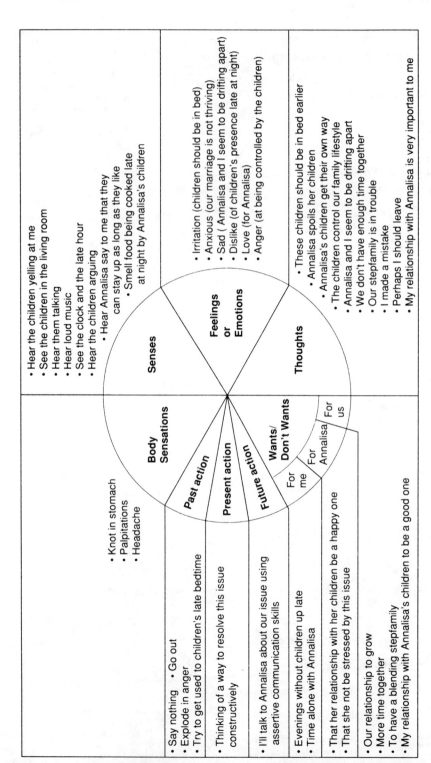

Fig. 7   Milton's self-awareness wheel for the issue of Annalisa's children's bedtime

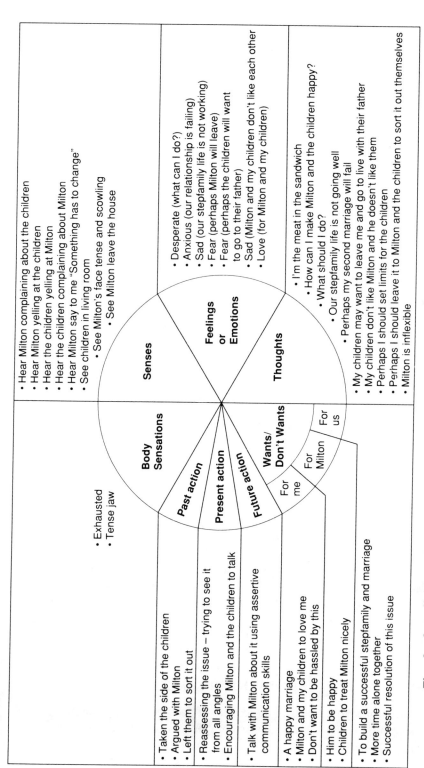

Fig. 8   Annalisa's self-awareness wheel for the issue of Annalisa's children's bedtime

- the time of day is appropriate
- they are having a relaxing dinner with a bottle of wine
- there are no interruptions or distractions
- the other person discloses

and more ...

Some people are hindered from self-disclosing when:

- there are constant interruptions and distractions
- emotionality is running high
- they are afraid of being criticized or yelled at
- they are afraid of being rejected
- they are afraid they will be thought stupid
- they don't know what to say
- they are tired
- they have, or the other person has, had too much to drink
- the other person keeps reading the paper or watching the television when they talk
- the children are listening
- other people are there
- the other person turns away

and more ...

Take time

What helps you open up and self-disclose? In your marriage, what does your spouse do that helps you reveal your innermost self to him or her? On the other hand, what does he or she do to make it difficult for you to do this? How do your children, stepchildren and other people encourage you to be honest with them? How do you encourage the people in your life to be honest and open with you?

Some inviting self-disclosure skills

If you know what helps your partner and other family members self-disclose, you can do a lot to help them open up and talk with you about themselves. In addition you can always help this process by using the following inviting disclosure skills:

Open and closed questions

One way to encourage (or invite) a person to talk is to ask an *open question*. This gives scope for a full response, for example:

- What do you think about our plans for this weekend when we have all the children with us?
- How do you feel about what I have just told you?
- What would you like to do?

Closed questions, on the other hand, are restrictive, yet commonly used. They require a short, definite answer, often "yes" or "no." For example:

- "Is it all right with you if we go for a picnic this weekend when we have all the children with us?"
- "Do you feel angry because of what I have just told you?"
- "Do you want to paint the house?"

Statements

Another communication skill that encourages or invites a person to talk is to use a statement, for example:

- "I'd like you to tell me what you'd like to do this weekend when we have all the children with us."
- "Tell me how you're feeling."
- "I'd like to know what you want to do."

(Notice these are statements—there is no question here.)

Prompting

Sometimes people seem to falter or get stuck for words, and a tactful prompt encourages them to keep on going, for example:

"When you look at me like that I feel ... um ... sort of ... well, I mean ... "

"Criticized?"

"Yes, that's how I feel, as though you are being very critical of me."

Accenting a word or words

This also can be a helpful way to encourage self-disclosure. It involves repeating a word or a few words to focus attention on them and perhaps get more information, for example:

> "Yes, I feel uncomfortable when I think you are being critical of me, it's as though I am a child and you are the parent ..."

> "Parent?"

> "Yes, that's how you come across, and it reminds me of the way my father used to look at me when he ..."

All of these skills are useful and you can practice them daily. Perhaps the most useful and most commonly used, however, are open questions and statements.

Take time

Think about patterns of communication in your family. How do you encourage each other to talk? To tell each other about your day? Or about what you are thinking or feeling? Is there much self-disclosure in your family? If there is, what has contributed to this? If there is not, what are the reasons?

(*Note*: Never expect anyone to open up and reveal everything about themselves. Everyone is entitled to their own private secrets—you are too!)

Sometimes it is appropriate to *set limits* on what you say *or* what others say. For example:

- "I'm prepared to tell you about a lot of my life before we married, but there are some areas I wish to keep to myself."

- "I'd love to hear about your life before I met you, but I respect your right to keep to yourself the more personal parts."

Too little or too much self-disclosure

A high level of self-disclosure contributes to a healthy relationship, but too little or too much prevents or destroys it.

> Lucille does not open up at all to Darren. Try as he might to get her to talk, she remains closed, aloof, distant and tight-lipped. Their marriage prospects are not good because she will not let him get to know her. She under-discloses.

> Cecil told his second wife, Helena, that her cooking was inadequate and he was sorry he'd left his first wife, who was a

better cook. He also told her, in a moment of anger, that her body was growing too fat and it repulsed him! In telling Helena this, he dropped two atomic bombs. The fallout led to the end of their marriage. Cecil over-disclosed.

Roberta gradually opened up to Gregory, her third husband, and revealed to him her innermost thoughts, feelings and desires. She did not rush this, but as the years unfolded he really got to know her and, as a result, valued her more and more. Roberta's self-disclosure was appropriate, open and honest and helped build a solid and loving marriage.

Using the skill of checking out

The skill of checking out is not used enough by most people. It involves making sure that you are *not making assumptions*. Here are some examples:

- "Did you say we'll all go together to the skating rink—or just you and your children?"

- "Right now you have that look on your face that makes me think you are disappointed in me. Am I right?"

- "You haven't given me a kiss tonight. Are you angry with me?"

- "I just wanted to check out with you: do you understand I'm not avoiding you—that I'm just exhausted?"

Much marital and family conflict could be prevented if people used this skill more frequently. It serves to clarify and prevent mind-reading, which discounts a person's right to think his or her own thoughts.

Take time

How often do you check your assumptions? If you do, how do you do it? If you don't, what stops you? Do other family members check out their assumptions with you? How do you know this?

Sharing a meaning

This is a skill that ensures *mutual understanding*. It can be used in many different situations for many different reasons. It helps create empathy, avoid misunderstandings and clarify messages and their intention.

It is also very helpful when people have differing views or opinions, as it can diffuse emotion. When two people are attempting to resolve an issue, they need to use this skill extensively.

Steps involved in sharing a meaning

Step 1:   One person, the sender of the message, says something which needs to be understood by the receiver. Either one can decide that it is important for them to share the meaning and needs to declare this by saying, for example:

Sender: I'm about to tell you something which I really want you to understand, so I'd like you to share a meaning with me.

What I just told you is so important that I'd like you to feed back to me what you think I said, so that I'm sure you heard me correctly.

Receiver: Wait a minute! *I'd* like to feed back to you what I think you said, just so I know I'm on the right track.

Step 2:   The receiver feeds back the sender's message, making sure not to add to it nor omit anything that was said. (*Note:* it does not have to be fed back in parrot fashion.)

Step 3:   The sender corrects this feedback from the receiver if it does not convey the original message she or he sent.

Step 4:   The receiver has another go at it—feeding back once again after receiving this new information.

Step 5:   Again! If it is not right, the sender corrects and assists again.

Step 6:   And so on … back and forth until the sender eventually says, "Yes! That's what I meant."

Rules

1. The receiver does not interpret by adding his or her own thoughts during this process.

2. The sender does not add new material but may, if necessary, give examples for the purpose of clarity.

(*Note*: This process is not meant to be stilted. The aim is for *both* people to understand what the sender is saying, and this means that language needs to be natural.)

Different styles of communication

Perhaps you have not realized it but you (and others) communicate in different styles, depending on who you are with and what your intention is:

Conversation style

You use this when you are chatting about your day, telling a story, giving an account of a movie you have seen or talking with your partner about what you plan to do over the weekend.

This style is sociable and safe. It feels safe because tension and conflict are absent. However, if it is used too much in a relationship, it is dangerous because it prevents people from really getting to know each other.

Controlling style

This style of communication involves lecturing, advising, teaching, selling, directing.

A little of this goes a long way. Many adults and children know the agony of always being lectured to and told what to do. People who use this style of communication too much have a need to be in control.

Many a dinner party has been ruined by the guest who is the "author" on every topic. It is a killer of relationships and too much of it often puts tempers on the boil.

Aggressive style

All of the aggressive behaviors that you read about in the previous chapter are included in this style. Apart from yelling at someone to keep out of danger, this style *has no place in the building of a happy stepfamily.* Eliminate it by using assertive skills instead.

Search style

This is a most valuable style, used especially in resolving issues. It involves being tentative, explorative, reflective and searching, for example:

- "I think a good way to do this may be ..."
- "How about this for a solution?"
- "My thoughts about this are ... What are yours?"
- "So you think that perhaps ..."
- "Perhaps we could ... "
- "Another approach might be to ..."
- "Maybe we could ..."

Do you pick up the tentative nature of this style?

Open style

Full and appropriate self-disclosure, using all the skills in this and the previous chapter, represents this style, but it is the disclosure of innermost feelings that makes it so different. It's as though a person opens up his or her inside and reveals what is really happening.

(*Note*: It's important to value and respect these open disclosures when you are privileged enough to receive them. Never use them against the person who opens up to you. Respect confidentiality. Some people think of intimate self-disclosure as being like a very beautiful and delicate flower, which bruises easily if mishandled.)

Preparing to discuss your issue

Step 1:   After you have identified your issue, decide *whose* issue it is. Decide who should be there when you talk about it. Only the people whose issue it is should be there. Usually, this involves two people only.

Step 2:   Now you need to make an "appointment" with the other person. You could say, "Sometime, I'd like to get together with you to discuss an issue that is bothering me. It is … " At this point say what the issue is but *don't* elaborate—just give the definition and leave all the discussion until later when you are going through the process of resolving it.

Step 3:   Arrange *when* you will meet. Make this a time when you can have peace, no interruptions or distractions and when you are not too tired or rushed.

Step 4:   Negotiate *how long* you will be together talking: half an hour? An hour? Any longer than this is usually too long.

Step 5:   Decide *where* this meeting is going to take place. Choose a place where you feel relaxed and that is conducive to this intimate interaction.

Step 6:   Each of you, having agreed on the issue, is to do your own awareness wheel away from each other. There is to be no discussion prior to the arranged meeting time.

Discussing and resolving your issue

When Milton and Annalisa resolved their issue, they went through the steps already outlined in this chapter and they then followed the steps outlined below.

(*Note*: The following steps need to be followed *strictly!*)

Milton	Annalisa
1. M. tells A. what he has written down in each section of his awareness wheel, *except the wants and future actions.*	2. A. shares a meaning as M. goes through, to make sure she understands what he is telling her.
	3. A. tells M. what she has written down in each section of her awareness wheel, *except the wants and future actions.*
4. M. shares a meaning as A. goes through, to make sure he understands what she is telling him.	
5. M. tells A. what he wants: a. for Annalisa b. for himself c. for the two of them.	6. A. shares a meaning.
	7. A. tells M. what she wants: a. for Milton b. for herself c. for the two of them
8. M. shares a meaning.	
9. M. tells A. what he is a. *willing* to do b. *not willing* to do.	10. A shares a meaning.
	11. A. tells M what she is a. *willing* to do b. *not willing* to do.
12. M. shares a meaning.	

13. They both engage in discussion, *using search and open styles of communication and all the other communication skills.* Each must be prepared to compromise, negotiate and seek a solution—until:

14. M. says what he *will or will not* do in the future.	15. A. says what she *will or will not* do in the future.

(*Note*: It is absolutely essential to stick to the rules. Each step must be completed, as the outline suggests.)

(*Warning*: **Stop** and continue later if emotions begin to run high and cannot be defused.)

A trap that many people fall into when they are trying to resolve an issue is to *get off the track* and start to discuss another issue. If you notice this happening, bring the discussion back to the issue.

Some of you may be asking "How long does this take?" or thinking, "This all sounds very boring and tedious."

You will probably be surprised to discover when you use these skills and procedures that, instead of being boring and tedious, you are (at last) having an intimate and constructive conversation, getting to know the other person *and* resolving something that has been a difficulty in your relationship!

One of the best ways to get to know another person is to work at resolving an issue. Members of stepfamilies help build healthy and lasting relationships when they resolve their issues in this way.

Conflict resolution breaks down tension and is a crucial building block of all stepfamilies.

Resolving your issues is an important key to blending your stepfamily.

Summary

In this chapter you have read about:

> Speaking for yourself
> Defining an issue
> The self-awareness wheel and how to use it
> Self-disclosure and inviting disclosure
> What helps and hinders self-disclosure
> Some inviting self-disclosure skills
> Too little or too much self-disclosure
> Using the skill of checking out
> Sharing a meaning
> Different styles of communication
> Preparing to discuss your issue
> Discussing and resolving your issue

19

We get along well with each other now

The reality that stepfamily life can match your dreams

In spite of the growing failure of second and subsequent marriages, there are many stepfamilies who have reached a point where family members can truly say they have achieved happiness. They usually acknowledge that the journey has had its ups and downs but, in spite of this, they may say: "We get along well with each other now! It's been worth it."

The real challenge is, as one woman put it, "to hang in there." This means that when it all seems too difficult and hopeless, you accept the fact that these times are inevitable and part of the growth of your stepfamily. Probably no marriage or stepfamily achieves perfection—ever. As long as the overall process is one of blending (in spite of pockets of curdling), you are on the right track.

How to use "pacing" to build solid stepparent-stepchild relationships

As we have discovered, one of the many mistakes that stepparents make is to believe they will be super stepmoms or super stepdads. Their confidence blinds them to the pitfalls that lie ahead. This often means that they fail to go slowly and instead race in and try to fill a parental role.

The dictum "go slow to go fast" is an important one in the building and blending of a stepfamily. Do not rush. Take time to learn and practice skills. Expect *gradual* improvement in stepfamily relationships—not instant results. Do not try to sort out all the issues at once. Approach them one by one and build on your successes.

Stepparents who go very slowly, who seem almost to be detached from their stepchildren, usually do better in the long and the short run. They allow time and space for the getting-to-know-you process. They aim to become friends rather than parents. They look for signs that they are liked or wanted and then respond accordingly.

This strategy seems to work best with children of all ages: a two-year-old may climb onto the stepparent's knee; a five-year-old might say, "Come and see what I made"; a ten-year-old may ask, "Are you coming to my school concert?"; a sixteen-year-old seeks help with homework; a twenty-year-old may offer to drive a stepparent to the bus stop. All of these are indicators that the children are ready to come a little closer to their stepparent. This is the time for the adult to respond with warmth and respect.

Here is a story about a stepmother and her young stepson:

> Lorraine's seven-year-old stepson refused to eat the school lunches she prepared for him and insisted that his father prepare them instead. His father went along with this, wisely, as there seemed to be no point in creating a major issue over a child's lunch.
>
> Lorraine made no comment and prepared lunch for the other children in the family, leaving this one for her husband to do. Eventually, her stepson asked her to make his lunch— Lorraine felt she had made great progress in her new stepfamily.

By holding back and not forcing herself on her stepson, Lorraine gave him the space and time to make the first friendly move himself. He liked the lunch she prepared that day and their relationship has been moving in a positive direction ever since.

(*Note*: Always try to be sensitive to the pace children set in their developing relationship with their stepparents.)

Positive relationships between stepparents and stepchildren

Given time, skills and patience, many stepparents and their stepchildren eventually find themselves actually liking, even loving, each other. It usually takes at least two years for a positive relationship to develop between stepparent and stepchild. A period of about five years is more common. In many instances it takes even longer for these two people to share in a relationship that could be described as close, or supportive and loving. This is irrespective of whether they live together permanently, on a part-time basis or not at all. Sadly, there are instances where this never happens, but with the skills and information outlined in this book, stepparents have every opportunity to develop long and lasting relationships with their stepchildren.

In many stepfamilies, stepparents and stepchildren become very important people to each other. Their lives are enriched as they learn valuable lessons about themselves and life from each other. A deep and lasting affection may be the end result of years of effort, patience and commitment to the blending process of stepfamily life.

> Brian and Ina experienced this in their stepfamily. At first, when Brian married into the family, Ina's daughters, ages 18 and 20, were rude and unwelcoming to their new stepfather. He decided to go slowly and give them time to get used to him. Ina decided also to give them space and time to become accustomed to her new partner. Ina's 16-year-old son was a little more accepting—but only just.
>
> It was not easy going and many times Brian seriously considered walking away from Ina and her children. Ten years later it is a different story. Brian is "Gramps" to his stepgrandchildren—and a much loved Gramps, too. His stepdaughters love him and can't imagine life without him. Ina's son is also married, and he and Brian are great friends.

This stepfamily is now one in which each member can truly say: "We all get along well with each other now—it's been worth it!"

One-to-one relating between stepparents and stepchildren

There is much value in stepparents and stepchildren having time alone together. Many a relationship has developed positively because of these opportunities.

> Keith never really felt comfortable with his 19-year-old stepdaughter, Mary Lee. Even though he had been part of her life for 11 years and had seen her grow up, finish school and commence employment, there always seemed to be a tension between them—until his wife had to take an overseas trip to visit a dying relative.
>
> Now Keith and Mary Lee were alone at home and had to make the most of each other. In spite of some trepidation

about how this would work, to their surprise it worked out really well. They found themselves chatting in a way they had not done before and gradually, as the weeks unfolded, a new and loving relationship developed between them.

When Keith's wife returned there seemed to be a cooling off on Mary Lee's part. She seemed to pull away again. Nevertheless, gradually Mary Lee was able to relate to her stepfather in the same way she had when her mother was away. Mary Lee, her mother and stepfather had found a new and comfortable balance in their interactions with each other.

Other stepparents, as mentioned earlier, take opportunities to drive stepchildren to sports and other activities, so as to have time to be alone with them.

Some stepparents and stepchildren experience guilt if they do not feel love, one for the other. They need to know that there is no rule that says they have to feel love. It is not something that turns on with a switch. Love takes time to grow and sometimes doesn't develop at all.

Positive relationships between children and two sets of parents or stepparents

Many children have two sets of parents. Sometimes they enjoy being with one more than with the other but even so, if they feel secure and loved, each parental grouping can play a significant part in the life of these children. When children in stepfamilies are given time to become accustomed to the changes in their family lives and believe they are understood and valued, their lives can actually be enriched by the newcomers.

Many children in these situations learn more about life and can be presented with opportunities not available in their first-time families.

Harry was 10 when his parents split up. For a while he lived alone with his mother and had regular contact with his father. Eventually his mother remarried and a whole new world opened up to him. His stepfather was a musician and it was undoubtedly because of this that Harry went on to become a talented musician himself.

When ex-partners are able to relate to each other and keep in touch because of their children, even when their lives have gone in different directions, the children are much more able to heal and get on with life in a positive way. This is a primary task for ex-partners: to learn to overcome past hurts and bitterness and relate with each other *for the sake of the children*.

Many ex-partners are able to come together for family occasions with their children. Most children report their appreciation of this, *if* there is an absence of tension. It helps them feel connected to their family roots and is a valuable lesson about life: that resentment and anger do not have to last forever and that forgiveness is possible.

Positive relationships between children and their absent parent

When children cease to live with one parent, the way they relate with that parent usually changes. This was talked about earlier.

Sometimes these relationships have to weather the storm of bitterness and resentment, but usually happier times are enjoyed again when these absent parents continue, in many different ways, to show their children that they are loved and valued.

Many grown-up children learn to draw close once again to the parent from whom they have been physically and/or emotionally distant. In some instances, as children grow and learn, they see their parent's relationship from a different perspective and come to understand more clearly the reasons for the disintegration of their earlier family life. All of this is part of the healing process of the past.

Positive relationships between stepsiblings

We've already said that stepsiblings can become great friends—in spite of earlier jealousy, distrust and dislike for each other. Here again, if parents and stepparents go slowly and do not try to force relationships within the stepfamily system, their respective children are much more likely to drop their defenses gradually and begin to value, trust, and like each other.

> Jason and Pete did not like each other at all when they first met and this dislike turned to hostile resentment before they completed their school years. Their parents did not try to coerce them into friendship or blame them for not getting on. Five years later, at the age of 23, they were great pals and planning to travel the world together.

While there is no foolproof formula for the positive growth of stepsibling relationships, it is more likely to happen if the respective parents follow three basic guidelines:

1. Help their children believe they are valuable human beings.

2. Do not triangle in on issues between stepsiblings.

3. Allow time for relationships between their children to develop at their own pace.

Positive relationships between children and grandparents and other relatives

In spite of initial difficulties with access between many grandparents and their grandchildren, these relationships, too, often find a way to flourish and grow as the years go by. Sometimes older children (or grandparents) initiate contact that has been lost for many years, and other times, parents and stepparents cooperate to bring this about.

In Chapter 13, we talked about the importance of maintaining relationships with relatives. Family ties *do* bind and contribute immensely to a person's sense of self-worth and identity—not to mention pleasure! So it is that many stepfamily members are able to enjoy their many relatives throughout their lives.

Joy in the step-couple relationship

As has been mentioned, the pivotal point of a stepfamily is the marriage of the step-couple. This relationship requires ongoing nurturing and tending for the blending process of stepfamily life to take place.

Many couples find in their second or subsequent relationship the happiness that matches their earlier dreams. Once they realize that marriage, like stepfamily life, is a process that is ever changing and growing, they are able to participate fully in the journey of their lives together.

> Five years after their marriage, Renata and Walter laughed when they recalled the many difficult and challenging times they experienced in their early stepfamily life. They were finally able to confess they both had fears and doubts about each other, and about their ability to cope with their new situation.
>
> Renata and Walter were now certain than their decision to marry had been the right one, and that their lives and those of their children had been greatly enhanced because of each other and the stepfamily they had created. They now felt sure they would never regret the path they had taken together.

Reaching into the future

Most people are resilient in life and continue to search for solutions and fulfillment, often in spite of adversity and difficulties. There is, in most of us, an optimism that drives us to keep trying in many different areas of our lives.

With respect to stepfamily life, what has been lacking for most people is direction as to how to bring their dreams and hopes into reality. There are many books, courses and videos designed to help people make a success of marriage and family life. Unfortunately, few people choose to seek out this knowledge until it is too late. Many people never take the opportunity to learn about themselves and others and *how to make relationships work.*

That it is possible to learn about and help ourselves and others is the reason for this book. There are people who have proved to themselves and their loved ones that they can change and grow. They are living proof that human beings are adaptable and positive in their intentions, especially when driven by a purpose or value.

The value of marriage, family and stepfamily life is one that most people hold. But when the going seems tough and the road ahead seems impossible, countless numbers believe there is no other option but to bail out.

Yet there *is* another way. And it involves you. It requires that you make a life decision to learn, to change. In the process of this journey, you and your loved ones will almost certainly reap great benefits.

Stepfamily Realities can be part of this journey. Use it, refer to it often and explore and experiment with new behaviors and attitudes. Stepfamily life can be all you ever dreamt of, all that you failed to have in your previous marriage or marriages ... it's really up to you!

Summary

In this chapter we have looked at:

How to use "pacing" to build solid stepparent-stepchild relation ships
Positive relationships between stepparents and stepchildren
One-to-one relating between stepparents and stepchildren
Positive relationships between children and two sets of parents or stepparents
Positive relationships between children and their absent parent
Positive relationships between stepsiblings
Positive relationships between children and grandparents and other relatives
Joy in the step-couple relationship
Reaching into the future

Further Reading

Bank, P., and M. D. Kahn. (1982) *The Sibling Bond*. New York: Basic Books, Inc.

Bradshaw, J. (1988) Bradshaw: *On the Family: A Revolutionary Way to Self-Discovery*. Pompano Beach, FL: Health Communications, Inc.

Durrell, D. (1989) *Starting Out Right*. Oakland, CA: New Harbinger Publications, Inc.

Einstein E., and L. Albert (1987) *Strengthening Your Stepfamily*. New York: Random House, American Guidance Service.

Fisher, B. (1981) *Rebuilding*. San Luis Obispo, CA: Impact Publishers.

Jansen, D., and M. Newman (1989) *Really Relating*. Australia: Random House.

Richardson, R., and L. Richardson (1990) *Birth Order and You*. Bellingham, WA: Self-Counsel Press.

Rosen, M. B. (1987) *Step-fathering: Stepfathers' Advice on Creating a New Family*. New York: Simon & Schuster.

Visher, E. B., and J. Visher (1982) *How To Win as a Stepfamily*. New York: Brunner/Mazel Publishers.

Cassette Tapes

Available at Relationship Development Center, 34 Oxley Street, Crows Nest 2065, Australia. (02) 436 3055 (008) 249 943

Becoming an Assertive Communicator, with Margaret Newman teaching and working with 14 participants. (3 tapes: 3-1/2 hours)

Self-Esteem, with David Jansen and Margaret Newman. (4 tapes: 6 hours)

How You Can Really Relate. David Jansen and Margaret Newman working with two couples on resolving conflict and developing intimacy. (1 tape: 1-1/2 hours)

Index

Italic numbers refer to pages with a chart, figure or table.

awareness of 44
cutting off 40
dealing with aggressive outburst 220
guidelines for dealing with 92
overreactivity 88
responses to separation 173-75
self-awareness wheel, 229, *230*
enmeshed families 28-29
expectations 1-7
self-awareness wheel 229, *230*
unrealistic 96
extended family *see* relatives

F

familiarity 9
maintaining 60-61
see also balancing behaviors, comfort
zone
family
conference 145
rules 105-6
see also stepfamilies
family of origin 41
child's position in 123
emotional glue of 30
influences from 24
money issues 205
unspoken rules in your 108
family system 9-14
maintaining balance 160-61
unspoken rules 106
fantasy stage 4
fear 78, 83-84
of change 85
of conflict 86
of losing contact with absent parent
84
of losing parental influence 170
of marriage failure 83
and money issues 212-13
of not belonging 85-6
preventing assertiveness 225
of punishment 134-35
of rejection 57-62, 113, 126, 173, 207-9
resulting in divided loyalties 85-86
resulting in jealousy 119
after separation 173
feelings *see* emotions
fighting 156-57
forgiveness 181

G

genetic inheritance 41
genograms 10-11, *12-13*
go-betweens 164-65
"goodbye" experiences 86-87, 175-76
grandparents
finding time for 167
relationship between grandchildren
and 178-81, 248
resentment of biological child 189
grief 77, 86-87, 174

over lost relationships 176-77
masked as anger 36
after separation 173
guilt 82-83
jealous feelings hiding 111
and money issues 207-8
over lost relationship 177
preventing forgiveness 181
after separation 173
gunnysack 219-20

H

habits 66-8
guidelines for living with different
75-76
hate 79
for a stepparent 116
hidden agendas
see unspoken contracts
home, boundaries with the 51-56

I

idealism 4
identity, sense of
establishing 11, 29-30
extending family contributing to 182
importance of values 72-73
strategies for personal growth 44-45
illusions, 4, 24
individual differences 18-21
boundaries and personal space 54
hidden or unknown 23
negative sameness behaviors 28-9
see also separateness
inner critic 216, 218
insecurity 112, 115
isolation as punishment 138
issues
defining 227
discussing and resolving 240-41
preparing to discuss 239-40

J

jealousy 83, 111-21
between half-siblings 187
of biological child 189
dealing with 119
different signs of 118
and money issues 208, 209
Johari Window 103-4, *103*

L

lifestyle
balancing 168
pie exercise 169, *170*
love 79
romantic 3, 23
withdrawal of 137
"love" child 189
lovemaking, restrictions on 193-96

M

money issues 204-13
    balancing 168
    how to resolve 212-13
mutual understanding 237-38
myths about stepfamilies 5-6

N

needs 4
    balancing demands of half-siblings
        186
    developing self-awareness 44-45
    see also wants
nonverbal aggression 221
nonverbal discipline 136

O

objects, withdrawal of 137
open style of communication 240

P

parents
    balancing time 167-68
    discipline by 140-44
    emotional effects of separation on 173
    father as go-between 165
    mother as go-between 164
    need for personal space 55
    as sole disciplinarian 144-45
    see also stepparents
passive aggression 221
payoffs 216, 217-18
peace, keeping the 74, 154-56, 217
    see also conflict, fear of
peacemakers 154-56
personal space 49-57
    sexual behavior between stepsiblings
        198
    strategies to maintain 157-58
physical boundaries 51-56
    stepparents as instant parents 134
physical punishment 138-39
previous marriage
    influences from 23
    unresolved anger from 81
privacy 60-62
privileges, withdrawal of 137
problem child 160
projection 15
    guilt and jealousy 111
prompting 235
pseudo self 4, 43-44
    and money issues 211
psychological boundaries 56
    feeling pushed out 82
    stepparents as instant parents 134
punishment, different forms of 136-38

Q

questions, open and closed 235

R

rationalization 15, 60
reaction formation 17
real self 43-44
reentry time 161-62
regression 16
reinforcement, positive and negative 148-49
rejection fear of 113, 126, 173, 217
    and money issues 207, 208, 209
    strategies to reduce 57-62
rejection of relatives 163
relationships
    changed nature of, in stepfamilies
        173-82
    learning about 249
    positive 243-49
    see also children, family system,
        siblings, stepparents, stepsiblings
relatives
    dealing with anger 83
    rejection of 163
    relationships between children and
        181-82, 248
repression 16
resolution stage 5
responsibility 217
rituals 20-21, 74-75
    guidelines for living with different
        75-76
role models 141-42
    communication skills 226
    for martial and parental relationships
        195, 202
    and money issues 208
rules 104-8
    differing in different places 148
    establishing 135
    setting limits 135
    for stepsiblings 166

S

sadness *see* grief
scapegoating 118, 162-63
search style of communication 239
self 33-47
    traps of nonassertiveness 219
self-awareness 44-45
    of anger 88
    exploring yourself not others 98
    wheel *230*, 229-30, *232, 233*
self-discipline 134, 140
self-disclosure 216, 234-37, 240
    too little or too much 236
self-esteem 45-46
    encouraging 119
    extending family contributing to
        181-82
    jealousy reducing 112
    and money issues 209, 211
    negative verbal discipline 136
    physical punishment 139

Other New Harbinger Self-Help Titles